ELUSIVE IDEOLOGY

Religion and Socialism in Modern Indian Thought

by

Mark Hager

DORRANCE PUBLISHING CO
EST. 1920
PITTSBURGH, PENNSYLVANIA 15238

Dorrance Publishing Co
585 Alpha Drive
Suite 103
Pittsburgh, PA 15238
Visit our website at *www.dorrancebookstore.com*

ISBN: 978-1-6480-4294-2
eISBN: 978-1-6480-4887-6

Contents

INTRODUCTION

This is a study of what could be called the ambivalent relationship between religion and socialism in modern Indian thought. It highlights
both congruences and antagonisms between religious and socialist ideas
in a handful of leading thinkers. It explores problems they encounter
attempting to reconcile religious and socialist concerns. It emphasizes
the general character of these problems by highlighting recurrence of
common themes. It also explores differences among these thinkers and
suggests that those variations create a pattern of distinguishable responses to a unified set of concerns. India is sometimes not recalled
these days as a haven for socialist thinking. Look again.

Attempts to restate traditional religious ideas and to juxtapose them
with Western socialist ideas are so pervasive in modern Indian thought
as to constitute perhaps its most distinctive and unifying characteristic.
In varying ways, leading figures weave together interpretations of socialist ideas and traditional religious ideas, often so as to imagine social
institutions and practices where spiritual values and economic organization might be mutually reinforcing.

It is not strange that socialism and religion should have an ambivalent relationship. On the one hand, their orientations tend to diverge.
Socialism concerns itself with problems of material production, while

religion devalues material concerns for spiritual ones. On the other hand, socialism generally and religion often translate concerns for human fulfillment into social visions of solidarity—sentiments of interdependence between private and general well-being. This resemblance sets religion and socialism apart from liberalism and capitalism, for example, which in their social theories typically de-emphasize solidarity. The commonality of religion and socialism tends to bring them into contact, but contrasting orientations can make that contact a tense one.

Ambivalence between religion and socialism has been especially acute in India, due largely to experiences of imperial subjugation. In the late nineteenth century, resistance to imperialism spawned a set of attitudes, including socialist and religious ones, which could be called the first Indian radicalism.

Imperialism, as it seemed, was first of all an experience of economic subservience and exploitation. The rise and triumph of industrial capitalism in Great Britain struck many as dependent on economic dominance over India, the impoverishment of which fueled Britain's enrichment. Indian thinkers learned to focus on capitalism's negative features. In imagining eventual liberation, they strove to imagine a system of non-exploitative production. They called it socialism.

Imperial subjugation was secondly an experience of cultural anxiety and doubt. Indian thinkers inhabited a twilight zone, feeling the attractions and repulsions of both Western and Indian cultures. Dominance of the West, combined with the apparently advanced nature of Western ideas, prompted an impulse to denigrate Indian culture. At the same time, dreams of liberation from imperial rule prompted impulses toward denigrating Western culture and exalting India.

The case for prompt liberation gained strength from asserting that Western culture was harmful to India's well-being but weakened under any sense that Western culture was superior or necessary to India's progress. Advocacy of Indian culture over Western culture involved sympathy toward religious themes.

Thus, radical resistance to British rule commonly linked up with advocacy of both socialism and traditional religion. Less radical anti-imperialism, by contrast, generally went with more muted economic critiques and less fervent allegiance to religion. This contrast exemplified itself in turn-of-the-century schism in the nationalist movement between "Extremists" and "Moderates." There was generally more of both explicit socialism and religious preoccupation in viewpoints of Extremists such as Tilak, Aurobindo, Bipin Chandra Pal, and Lala Lajpat Rai than with Moderates like Ranade and Gokhale.

Modern Indian radicalism then, originated with intense symbiosis of religion and socialism, a symbiosis that ironically remained ambivalent. Born from experiences of imperial subjugation, this ambivalent symbiosis later fed upon the increasingly negative example of Soviet socialism. Some admired early Soviet developments while others frowned from the start on communist atheism and violence. Criticism mounted as the Soviet system grew increasingly autocratic, bureaucratic, cynical, and repressive. This did not, however, induce leading Indian thinkers to ignore problems of Western hegemony or to embrace the developed West as savior of the "free world." They developed instead a critique of both Western and Soviet systems culminating in Nehru's sponsorship of a Non-Aligned Movement for the "Third World." This Third World consciousness reinforced India in its anti-imperial impulse to seek out virtues in its own heritage. Rejection of Soviet socialism struck some as leaving no option but to develop a socialism rooted in India's distinctive heritage of flourishing religious sensibility.

For several reasons then, juxtaposition of religion and socialism lies at the heart of modern Indian thought's most characteristic failures and achievements. It can therefore stand as an axis around which to interpret that thought as a unified intellectual tradition. This tradition drills down on a distinctive "problematic": to interweave socialist ideas with Indian religious ideas in pursuit of a sound and worthwhile ideology. By "problematic," I mean a persistent pattern of interrelated questions defining the subject matter for a system of inquiry. By "ideology," I mean simply some picture of a better society combined with ideas on how to achieve it. As will become clear, the problematic explored here is an elastically-defined intellectual universe. It is by no means a unified answer to a single question, but rather a cluster of questions and proposed answers driven by a distinct and persisting sense of moral and intellectual unease.

By framing my analysis in terms of a problematic, I hope both to highlight its centrality and to suggest a certain logic in its unfolding.

Particular controversy may emerge from my treatment of thinkers within the problematic as "failures" or "successes." By "failure" and "success", I mean something quite particular: the degree to which various thinkers, in their deployment of religious and socialist ideas, manage to remedy the complementary weaknesses of each.

Religion's typical weakness as ideology is failure to visualize practical institutions to embody and express its values in all spheres of activity. Religion is often especially weak in reconciling aspirational values with demands of productive activity. Socialism's frequent weakness lies in failure to investigate and cultivate spiritual virtues needed in any worthwhile system of socialized production. Socialism's frequent and erroneous conceit holds that achieving socialized production—common and roughly equal ownership of productive resources—itself ensures moral regeneration. Even when it does focus on spiritual regeneration it often treats those concerns as secondary to socialized production.

Modern Indian thinkers have tried to steer a middle course avoiding typical failings of both socialism and religion. They by and large reject what may be called "materialist socialism," which imagines either that right economic organization must precede cultivation of fraternal social relations or will yield such relations automatically afterward. These thinkers also by and large try to avoid what may be called "pure religious ideology," which imagines that spiritual transformation can usher in a harmonious and just society prior to or without need of transformed productive organization. With one interesting exception they grope to articulate an ideology of mutual dependence and reinforcement between spiritual growth and socialist productive arrangements.

Within this problematic "success" lies especially in emergence and refinement of Gandhian socialism. Gandhian socialism maintains a simultaneous focus on cultivating virtue and socializing productive arrangements. Widespread practice of moral virtue and progressive socialization require and reinforce each other, pursued in tandem not isolation. These insights, crucial to Gandhian socialism, characterize the entire tradition examined here, with Ambedkar as the interesting exception. What distinguishes Gandhian socialism from "failures" within this tradition is its clarity in perceiving the issues and coherence in solutions offered.

In a sense, therefore, this is a study of the background and development of Gandhian socialism. In contrast to many Gandhian studies, it seeks to locate Gandhi in a particular intellectual-historical framework. It seeks to understand the context of ideas in which Gandhi's thought evolved as well as the pivotal impact of his thought upon that context.

Part I examines Vivekananda's thought as the problematic's first full-blown articulation. The protean character of this thought will be evident throughout the study as it explores themes, problems and vicissitudes that Vivekananda first raises somewhat awkwardly.

Part II explores "failures" within the problematic: formulations which, though steeped in its peculiar concerns, resolve those concerns in ways not conducive to innovative thought and progressive action. Part II classifies these "failures" in terms of differing attitudes toward the Hindu tradition. Bhagavan Das formulates a "backward-looking" Hindu socialist ideology based on the specific classical social scheme set out in Manu, the ancient text of legal and religious orthodoxy. Bipin Chandra Pal and Sri Aurobindo, by contrast, formulate "forward-looking" Hindu socialisms, de-emphasizing Manu's specific framework and stressing instead notions of social order they find implicit in certain Hindu themes. While Aurobindo emphasizes *Advaita*, inquiry into the "non-dual" or "non-divided" nature of reality. Pal, stresses *Bhakti*, theistic devotionalism. B. R. Ambedkar, finally, represents complete rejection of Hindu tradition as any source of progressive social ideas. Though he repudiates Hinduism, he maintains identification with Indian spiritual culture by embracing and interpreting Buddhism, treating it as chief historical antagonist to Hindu social values.

For differing reasons, all these formulations represent "dead ends" within the problematic. Though rich with interesting and provocative conceptualizations, they lack the ideological fecundity of Gandhi's thought. In various ways, thinkers examined in Part II paint themselves into ideological corners.

Part III inspects Gandhi's thought, focusing especially on the evolution and revision of certain key ideas. It highlights how, despite serious problems in his thought, Gandhi lays the foundation for a self-consistent and plausible, innovative, and progressive theory of a worthwhile society and how to build it. Though Gandhi's concept of wealth "trusteeship" is unpromising, two corollaries of his non-violent philosophy become cornerstones of India's distinctive political vision: "Gandhian socialism." One is *sarvodaya,* construction of egalitarian village communities. The other is *satyagraha*, non-violent confrontation as method of social change.

Parts IV and V trace the impact of Gandhi's ideas upon Indian socialists rooted in Marxism. Here lies the emergence of a distinctive school of thought that can be called "Gandhian socialism." Part IV explores "partial" Gandhian socialism by way of Asoka Mehta, Narendra Deva and Jawaharlal Nehru. "Partial" implies not inferior thought, but rather a somewhat piece-meal way of fusing Gandhian notions with socialist ones.

Part V explores "thorough" Gandhian socialism by way of Ramanohar Lohia and J. P. Narayan. These two differ from those in Part IV by the self-consciousness and ambitiousness with which they set about articulating a Gandhian socialism. They are also distinct in their strong emphases on religious themes, issues and ideas.

The Conclusion briefly considers some previously unaddressed questions on Hindu-Muslim conflict and on the emergence, shortfalls, limits and significance of Gandhian socialism. There are two reasons for study of modern Indian thought in terms of the patterned problematic outlined here. It serves to clarify the distinctive concerns and ambitions of the thinkers involved, both individually and collectively. It also augments our own thinking about social matters, underscoring crucial issues and making accessible some serious reflection on them. The study's ultimate purpose is to emphasize interdependence of the material and the spiritual in social matters. This theme raises analogies both Marxist and theological that may warrant brief comment.

A Marxist analogy arises from my bisection of social matters into a "material" realm of productivity and a "spiritual" realm of religion, culture, and values. This may recall Marx's distinction of economic "base" from ideocultural "superstructure." Marx sees causal linkage from productive arrangements to religious and cultural values. The tradition explored here departs from dogmatic versions of that paradigm, ones that portray ideocultural superstructure as causally determined by a dominant material base. To thinkers examined here, such views underestimate both possibilities for ideological change within an existing productive order and the necessity of such change in creating new ones.

The theme of spiritual-material interdependence may also bring to mind a theological analogy: incarnation. Gandhi's thought implicitly entails a theory of incarnation—penetration of the material by the spiritual. For Gandhi, incarnation is no single event or series of events, but rather an ongoing transfiguration of the material by the spiritual, through which human affairs grow progressively moralized. This spiritualizing process reaches into the material sphere of production and presses for moral transformation there. Incarnation thereby "embodies" spiritual values in the material sphere, replacing exploitational arrangements by moralized ones. Gandhi's thought rebukes doctrines of incarnation that fail to seek moralized productive arrangements.

PART I

ORIGINS OF A PROBLEMATIC

CHAPTER 1

Vivekananda: Socialism and the Reconceptualization of Hindu Religion

Uninvited walk-on rock star at the World Parliament of Religions, Swami Vivekananda (1863-1902) was born in Calcutta with the given name Narendranath Dutt. He was the son of a successful attorney. In 1881, during his college education in Calcutta, Vivekananda first encountered the ecstatic mystical prophet Ramakrishna. Vivekananda's relationship with Ramakrishna deepened after Vivekananda's college education, upon the death of Vivekananda's father in 1884.

Between 1884 and 1893, Vivekananda divided his time among his discipleship to Ramakrishna, work at various jobs to support his family, and wanderings throughout India. In 1893, he addressed Chicago's World Parliament of Religions, where his speech brought him instant celebrity. He toured the United States lecture circuit until 1895, then travelled by way of England, continental Europe and Ceylon (Sri Lanka) back to India, arriving in 1897. It was in 1897 that Vivekananda launched a social service organization known as the Ramakrishna Mission. In 1899, he voyaged again to the West, returning to India fatigued and ill the following year. He thereafter remained in India, lecturing and writing insofar as his health permitted until his death.

His journey to the West in 1893 represented a mission unprecedented among Indian social reformers. He sought both to propagate Indian religious ideas and to secure funding for relief programs targeting the plight of India's downtrodden masses. His subsequent shuttling between India and the West exemplified a turn in modern Indian sensibilities, and his writings mark a new era in Indian thought.

Throughout most of the nineteenth century, Indian thinkers had investigated a broad range of religious and social issues, motivated by desire to purge Hindu society of beliefs and practices inappropriate to contemporary challenges or to their conceptions of Hinduism's essential genius. Arguments flared and movements emerged in a surge of visionary activity unprecedented since the days of medieval Bhakti. Issues various and vital demanded attention: the meaning or meaninglessness of ritual, the true nature of caste, the oppression and liberation of women, for example. It remained, however, for Vivekananda to focus on one of India's most glaring ills: poverty, degradation and subjugation among most of India's vast population.

"I am a socialist" proclaimed Vivekananda,[1] the first major Indian social thinker to do so.[2] He devotes great attention to the misery of India's "masses." No Indian thinker before him had stressed, as he did, urgent need to eradicate mass poverty.[3] After Vivekananda, no Indian thinker could ignore issues of poverty, exploitation and socialism.

It was not merely the fact but also the manner of this new concern that made Vivekananda's career paradigmatic. His travels between India and the West manifested fervor to forge some synthesis of Indian spiritual and Western material cultures. The way forward for India and perhaps all humanity lay in achieving a progressive material culture harmonizing rather than conflicting with Indian spirituality. Vivekananda's dream was to become the dream of an entire era.

THE AMBIGUOUS SIGNIFICANCE OF SOCIAL ACTION

One striking feature of Vivekananda's thought is its ambivalence on the religious meaning of progressive social action. Vivekananda pays official allegiance to certain classical Indian conceptions of religious life. The ultimate religious task, he claims, is personal spiritual liberation, conceived as escape from a meaningless conventional world into a transcendental dimension of awareness. Escape from the conventional world is, among other things, an escape from society, conceived as a realm of transient, illusory and ultimately meaningless relationships. He rejects the notion of social progress: how could there be "progress" in such a transient and meaningless realm? The balance of social ill and good remains forever constant, despite manifold apparent changes. Social "evil" and social "good" reflect aspects of worldly *maya*, matters of illusion and ultimate irrelevance from the standpoint of true spiritual insight.[4]

Why then should anyone engage in any kind of social action? Vivekananda suggests that the value of social action lies exclusively in contributing to personal spiritual liberation. The most captivating aspect of conventional reality or maya is preoccupation with concerns of one's worldly self. Social action entailing personal sacrifice helps the individual achieve liberation from such bonds of worldly ego-centricity. Vivekananda repeatedly speaks of the world as a moral "gymnasium" in which individuals can strengthen their spiritual natures through exercises of self-sacrificial social action.[5]

Vivekananda seems on the surface unaware of any contradiction in advocating self-sacrifice for a society that cannot thereby benefit. "Self-sacrifice" implies a preference for a wider social good over a narrower personal one. This makes no sense if the possibility of wider social good is denied.

Though Vivekananda may not see the contradiction logically, he surely feels it existentially. He could not devote so much concern to alleviating social miseries without feeling positive transformation to be both possible and intrinsically worthwhile. He cannot, despite himself, resist the notion that the very pinnacle of religious life lies in social action. "I have realized…" he writes at one point, "that altruistic service only is religion, the rest…are madness—even it is wrong to hanker after one's own salvation." (sic).[6] It is rare for Vivekananda to voice this viewpoint so explicitly. Far more typical are comments that "[O]ne must completely mold one's religious life in solitude," and that "All the work you do…is done for your own benefit."[7] He endorses classical notions of a sharp divide between social engagement and the highest religious life. Occasional comments, however, along with the sheer scope of his social concern, indicate Vivekananda wrestling with radical notions: that the true meaning of religion is society and that the highest religious life lies in working for progressive social change.

SOCIAL CHANGE BY AND FOR THE DOWNTRODDEN

Vivekananda's writings contain curious passages in which he rails against Indian advocates of "social reform." Such passages at first appear reactionary, but in fact they represent a radical new approach to Indian social change. The problem with so-called "social reformers," according to Vivekananda, is that they merely criticize specific ills in hopes of provoking changes in habits. Vivekananda finds this approach naïve: people do not change their practices just because they have been plausibly criticized. "A few men who think that certain things are evil will not make a nation move," he writes.[8]

Social change, he thinks, can be catalyzed, but not engineered. Masses of people must, through their own experience and reflection, create new ways of organizing their lives. True social reform requires augmenting the power of the "masses" to reflect and to act. Vivekananda writes:

> It takes time, quite a long time, to make a healthy, strong, public opinion which will solve its own problems… The whole problem of social reform, therefore,

resolves itself into this: Where are those who want reform? Make them first... First educate the nation... First create the power, the sanction from which the law will so ring.[9]

The masses require education and power. Hence, for Vivekananda, meaningful reform requires revolutionizing society's fundamental order, an order of hierarchical exploitation:

To the reformers I will point out that I am a greater reformer than any one of them. They want to reform only little bits. I want root-and-branch reform. Where we differ is in the Method... Most of the reforms that have been agitated for during the past century have been ornamental. Every one of these reforms only touches the first two castes, and no other. The question of widow marriage would not touch seventy per cent of the Indian women, and all such questions only reach the higher castes of Indian people who are educated, mark you, at the expense of the masses. But that is no reformation. You must go down to the basis of the thing, to the very root of the matter. That is what I call radical reform.[10]

Vivekananda seldom misses an opportunity to emphasize the plight of India's poor or to condemn systems of exploitation that oppress them. "The one thing that is at the root of all evils in India is the condition of the poor," he writes,[11] as he describes their condition:

(C)lusters of huts, with crumbling mud-walls... (M)oving about...emaciated figures of young and old in tattered rags, whose faces bear deep-cut lines of the despair and poverty of years...the pitiful gaze of lustreless eyes of the hunger-stricken… Devastation by violent plague and cholera; malaria eating into the very vitals of the nation; starvation and semi-starvation as second nature; the Kurukshetra (battlefield) of malady and misery… A conglomeration of three hundred million souls, resembling men only in appearance, crushed out of life by being downtrodden by their own people and by foreign nations…[12]

Vivekananda points to the caste system and imperialism, "priest power and foreign conquest," as twin causes of mass impoverishment.[13] In Marx-like fashion, he analyzes both caste and imperialism as systems of exploitation in which the downtrodden produce wealth but do not own or enjoy it. He writes of the "tyranny of the higher castes,"[14] in which:

The cultivator got almost nothing… The protector came to be known as the king; he who took the commodities from one place to another was the merchant. These two did not produce anything—but still snatched away the best part of things and made themselves fat by virtually reaping most of the fruit of the cultivator's toil and labor.[15]

Elsewhere, he writes of "the peasant, the shoemaker, the sweeper, and such other lower classes of India, who through the ages have been producing the entire wealth of the land," while non-producing classes "have taken the substantial part of the fruits of their labour."[16]

A similar analysis applies to British rule, of which he writes "the main idea is blood-sucking."[17] "Indian labor and produce" could support the entire nation in material comfort, "if the whole thing is not taken off from them."[18] Instead, India suffers at the hands of the British, who have "carried away with them millions of our money, while our people have starved by villages and provinces."[19] Vivekananda argues that though famine seldom visits parts of India still free from British rule, it occurs as the "inevitable consequence" of exploitation in British-ruled India.[20]

Keen to alleviate the plight of India's poor masses, Vivekananda organizes resources and activities of the Ramakrishna Mission. He urges followers to "devote heart and soul to this one duty—the duty of raising the masses of India."[21] Borrowing from ancient religious notions of foreswearing normal pursuits in favor of spiritual seeking, he urges a life of *sannyasa* (renunciation) for his followers, who should subdue all private desires in order to serve the masses: "Vow, then, to devote your whole lives to the cause of these three hundred millions."[22]

Less than clear as to what activities these *sannyasins* of service should pursue, Vivekananda focuses most concretely on education. He imagines bands of "disinterested sannyasins, bent on doing good to others," going from village to village, "disseminating education and seeking in various ways to better the condition of all…"[23] The instruction should emphasize religion, as well as the "arts of life."[24] His images of instruction to offer seem sketchy:

> Make an organized plan. A few cameras, some maps, globes, and some chemicals, etc., are needed. The next thing you want is a big hut. Then you must get together a number of poor, indigent folk. Having done all this, show them pictures to teach them astronomy, geography, etc., and preach Sri Ramakrishna to them.[25]

Along with abstract learning should go enhancement of productive skills: the discovery of "new avenues of production" through "exertions aided by Western science," enabling villagers to "produce food and clothing for themselves."[26]

Vivekananda imagines that such efforts will spark mass movements so as to "revolutionize the whole country."[27] Villagers will join the educational movement, accelerating expansion of knowledge and problem-solving capacity.[28] Vivekananda's philosophy of change includes almost no analysis of specific problems or how to solve them. He explains his entire approach with a formula: "(E)ducate our people, so that they may be able to solve their own problems."[29] There is undoubted naïveté in this vision of mass liberation through mere education. In discerning the need for village mobilization, however, Vivekananda points out an approach which, in the hands of Gandhi and some of his followers, becomes a rich philosophy of transformation.

Exploitation, Vivekananda thinks, will ultimately cease with the triumph of socialism. In Marx-like fashion, he associates socialism with rule by the laboring class or *Shudras*. Like Marx, he sees the triumph of labor historically destined: "(A) time will come when…the Shudra class *with their Shudrahood*…will gain absolute supremacy in every society."[30] Again like Marx, he sees labor's impending triumph as the crowning phase in an historical succession of rule by different classes. For Vivekananda, these correspond to the four *varnas* (caste groupings) of classical Indian social thought: "(H)uman society is in turn governed by the four castes—the priests, the soldiers, the traders, and the laborers."[31] He thinks of capitalism as rule by the commercial or *Vaishya* caste, "awful in its silent crushing and blood-sucking power…"[32] He associates British imperial rule with Vaishya hegemony.[33]

"Last will come the laborer rule," writes Vivekananda, and he applauds this as the end to economic exploitation.[34] Yet he is less than fully enthusiastic about this triumph of socialism. He sees socialism as a system or doctrine with something important missing. "I am a socialist not because I think it is a perfect system, but half a loaf is better than no bread."[35] Nowhere does he articulate in detail what he means by the "half a loaf" that socialism fails to provide. He indicates, however, that socialism—though essential from a purely economic standpoint—lacks moral or spiritual dimensions crucial to worthwhile social life. Of socialism he writes: "Its advantages will be the distribution of physical comforts—its disadvantages, (perhaps) the lowering of culture."[36] By "the lowering of culture," he means decline in morality, which is decline in essential religion:

> Everything goes to show that Socialism...is coming on the boards. The people will certainly want the satisfaction of their material needs, less work, no oppression, no war, more food. What guarantee have we that this civilization will last, unless it is based on religion, on the goodness of man? Depend on it, religion goes to the root of the matter. If it is right, all is right.[37]

Vivekananda insists that ancient *Vedantic* (philosophically scriptural) Hinduism is the "right" religion for socialism: "(E)qualising theories must have a spiritual basis, and that spiritual basis is the Vedanta only."[38] To understand this, we need to explore his interpretation of Vedanta. This will prove helpful when we touch on other thinkers as well.

KANTIAN ADVAITA AND SPIRITUALIZED SOCIALISM

Vivekananda's Vedanta centers on *Advaita*, the philosophy of universal non-dualism, explanation of which occupies much of Vivekananda's effort. It is crucial to understand the Advaitic doctrine of selfhood as Vivekananda interprets it.

Advaita, he observes, asserts a non-dual theory of selfhood. There may appear to be a plenitude of selves in the world, but this is an illusion. There is, in reality, only one unitary and universal Self, in which all the many separate and particular "selves" merely participate.[39]

Classical Advaita, it has often been claimed, makes no strong pronouncements in ethics and morals. The goal is private salvation, not the well-being of others. Liberation, insight on the non-duality of Selfhood, consists in gnosis, or knowledge, not moral action. Vivekananda's striking reinterpretation links the Advaitic doctrine of Selfhood with a theory of morality.

Morality for Vivekananda concerns two basic questions: what is moral action? and why should one practice it? His simple answer to the first question is : "(T)he only definition that can be given of morality is that: That which is selfish is immoral, and that which is unselfish is moral."[40] His answer to the second question involves Advaitic interpretation of "selfish" and "unselfish." Selfishness, concern for private well-being over general well-being, self-defeatingly posits an illusory, separate, and particular "self," over the true and universal Self. In reality, however, there is no well-being apart from general well-being. Unselfishness pursues general well-being, the only true well-being. We learn why one should act morally: because only moral action promotes true well-being.[41] True well-being, general well-being, advances only through unselfish action.

Borrowing from classical Advaitic philosophy, Vivekananda explains how humans naturally but mistakenly identify their well-being with illusory private selfhood. An illusion of isolated and particular "selfhood" arises from entanglement of universal Selfhood in the material world. There the Self inhabits particular bodies creating illusion of distinction and separation. The universal Self makes contact with nature through the sense experience of these illusory selves. This entanglement with nature, the sense experience of illusory separate selves, is root cause of selfishness. Well-being mistakenly seems identified with the body's sensual enjoyment in the world of nature.[42]

If pursuit of private well-being is illusion, it is also unfreedom. Selfishness is a life of slavery to sense experience, desire, and satisfaction. Vivekananda's interpretation of Advaita owes much to Kant. For Vivekananda as for Kant, morality and freedom are one and the same. Like Kant, Vivekananda conceives of nature as a realm of determination and unfreedom. In nature, events follow laws of causality that allow no variation. There is therefore no freedom in the world of nature. Human beings, through their bodies, inhabit this enslaved realm, part of nature and therefore subject to determined causality. Human action tied to nature through the body can never be free.[43] In particular, human action is unfree if determined by sensual imperatives of the illusory separate self. Sensually determined action, selfishness, unfreedom: these are equivalent.

Freedom, by contrast, lies in control of the sensual passions by the will, which is spiritual. Freedom lies in action not dictated by nature.[44] Free action is moral action, aimed at general rather than private well-being. "That action is moral which frees us from the bondage of matter and vice versa," writes Vivekananda.[45] Pursuit of private well-being can yield only frustration because sensual desire is ultimately insatiable, only inflamed by temporary satisfaction. "Desire is infinite, its fulfillment limited," Vivekananda writes.[46] "The satisfaction of desire only increases it, as oil poured on fire but makes it burn more fiercely."[47]

To Vivekananda, true well-being implies a liberation from nature. This requires restraint upon sensual passions and material enjoyment. As with Kant, freedom requires self-restraint, exercise of power by will over nature. "No freedom without renunciation," writes Vivekananda.[48] As also with Kant, this freedom is equivalent to morality.

Vivekananda's interpretation of Advaita provides socialism with an appropriate "spiritual basis." Socialism seeks an end to exploitation. Exploitation and social inequality, thinks Vivekananda, are ultimately rooted in "selfishness," slavery to inherently limitless material desire:

> There is a limit to the working power of human beings, but no limit to desire; so we strive to get hold of the working power of others and enjoy the fruits of their labors, escaping work ourselves.[49]

By explaining roots of selfishness in Advaitic terms as spiritual error and its consequences in Marxist terms as drive to command the labor of others, Vivekananda shows the mutual relevance of Vedantic religion and socialism.

To Vivekananda, the main shortcoming of most socialist doctrine lies in failure to identify and attack exploitation at its root: spiritual error. Advaita, urging restraint on material passions and preference for general well-being, attacks the root of exploitation and motivates effort to build a socialist order. Sannyasins of service exemplify Advaitic renunciation as they work for social transformation.

If Advaita is crucial to actualizing socialism, the reverse is also true. Vivekananda tirelessly insists on the emptiness of spiritual values not exemplified and fostered by concrete social institutions. He writes, "That society is the greatest, where the highest truths become practical."[50] His thought weakens, however, when he tries to imagine the incarnation of non-exploitation in "practical" arrangements.

AMBIVALENT SOCIOLOGY

Vivekananda's exploration of the "practical" consists primarily of scattered commentaries on Indian and Western social arrangements. The bulk of these consists of two overlapping types: 1) contrasts of Indian and Western society; and 2) discussions of caste.

Societies, holds Vivekananda, can be distinguished from each other based on particular aptitudes for exploring and solving different sorts of problems. Hence every society displays a distinctive genius accounting for much of its overall character.[51] To Vivekananda, the crucial distinction lies in contrast between Indian and Western societies. Indian society, he urges, is essentially spiritual, Western society primarily materialistic. India specializes in spiritual progress, the West in material progress.[52]

Western materialism, thinks Vivekananda, inevitably fosters both exploitation and dissatisfaction. He sees Western capitalism as the apotheosis of exploitation and dissatisfaction rooted in a materialist approach to life. Capitalist wealth has "not solved the problem of want, but only made it keener."[53] Pursuit of material enjoyment brings no satisfaction, but only a greater quantum of desire.[54] Accumulations of capital and productive power merely expand the power of selfish impulses. Hence, capitalism achieves record heights of exploitation and antagonism:

> The material tyranny is tremendous. The wealth and power of a country are in the hands of a few men who do not work but manipulate the work of millions of human beings. By this power they can deluge the whole earth with blood…[55]

Vivekananda maintains that the West cannot alleviate this appalling state of affairs through its own spiritual resources. Many Westerners, he maintains, have grown weary of the "competition," the "struggle," the "brutality of their commercial civilization." He presumably has socialism in mind when he writes that "they are looking forward towards something better," calling for "political and social changes" as "panacea" for capitalist ills.[56]

Vivekananda finds little promise in what he sees as the narrowly institutional approach of most socialists, who expect progress from mere "political or social manipulation." It is "spiritual culture and ethical culture," he thinks, that the West needs in order to remedy its civilizational defects.[57] Only India, with its rich reservoir of "spiritual culture," can provide Western culture what it needs. "The nations of the West are coming to us for spiritual help," he writes.[58] The West must "learn from India the conquest of internal nature."[59]

India meanwhile stands in danger of infection by Western materialism. The "curse of the West—the senses," has been "creeping into India," contaminating Indian culture with "luxurious ideals," he writes. India must "keep a firm hold on spirituality." To adopt the "materializing civilization of the West" courts moral ruin.[61]

Despite these moral hazards, Vivekaranda insists that India embrace greater materialism. What is most dangerous is also most necessary.

India's poverty and exploitation cannot be alleviated without massive attention to problems of production:

> We talk foolishly against material civilization… Material civilization, nay, even luxury, is necessary to create work for the poor. Bread! Bread!… India is to be raised, the poor are to be fed, education is to be spread, and the evil of priestcraft is to be removed. No priestcraft, no social tyranny! More bread, more opportunity for everybody.[62]

There is obvious perplexity in Vivekananda's mind as he alternately condemns and praises "luxury" and "material civilization." Socialism's practical requirements clash with its spiritual ones. Vivekananda attempts to resolve this dilemma through formula and conceptual compromise. In order to reap benefits while avoiding pitfalls, he advises that "material civilization" be adopted in moderate amount: "A little of it, perhaps, is good for us."[63] The notion of moderate materialism is a fertile one, but only insofar as it transcends Vivekananda's quick Goldilocks epiphany. Some thinkers explored below improve on this at least somewhat, offering spiritual discussions and productive proposals around themes of moderate materialism. On a related note, Vivekananda imagines a sort of hybrid of India and the West, producing a society progressive both materially and spiritually. "Can you make a European society with India's religion? I believe it is possible, and must be."[64] A blend of Indian spirituality with Western material culture becomes a paradigm for later thinkers. Vivekananda articulates the paradigm but does not go far in applying it.

Vivekananda's dilemmas grow more convoluted when he turns to the issue of caste. Caste, according to Vivekananda, is a system of exploitation. It is also Vedantic religion's most prominent social feature. Hence, caste is an obvious embarrassment for asserting Vedantic religion as key antidote to exploitation.

The simplest evasion is to deny any link between Advaitic spirituality and caste. "In religion," Vivekananda writes, "there is no caste; caste is simply a social institution."[65] Caste is nothing more than hereditary division of labor, comparable to networks of trade guilds.[66] It is a mere practical arrangement, devoid of religious meaning. Vivekananda warns that exaggerated ritual aspects of caste have nearly destroyed religion. "What more degradation can there be," he writes, "than that the greatest minds of a country have been discussing about the kitchen for several hundreds of years, discussing whether I may touch you or you touch me, and what is the penance for this touching!"[67] Vivekananda bemoans these bizarre preoccupations:

> We are neither Vedantists, most of us now, nor Pauranics, nor Tantrics. We are just "Don't touchists." Our religion is in the kitchen. Our God is the cooking pot, and our religion is, "Don't touch me, I am holy." If this goes on for another century, every one of us will be in a lunatic asylum.[68]

Vivekananda wavers, however, in separating religion and caste. He seeks in various ways to portray caste as an element in Vedantic religion's moral and anti-exploitative genius. He portrays caste, for example, as an orientation in social life toward general well-being in communities rather than private well-being as individuals. Caste therefore exerts a moralizing influence in contrast with Western culture's encouragement of selfishness:

> You Western people are individualistic. I want to do this thing because I like it; I will elbow everyone. Why? Because I like to. I want my own satisfaction... So what is the basis of India's social order? It is the caste law. I am born for the caste, I live for the caste. Born in the caste,

the whole life must be lived according to caste regulation. In other words...the Western man is born individualistic, while the Hindu is socialistic—entirely socialistic.[69]

In discouraging selfish individualism, the "socialist" spirit of caste protects the weak from exploitation. This it does by fostering cooperative rather than antagonistic economic relationships:

> Competition—cruel, cold, and heartless—is the law of Europe. Our law is caste—the breaking of competition, checking its forces, mitigating its cruelties...[71]

The notion of caste as protector of the weak departs strikingly from Vivekananda's portrayal of caste elsewhere as a system of exploitation. Contradiction emerges even more sharply when Vivekananda pictures caste as a hierarchy of renunciation, with higher-placed groups cultivating morality and spirituality through material self-restraint:

> The higher the caste, the greater the restrictions. The lowest caste people can eat and drink anything they like. But as men rise in the social scale, more and more restrictions come...[72]

This hierarchy of material renunciation culminates with *Brahmins*, "the poorest of all the classes in the country," says Vivekananda, "who never covet wealth."[73] Vivekananda's sociology breaks down in his attempt to defend Vedantic religion as a source of moralizing and even "socialist" institutions. Caste as a hierarchy of renunciation integrates poorly with caste as a hierarchy of exploitation.

This contradiction in Vivekananda's doctrine of caste points toward subtler problems in his theories of social change and democracy. With such contradictory views on the nature of caste, Vivekananda cannot help but equivocate on the question of eradicating it. In one voice, he argues that caste is "bondage," and India's "greatest dividing factor."[74] Caste is "a barrier to India's progress. It narrows, restricts, separates."[75] In another voice, he insists that, "caste is a very good thing,"[76] "one of the greatest social institutions" ever devised.[77] For India, "caste is the plan we want to follow,"[78] because it is "destined to lead Indian humanity to its goal."[79] Though Vivekananda's views are deeply unsettled, he occasionally hints at a reconciliation. He imagines preserving caste as division of labor but destroying it as a system of exploitation. The division of labor will operate without such "privileges" as allow higher castes to "trample" on lower ones.[80]

Eradication of exploitation does not, for Vivekananda, necessarily imply eradication of hierarchy. There will, it seems, be some castes to rule society and do its intellectual work, others to do its menial work.[81] Though somewhat ambiguously, Vivekananda supports the notion that such divisions be based on aptitude and merit rather than birth.[82]

Vivekananda envisions a sort of hierarchical socialism in which power differentials exist, but without exploitation. Such is his picture of the ancient caste system, prior to corruption by high-caste oppression and exploitation.[83] He imagines a revival of that old order, such that Brahmins would once again exemplify renunciatory values and virtues, while tutoring lower groups progressively in them:

> The plan in India is to make everybody a Brahmin, the Brahmin being the ideal of humanity. If you read the history of India, you will find that attempts have always been made to raise the lower classes. Many are classes that have been raised. Many more will follow till the whole will become Brahmin. That is the plan. We have only to raise them without bringing down anybody. And this has mostly to be done by the Brahmins themselves…[84]

One difficulty with this hierarchical vision is that it contradicts Vivekananda's other model of progress: mass action by the dispossessed, culminating in a Shudra regime of popular self-rule. Vivekananda the revivalist is at odds with Vivekananda the revolutionary. To be sure, Vivekananda hints that a truly egalitarian order would perhaps emerge from the system of hierarchical socialism and elite-managed change.[85] Moreover, the two models can partially be reconciled through his notion of elite-sponsored education transmitting spiritual and material wherewithal that the downtrodden require so as to improve their own lives. The moral ascendancy of Brahmin-hood dovetails with the social ascendancy of Shudra-hood.

There is, nevertheless, a disturbing paternalistic flavor to Vivekananda's hierarchical socialism, a flavor poorly concealed by his naive faith in the liberating power of mere education. Education initiated by the elite will "slowly and gently" alleviate oppression.[86] Meanwhile, there must be no direct attack upon exploitational arrangements. Vivekananda admonishes activists to "take care not to set up class-strife between the poor peasants, the laboring people, and wealthy classes."[87] No direct attack is needed because the exploitative order is historically destined to disappear through the activity of the upper classes.

Vivekananda argues that the historical role of a ruling class is to "dig its own grave"—pave the way to its own demise and toward eventual end of exploitation.[88] This seems to borrow from Marxism, but there is a crucial difference between a Marxist formulation and Vivekananda's. In Marxist theory, there is a cunning to history by which a ruling class, precisely through pursuit of selfish class-bound interests, unwittingly creates conditions leading to its own demise and replacement by a successor dominant class. Vivekananda, by contrast, imagines ruling classes consciously pursuing their own demise as rulers by lending generous assistance to lower classes.[89] Though the Marxist theory may be untrue, it is certainly more plausible than Vivekananda's naivete.

The sophistication Vivekananda brings to bear when criticizing piece-meal approaches to social reform deserts him when he envisions the moral regeneration of India's ruling classes. As Vivekananda himself notes, groups do not yield their ways of life simply because reformers have criticized them.

ELEMENTS OF DEMOCRACY

There is, fortunately, a strong democratic thrust to Vivekananda's thought that perhaps outweighs his hierarchical fancies. Contrary to his hierarchical socialism, Vivekananda also puts forward a vision of democratic self-rule, with strong and widespread popular participation at its core. In this voice, Vivekananda rejects an ideology of benevolent hierarchy:

> Being always governed by kings of godlike nature, to whom is left the whole duty of protecting and providing for the people, they can never get any occasion for understanding the principles of self-government.[90]

At least three interrelated ills flow from this shortfall of popular self-government. First, it stifles initiative, that "inherent strength and energy" needed to solve common problems. Second, it dilutes morality, constraining active popular concern with and pursuit of the "common good."[91] Third, it blocks the downtrodden from acquiring power they need to fend off exploitation. On this third point, Vivekananda asserts a democratic sentiment that all should "gain the right of representation in the control of State revenues and expenditure," which are after all collected by the government from the people.[92] Democratic rule, he suggests, succeeds better than even the most benevolent hierarchy in maximizing initiative and morality and in minimizing exploitation.

Vivekananda worries about the feebleness of democracy in Indian civilization:

> Neither under the Hindu kings, nor under the Buddhist rule, do we find the common subject-people taking any part in expressing their voice in the affairs of the State… (T)he subjects… have no direct voice in the supreme government. The power of the populace is struggling to express itself in indirect and disorderly ways without any method. The people have not as yet the conscious knowledge of the existence of this power. There is neither the attempt on their part to organize it into a united action, nor have they got the will to do so…[93]

This lack of democracy troubles him in particular because it blurs his notion of India's special genius in promoting spiritual virtue. With caste, his problem is explaining the moral and anti-exploitative genius of a prevailing institution. With democracy, his problem is to deal with absence of a presumably moral and anti-exploitative institution.

Vivekananda attacks the latter problem by insisting that Indian culture is not totally devoid of democratic experience:

> "That the government of the people of this country must be by the people and for the good of the people"—cannot however be said to have been totally unrecognized in ancient India. The Greek travellers and others saw many independent small States scattered all over this country, and references are found to this effect in many places of the Buddhistic literature. And there cannot be the least doubt about it that the germ of self-government was at least present in the shape of the village Panchayat, which is still to be found in existence in many places of India… In the religious communities, among Sannyasins in the Buddhist monasteries, we have ample evidence to show that self-government was fully developed.[94]

Here Vivekananda identifies three distinct strands of "ancient democracy," which subsequent thinkers also highlight in similar effort to prove India's democratic genius. There is, first, "ancient republics": small, independent states that existed primarily in Mauryan and Gupta times, practicing a form of democratic government through periodic citizen assemblies. There is, second, the notion of democratic village self-government in pre-British times by *panchayats*, councils or representatives chosen by residents. There is, third, democratic habits and procedures within organized settlements of ancient heterodox religious movements, especially Buddhism. Elsewhere, Vivekananda adds a fourth element, lending a "socialist" dimension to his picture of ancient democracy:

> All the land from time immemorial was nationalized, as you say—belonged to the Government. There never is any private right in land. The revenue in India comes from the land, because every man holds so much land from the Government. This land is held in common by a community, it may be five, ten, twenty, or a hundred families. They govern the whole of the land, pay a certain amount of revenue to the Government, maintain a physician, a village schoolmaster, and so on.[95]

Though anxious to make the case for India's democratic talents, Vivekananda frankly concedes their limitations:

> (T)he germ of self-government…remained forever the germ; the seed though put into the ground never grew into a tree. This idea of self-government never passed beyond the embryo state…and never spread into society at large.[96]

Later thinkers, especially Aurobindo, show less modesty in claims about India's "ancient democracy." Significantly, Vivekananda's ancient examples—the intimate republic, the village, and the religious settlement—all feature democracy in contexts of smallish community. Later thinkers will highlight this, developing the notion that though pre-modern India never experienced Western-style national democracy, it harbored genius in what some might call "decentralized democracy."

PART II

Contested Hinduisms and Failed Syntheses

CHAPTER 2

Bhagavan Das: Theosophy and Guild Socialism

Learned Theosophist and Manu revivalist, Bhagavan Das (1869-1958) was born in Benares (U.P.), son of a scholar and founder of various voluntary organizations and schools. By 1885, Das had earned bachelor's and master's degrees from Calcutta University through Queen's College, Benares. He joined government service in 1890 and resigned in 1898, thereafter pursuing a career in scholarship and civic activity.

In the course of his career, Das published a number of works interpreting and applying ancient Hindu religious and philosophical learning. In his early career, Das's interests brought him into close association with the Theosophical Society. In 1916, he helped establish Benares Hindu University and in 1921, he founded the Kashi Vidyapith, becoming its first Chancellor and serving also as Professor of Philosophy. Also in 1921, he was sentenced to a one-year prison term for participation in boycott activity surrounding a visit by the Prince of Wales to India. Though popular agitation secured his early release in 1922, Das elected to maintain self-detention at Kashi Vidyapith for the remainder of his term.

Das retired from daily responsibilities in 1925 but continued his scholarly pursuits and civic activities for the rest of his life. During this period, his concerns included work to improve Hindu-Muslim rela-tionships and to secure humane treatment of Untouchables.

Das's thought embodies the best and worst of early twentieth-cen-tury Theosophy. It is impressively erudite and shows influence of wide reading. On social issues, in particular, there is considerable familiarity with contemporary Western thought and thorough expertise in Manu's legal doctrine, *dharmasastra*. There is, as is typical with Theosophy, a synthetic character to the thought that sometimes borders on the gran-diose and a cosmopolitanism that borders on credulousness. Das loads his writings with extensive quotations from books that attract him. These quotes reveal much about the nature and range of ideas he tries to incorporate. They also help highlight the problematic character of his synthetic endeavors. He tries to harmonize radically incompatible clusters of ideas. He typically shows little critical awareness of such in-consistencies, with the result that they get ignored, glossed over or re-solved in formulaic ways that strain plausibility.

ILLUSORY ESCAPE FROM PURE RELIGIOUS IDEOLOGY

Das's social thought, written mostly during the 30s, appears primarily in two major works: *Ancient versus Modern "Scientific Socialism"* and *The Science of Social Organization*. These two works comprise a unified ar-gument that modern social problems can best be resolved through re-vival of ancient principles contained in the Laws of Manu. Das sees Manu as a complete and self-sufficient repository of social wisdom. Other social ideologies, through ignorance of Manu, display inevitable quotients of error.

In the opening pages of *Ancient versus Modern "Scientific Socialism,"* Das conceptualizes his task explicitly in terms of what I have called the problematic. He repudiates pure religious ideology, insisting that ac-tualization of spiritual goals requires creating appropriate productive and social organization:

It is not enough to Subjectively and sentimentally *feel* Universal Brotherhood. Nor is it enough even to see that the Golden Rule of Ethics… enunciated by the scriptures of all the great religions, describes the *practice* of which Universal Brotherhood is the *theory*. It is necessary to work out a fresh *Technique*, a modified old or wholly new *Scheme of Social Organization*… This technique must be such as would make it possible for the Golden Rule to become objectively and actually operative, as would make Universal Brotherhood *practicable*, would make it *feasible* to change Society, under the existing industrial, mechanical and urban conditions (assuming, as we must, that they cannot be wholly abolished so as to leave behind only pastoral, agricultural, and rural ones) from its present basis of grossly iniquitous and excessively individualist capitalism and the subservient militarism and imperialism, to the basis of a really equitable (not any impossible *equal or exactly similar*) sharing, by all and each, in the world's work as well as the world's good things, its necessaries, comforts, luxuries, and enjoyments.[1]

After so stating the problem, Das proposes Manu's *varnashrama*, caste and life-stage, social scheme as its solution. Critical of vague spiritualities in visualizing reform, Das characterizes Manu as a precise, concrete, timeless and gapless scheme of social relations. Unlike, for example, five-year plans applicable to a particular society at a given moment, Manu provides a "permanent" plan, applicable to "the whole of the Human Race" at all times. Neither partial nor incomplete, Manu's scheme is humanity's only "systematic and complete Plan" for social organization.[2] Insistence on Manu's gapless character weakens Das's thought, provoking strange interpretations and insupportable assertions. Repudiating spiritual vagueness, Das steers into an opposite ditch—exaggerated concreteness glued to Manu's detailed formulas. From there he over-corrects again, back toward disembodied spirituality. While criticizing pure religious ideology, Das also rejects materialist socialism. "(G)enuine socialism," he contends, is "helplessly *rooted in genuine Religion*."[3] Rather than pin itself to material issues, socialism should embrace even mysticism, religion's most metaphysical aspect. "For Socialism to quarrel with Mysticism is to deny its parent," writes Das. "There is no Socialism possible without Universal Brotherhood; and there is no Universal Brotherhood possible without the Universal Self—the recognition of which is the acme of Mysticism."[4]

For Das, Manu's varnashrama society represents a "spiritual socialism," inspired equally by religious insight and practical wisdom. He sets about elucidating the spiritual and practical advantages of varnashrama over modern ideologies.

One difficulty is to imagine social processes that might bring varnashrama to actuality. Das offers little except cultivation of a moral and spiritual elite that would teach and legislate in accord with right values.[5] He makes no attempt to show how contemporary groups might solve practical problems through varnashrama. Such scenarios, if offered, would suffer from implausibility, which is perhaps why Das avoids them. Unable to connect it with any program for practical transformation, he articulates varnashrama only as an end product. Transformative action lies exclusively in cultivating sound values within a spiritual elite and transmitting them through society. This theme echoes Vivekananda and gets repeated by other thinkers examined here, especially Aurobindo, who also proposes a spiritual elite as primary motor of social progress.

Das is, despite himself, driven back into pure religious ideology. Social transformation depends predominantly on transmission of right spiritual attitudes. Das in fact insists that right spirituality, pursued through education, can eliminate social injustice:

> The men and women, all over the world, who are devoted to the worship of the Divinity of Wisdom, Science,

Learning, and are engaged in that noblest of all vocations, the vocation of teaching, of implanting right knowledge and developing righteous character...have only to add to their achievement and their work, their *vidya*, their *ilm*, the virtue of *tapasya, zohd*, resolute public spirit and philanthropy, and the holiness of asceticism and its inseparable will-power, its moral force, its spiritual all-subduing energy. As soon as they do so, the disease of the world would be cured—in a single day; the devils of greed, pride, lust, vice, would all be exorcised at once, and would take flight in fear and trembling from the hearts of the rulers, who would then become true public servants; the human world's atmosphere would be disinfected of the foul odours of Hate and become suffused with the sweet fragrance of Love, and Mankind be retransformed from "Oppressors and Oppressed" into "Protectors and Protected."[6]

Like Vivekananda, Das lays great stress on education, devoting hundreds of pages to it in *The Science of Social Organization*. His heavy emphasis on spiritual transformation through education is flip side to his failure to examine problems of practical transformation—a deficiency he claims to criticize.

Radical change from Individualism to Socialism...cannot be brought about at one stroke... but can only be gradually secured by: first the thorough education of the whole population, rulers and ruled, in the fundamental fact of non-separateness, the Unity of all Life...by the consequential change, for the better, in the general tone and spirit of each towards all...by the education of the soul of the nation in short. Then only will become

> healthily possible a redistribution of work and leisure, a
> new division of labor and the proceeds thereof...[7]

Das seems to maintain that practical transformation must await completion of spiritual transformation.

SPIRITUALITY IN THE TRUE SOCIALIST ETHOS

Like Vivekananda, Das divides human nature into two opposed motives or orientations. Materialism, egoism and individualism contrast with spirituality, altruism and socialism.[8] For example, he divides Manu's four *ashramas* or life stages into two halves. The first two ashramas, student and householder, address materialist and individualist concerns, while the second two, elder and renouncer, address spiritual and socialist ones.[9] Das likewise views family life as transmutation of physical and egoistic passions into spiritual and altruistic sentiments.[10]

Das peppers his writings with stinging rebukes of capitalist society. Capitalism is cruel, exploitative and plutocratic. It comes from individualism and materialism,[11] in contrast with socialism and spirituality. Das's thought suffers from a tendency to view capitalism more as an ethos than as a distinct productive system. Marxists might say he portrays capitalism as a mere excess of vice and greed, rather than a system of wealth accumulation by some who own productive resources, utilizing wage labor from others who do not. Hence Das fails to scrutinize the linkage of capitalist ethos and capitalist production. This yields failure to integrate notions of socialist ethos and socialist production.

Das has much to say about socialist ethos, equating it with altruism and spirituality. Socialism, he thinks, cannot long endure without an "exaltation of mood" manifest as an "ardent longing for, equality, equity, justice, fair play, non-exploitation, for all human beings..."[12] This exalted mood, essentially a spirit of "self-sacrifice," energizes socialism's "will to equitability."[13] It amounts to a "great religion" of "all-conquering faith."[14] It cannot sustain itself as mere allegiance to material progress. Socialism therefore requires direct cultivation of spiritual insight and desire.[15] Das calls for a "*systematic* cultivation, exercise, and social direction of Altruistic impulses."[16]

In this light, Das worries lest Western socialism be corrupted by excessive materialism. Springing from a distorted "materialist interpretation of history,"[17] Western socialism adopts an outlook "crassly materialist."[18] Such "mammonism" Das links with "individualism" as inimical to the "spirit" of socialism.[19] Western socialism is therefore insufficiently "socialistic," due to materialist bias. "Genuine socialism" would avoid this.[20]

Das offers a second criticism of Western socialist ethos, puzzling in light of the first. Western socialism, he thinks, is excessively hostile to individualism. He argues that there is a legitimate egoism, instinctive to human nature, that cannot and should not be suppressed.[21] Western socialism, especially as manifest in the Soviet Union, errs by attempting too radical a suppression of egoistic feeling and behavior. Manu, by contrast, makes room for legitimate egoism in two ways. First, it encourages appropriate private enterprise.[22] Second, it sets aside half of life, the first two ashramas, for pursuit of materialist and individualist goals.[23] In both ways, Manu provides what Das calls "a truly scientific combination of individualism and socialism."[24]

It is hard to make clear sense of Das's criticisms of Western socialism as both insufficiently and excessively "socialistic" in ethos. He distrusts the "individualist" spheres he seeks to preserve. He wavers on whether individualism should truly dominate its preserved spheres at all. Altruism should ultimately prevail over egoism in production as well as personal life. Hence, private entrepreneurs should manage their wealth "not in the individualist but the co-operative spirit"[25] (an idea Gandhi makes much of, as we shall see). People should deem egoism legitimate only insofar as it stays subservient to altruism. They should strive to "promote Altruism" within themselves, enabling it "to prevail over and regulate and guide Egoism."[26] The puzzle again is that Das insists on altruism while simultaneously protecting egoism.

It is perhaps not egoism Das wants to protect so much as the free character of altruism. Forceful assaults upon egoism may yield only a false altruism, spiritually polluted by a buried yet recalcitrant egoism. It is best not to stifle egoism, but to recognize it and encourage its gradual free abandonment even if it never wholly disappears.[27]

Das fears overuse of the state in building socialism. State socialism, exemplified by Soviet bureaucracy, represents an overly coercive approach to curbing egoism. As an alternative, he imagines growth of non-coercive cooperative institutions, operating with relative independence from state bureaucracy. He contrasts "self-organized" institutions following principles of "voluntary cooperation" with organizations which are "other-organized,"—by the state for example—following principles of "compulsion."[28] He advocates building socialism through voluntary organization, more tolerant of egoism in the short run but surer to curb it in the long run.

Voluntary association makes possible a more genuine socialist ethos, characterized by "inner impulsion," not "external" compulsion, more stable than anything state socialism could produce.[29] The artificial altruism of state socialism crumbles all too easily into egoistic strife and exploitation. State socialism is a "dead machine requiring constant attention and perpetual artificial cleaning." By contrast, socialism based on free altruism is a "living organism."[30]

Das's critique echoes in thinkers examined below. Questions about using the state in building socialism become a major theme in modern Indian thought. Suspicion of statist socialist transformation is both strength and weakness in that thought.

ASHRAMA AND THE CRITIQUE OF SANNYASA

In Das's guarded defense of egoism lies an implicit critique of Vivekananda's sannyasa ideal. It is common in Indian religious thought to distinguish between two ways of life or spiritual paths: that of the householder who observes varnashrama structures and that of the sannyasa who renounces them. Das links his socialist ethos more with householder than with sannyasa. His householder socialist ethos seems more promising on several counts than Vivekananda's sannyasa approach.

Vivekananda imagines a socialist ethos founded upon thorough-going renunciation of materialist and individualist passions. It seems implausible that heroic sannyasa-style renunciation could generalize itself widely. On the other hand, if confined to a spiritual minority its transformative power would be limited by small numbers. There are other problems as well. Vivekananda often associates heroic renunciation with mystical experience of non-dual insight. This may be too abstract, since most people seldom achieve such gnostic insight. Moreover, there is anomaly in Vivekananda's stress on renouncing material passions while simultaneously emphasizing socialist ambitions for material prosperity.

Das imagines a socialist ethos less heroic than Vivekananda's but more generalizable. He envisions gradual and partial renunciation rooted in commonplace life experience. By means of the four ashramas or life stages, each person may complete a lifetime transition from egoistic to altruistic preoccupations. As indicated, the first two ashramas, student and householder, are more "individualistic," while the second two, elder and renouncer, are more "socialistic."[31] Ideally, however, each ashrama should provide experiences that foster abandonment of egoism and growth of "socialist" consciousness.[32] Egoism is not so much renounced as transmuted by everyday experience where lessons of cooperative effort get absorbed.

It is crucial then for Das that mundane material life be organized so as to emphasize cooperative virtues. The productive life of the householder he sees as inevitably anchored in material and egoistic concerns. He thinks it possible, however, to structure that life such that its inevitable materialist, egoist concerns grow penetrated by spiritual, socialist ones. One example Das finds in family life itself. "Every true Home is a moral laboratory," he writes, in which the "base metal" of passionate egoism is alchemized into "the spirit of the best and highest socialism."[33] Even more than on family life, however, Das focuses on wider productive arrangements in which householders join. He argues that Manu's division of society into four distinct varnas provides the ideal framework for transfiguring egoism in productive life by socialism. His conception of varna resembles in some ways thinkers like Durkheim and movements like guild socialism that call for modified revival of medieval "occupational guilds" in organizing production.[34]

VARNA AND SOCIALIST PRODUCTION: FAILED RECONCILIATION

Manu's varna system, as Das portrays it, sorts society into four "guilds" with different functions in production and management. Das describes these functions differently at different times, which makes for some confusion. In general, however, he imagines Brahmins engaged in educating, advising, and legislating, Kshatriyas engaged in political administration and Vaishyas engaged in wealth production and management. He imagines Shudras engaged in menial labor, servicing the other three varnas.[35]

Like Vivekananda sometimes, Das sidesteps aspects of caste involving hereditary exclusivity and hierarchical exploitation. He argues that caste was originally a four-fold occupational division based upon individual aptitude. The purpose of this division, he writes, was equitable "partitioning of the means of livelihood," so as to "minimize the evils of unregulated frantic competition" in productive life.[36] Members could work only in occupations appropriate to their respective varnas and were forbidden to "encroach" upon livelihoods of other varnas. By regulating competition in this way, the system ensured an "equitable distribution of work and wages, leisure and pleasure," as well as helping "reduce unemployment."[37] In early times then, the varna system was a "cohesive centripetal force" at the core of a basically cooperative productive order.[38] Modern hierarchical and exploitational caste represents decline rooted in neglect of wise ancient principle:

> It is the neglect of the fundamental principles underly-
> ing the scheme, distorting and misinterpretation of
> them, excessive exaggeration of the principle of hered-
> ity…and grabbing of all rights and shirking of all duties
> by the strong and cunning, which has brought about
> degeneration of the vocational-class-system into the
> current caricature of it, in the shape of between two and
> three thousand mutually exclusive, even repellent,
> castes and sub-castes and sub-sub-castes…[39]

Das offers no historical theory or account of this caste system decline. He mentions the rise of heredity membership as a factor exacerbating exclusivity and economic antagonism.[40] Beyond this, however, he cites only a disintegrated "spirit," of the ancient system.[41] By portraying contemporary social ills as a decline of ancient "spirit," Das implies that they can be remedied through simple spiritual revival.

Das proposes that Manu's four-fold scheme of occupational varnas be revived as a contemporary production system. He sees Manu's scheme as uniquely workable because it rests upon a deep psychological law of human nature: division into four distinguishable temperaments or types. Every person manifests one of the four temperaments and can on that basis be assigned to the right varna.[42] Proper use of Manu's psychological science can foster return to the righteous caste structure of old.[43] Das faintly recognizes the implausibility of Manu's four-fold human psychology. "There are no hard and fast divisions…" he writes. "Everything overlaps and merges into its surroundings, by means of fringes of varying depth, and in impalpable gradations."[44] Despite caveats, however, he insists that people can be classified within Manu's four-fold scheme by the "predominant feature" in their temperaments.[45]

Das must endorse Manu's four-part psychology because without it dividing society into four occupational varnas seems arbitrary. Das wants to eliminate vast numbers of existing castes (called *jatis*), though he recognizes in candid moments that they lie closer to the notion of "occupational guilds" than do the four classical varnas.[46] The problem is that the proliferation of largely occupational jati castes does not appear in the "old books," and therefore cannot form the core of an ideal order.[47] Das denigrates actual occupational castes in favor of Manu's scriptural varnas, while extolling an occupation-based social order. In ignoring the contradiction, he commits himself to Manu as supreme repository of social wisdom. Though he sometimes imagines retaining actual occupational castes as "branch Guilds," emphasis remains on the four scriptural varnas.[48] This emphasis and his characterization of specific varnas carry negative implications for the socialist nature of Das's thought.

Though Das portrays Manu's four-varna order as fostering a socialist productive ethos, he is far from explicit on how this is so. He describes a varna order of autonomous functional "guilds" coordinated by an Executive and a Legislature comprising representatives from each. Each guild performs distinctive functions in social production and management.[49] Members of each guild are equitably compensated.[50] Das posits this division of labor and equitable reward system as the sum and substance of socialized production. It achieves "the best possible reconciliations between the egoistic and altruistic instincts of the human being, the wisest compromises between the rival claims of Individualism and Socialism...." The varna system tolerates a measure of egoism in productive life but acts as a "force of integration" so that "excessive individualism" gets replaced by more socialist attitudes. The outcome is a "spirit of true socialism."[51] He advances several vague arguments to support this view, each of them unsatisfactory.

Das argues that economic inequity is prevented by a strict division of labor, forbidding attempts to augment income by doing work reserved to another varna.[52] This argument is hard to take seriously: suggesting that economic inequity is caused mainly by people who perform two jobs so as to maximize income. Manu's varna order would ensure "an equitable distribution of work and wealth and leisure, because no person would be allowed to make money by more than one means of livelihood."[53] It seems silly to blame systemic economic disparity on the greedy practice of earning double incomes. Das notes that occupational castes are "jealous of newcomers, for economic reasons."[54] Such "newcomers," however, would presumably not attempt occupational mobility unless dissatisfied with current incomes and convinced that mobility promised improvement. Das does not worry that preventing mobility could freeze low-income people into fixed positions.

On another note, Das stresses that regulation of occupational incomes under the varna system would ensure that income disparities remain "strictly within the limits of equitability." The system would prevent "extreme differences" in wealth.[55] No socialist would quarrel with more equitable reward. But Das forgets to specify the institutions, principles or processes ensuring it. He advocates a socialist outcome but provides no sketch of socialist production or management systems to bring it about.

Another point Das stresses is that the varna system divides socially powerful functions from each other. Brahmin educational and law-making functions stand strictly segregated from Kshatriya administrative and executive functions and both of them from Vaishya wealth-production, accumulation and management functions.[56] Das warns that "combination of several powers in the same hands" inevitably produces a "tyrannical misuse of unrestrained power."[57] This warning calls for sharp separation between wealth and political power, a promising step for socialism. One problem, however, is that this oversimplifies the connection between economic power and political power, which is not caused only by predominance of rich people in public life, though that is a factor. It stems also from superior organizational faculties of wealthy over non-wealthy interests, facilitating disproportionate sway over political institutions and decisions. Weakening links between economic and political power may require radical de-concentrations of each. It certainly requires more than merely separating those wielding political power from those wielding economic power.

The separation formula also ignores the fact that wealth exercises power beyond formal politics. Das loses socialist relevance by overlooking such power.

There are, in short, problems with effort to show how Manu's institutional order would foster or embody socialism. Moreover, Das's institutional arguments seem but dimly related to creating a socialist ethos or spirit. Das does not explain how Manu's institutions would help socialist ethos infiltrate productive life. Yet it is crucial for Das to suggest that such infiltration would occur. This provokes him toward images of moral and spiritual hierarchy, with virtue radiated downward from exemplary elites through society.[58] Still, he wants to show that Manu's productive system would directly nourish socialist virtue. This drives him to another, quite distinct, line of argument. He works out an extended analogy between Manu and the "guild socialism" much-discussed in the West during the early twentieth century.

Das's discussions of guild socialism help illustrate the kind of productive system he deems desirable. They also reveal significant gaps between Das's Manu and genuine socialist ideology.

To Das, Manu and guild socialism represent an alternative to the repression and inefficiency of bureaucratic state socialism. Though full of praise for contemporary Soviet achievements in education, health and industrialization, he rebukes the Soviet Union as epitome of over-centralized statist socialism. Excessive state control, he maintains, yields both productive inefficiency and futile repression of legitimate egoism. He describes Manu's system as "a 'Guild-State of Four Guilds,' each with a flexible and largely self-governed organization of its own…"[59] Each guild enjoys autonomy in managing itself and in performing its distinctive functions. This operational autonomy, together with the four-fold division of function, ensures greater efficiency and higher voluntary cooperation than state socialism allows.

European guild socialism offers a critique of statism broadly congruent with Das's. It holds that state socialism, like capitalism, gives workers no effective voice in productive life. It re-imagines productive life as voluntary cooperation and participatory collective self-management. Workers decide democratically amongst themselves how to organize direct productive activities. Aligning with slogans of "industrial democracy," guild socialism envisions all productive decisions made through democratic processes, with the entire polity constructed from functional units, not geographical ones.

Central to guild socialism is a doctrine of rough equality in wealth. Equal ownership fosters voluntary cooperation in which self-interest and altruism coalesce. As Das sees it, guild socialism is "not a mere rearrangement of the social machinery but an attempt to express a rearrangement of human ideals."[60] Private well-being and communal well-being emerge simultaneously, in and through effective cooperation.

Reduced bureaucracy, organization by function, non-coercive co-operation, non-repressive transfiguration of egoism by altruism: these are aspects of guild socialism that Das admires and wants to attribute to Manu. He labels Manu's system "Ancient Scientific Guild Socialism."[61] The appendix to *Ancient versus Modern "Scientific Socialism"* is an extensive discussion of guild socialism, laden with quotes from Western books. By aligning with guild socialism Das hopes to show how Manu is a socialist system reconciling egoism and altruism in productive life. The problem is that his understanding of guild socialism is in key ways superficial.

First, as mentioned above, there is a big difference between "varna" as Das conceives it and "guild" as conceived by guild socialism. "Varna" classifies broad types of work—intellectual, administrative, mercantile and menial. "Guild," by contrast, classifies by specific occupation—high school teachers, cabinet makers and electricians, for example. This makes it at least somewhat plausible that productive technique and ethos could emerge through democratic worker self-government. Das makes no effort to show how varna might contribute to democratic regulation of productive life. This is partly because he does not really believe in it.

Secondly, Das fails to grasp guild socialism's dependence on equitable worker ownership of productive property. Wage laborers without ownership face impositions by owners because their interests diverge. Guild socialism requires either a system of worker-owned firms or one of public ownership with self-management rights granted to workers—or perhaps some blend of the two. Widespread participation in ownership and management helps transmute egoistic impulses into altruistic ones: one helps oneself through close cooperation with others.

OWNERSHIP AND INEQUALITY IN MANU SOCIALISM

In portraying Manu's system, Das sketches out complex and often contradictory notions of ownership. In general, he envisions a mixture of private and public enterprise. He makes no consistent effort to link this up with guild socialism. He links instead with varna in ways quite distinct from guild socialism or any other kind of socialism.

Das nominally endorses socialist ownership, writing for example that, "Means of production, land, mines, forests, and other natural sources of raw materials and wealth, should be owned by the State..."[62] Manu, he claims, condemns large-scale capitalist enterprise and insists that "large machinery and factories...should be under State-control."[63] Though favoring state ownership of resources and large-scale capital, Das also favors minimizing actual state enterprise. "State factories might be opened as necessary," he writes, but they should not become the dominant pattern.[64] He strikes an anti-bureaucratic note superficially reminiscent of guild socialism, speaking of "great socialized public works and services, mines and factories, worked, not so much directly by State servants (whence all the well-known evils of Bureaucracy) as through Trusts, Association, Companies, Guilds...with profits or remunerations carefully limited, regulated, controlled by the state."[65] He envisions exercise of actual production responsibility by non-state institutions. When it comes to specifying those institutions, however, guild socialist principles scarcely appear.

Das occasionally hints that state enterprise be "handed over…to be worked by the employees."[66] More prominent, however, is a notion that exploitation of public wealth should be entrusted "as far as possible" to capitalist firms.[67] There is no suggestion that workers in such firms would share ownership or managerial rights, as in guild socialism. In fact, Das seems to imagine traditional capitalist arrangements in firms utilizing public resources.[68]

In convoluted ruminations, Das conjures arrangements that could be called state socialism, state capitalism, regulatory capitalism and much else. Das's sporadic comments suggest a system falling somewhere in a grey area, combining diverse and perhaps divergent elements. Das speaks of "restriction and regulation," as well as "supervision" and "general direction" by the state.[69] He hints that for efficiency's sake "financial and economic" decisions should be controlled by capitalist firms.[70] In some passages, this seems to mean outright private ownership, despite advocacy elsewhere of state ownership.[71]

It seems unfair to blame Das for ambivalence and uncertainty alone. But his equivocal formulations may indicate that he lacks much interest in issues of ownership. He repeatedly emphasizes, after all, his commitment to a system which combines egoism and altruism, capitalism and socialism.[72]

Das aspires to encourage egoism's transfiguration by altruism. This sends him looking for a system where this transfiguration would be embodied and fortified in productive life. This in turn yields his idiosyncratic analogy between Manu and guild socialism. He wants this analogy to do the work of his sought-for altruistic transfiguration. Ambiguities about ownership do not bother him, because he fancies that Manu's system eliminates conflict between public welfare and private wealth. Altruistic transfiguration of private capitalism takes place partly by means of state supervision. More important, however, is altruistic transformation of capitalists themselves into conscious public servants.[73]

It is possibly from Gandhi that Das borrows the notion of private capitalists utilizing their wealth as "trustees" for the public good. Trusteeship or altruistic capitalism plays a pivotal role in Das's image of a productive system transfiguring egoism with altruism.[74]

Manu's mythical Vaishya (merchant) provides Das with his model of the altruistic capitalist. "Manu's Vaishya," he writes, "gathers and holds wealth as trust only for use of others, not for his own luxury…"[75] Decisive economic power can safely be entrusted to the Vaishya, who manages private productive wealth "in the spirit, not of the private owner and enjoyer, but of the public treasurer and almoner."[76] Vaishya virtue makes public ownership superfluous, even for large-scale enterprise. The Vaishya will manage his private enterprise "not in the individualist but the co-operative spirit, as if it were a state-business, not his own."[77] Public ownership and control yield to a "spirit" of service in enterprises run "as if" they were public. Socialism dissolves into idealized capitalism.

Das's attempt to imagine the capitalist as virtuous Vaishya rests on a fatal misunderstanding of capitalism as a system. Again Das blames capitalist ills entirely on the moral turpitude of capitalists. To contrast with the virtuous Vaishya, he pictures the "greedy grasping capitalist," whose "swindling" accounts for all depravities.[78] Again he seems without grasp that capitalist actions proceed within a *system*, where sums of wealth compete for profits needed to expand and even survive. A capitalist may wish to act as public benefactor, but if she fails to ensure healthy profit flow, she will lose out to those with keener eyes on the bottom line and will eventually lack enough wealth to remain a capitalist at all. It is the scramble for profit that drives even capitalists in the low range of venality to deploy wealth in ways neglectful of general well-being.

Das sets out to imagine a system in which altruistic action, no longer dependent on mere spiritual aspiration and exhortation, emerges from the practical logic of productive arrangements. He wanders astray from this goal through inadequate scrutiny of ownership issues and market behavior and through exaggerated loyalty to Manu and a romance of the virtuous Vaishya. Though he claims to frame his analysis within actual productive constraints,[79] his linchpin turns out to be capitalists exercizing virtue in defiance of real-life productive and competitive logic. Despite his stated intent of transcending pure religious ideology, Das again falls into it.

It is fitting, as he insists, that Vaishyas own and manage nearly all social wealth. This is because they perform "productive" functions in society.[80] As the "wealth-makers," they merit control of wealth and predominance in enjoying it.[81] This is strange "socialism" because it specifies the wealth-owning class as the "productive" one. Marxism, by contrast, identifies labor, not ownership, as true source of productivity. Even pro-capitalist economic theory acknowledges a role for labor productivity. In zeal to assert Manu's ideology, Das downplays labor's merit in productivity and claim upon wealth.

This tendency emerges the more sharply when Das presents a specific program for reformed income distribution. He often decries mass poverty and insists that Manu's scheme favors more equal distribution.[82] But he sees no reason to press redistribution beyond eliminating "extreme inequality."[83] His proposal represents triumph of Manuist over socialist sensibility. Vaishyas should make much more than Brahmins and Kshatriyas, while Shudras should make less than all.[84] He justifies this income scheme in terms of Vaishya productivity and the notion that Shudras would receive free "amusements" appropriate to their child-like natures.[85]

Das's "socialism" rings most hollow when he comments on the nature and role of Shudras. He loses all trace of guild socialist sensibility in his portrayals of Shudras as incapable of skilled work, productive self-management or moral growth. Because of their "limited grasp" and "uneducable child-minds," Shudras can perform only "unskilled' or "little-skilled" labor.[86] They cannot handle "heavy responsibilities" and must therefore remain "subservient" in production and society, doing only what they are "told to do."[87] Das buttresses these points with results of "scientific investigation and experiment" purporting to measure intelligence comparatively.[88] One might expect a socialist to question the validity and significance of such tests, especially if they find that intelligence tracks social class, but Manuism predisposes Das otherwise.

Even more disturbing than his view of Shudras as intellectually backward is his portrayal of them as a distinct and inferior species of moral being. Largely "incapable of introspective consciousness," Shudras cannot grow or transform themselves morally.[89] Opposite but complementary implications follow from this. On the one hand, Das portrays Shudras as vicious creatures, "fond of hurting others, avaricious, ready to do anything without thinking of consequences…"[90] On the other hand, he portrays them as natural saints who "can do no wrong" if properly ruled because they lack that "conscious egoism" that produces selfish impulses.[91] Whether as beast or as self-sacrificing imbecile when properly managed, Shudras are fit only for subservience. To be sure, Das stipulates that caste should properly reflect personal temperament, not preset inheritance.[92] It is telling nonetheless that he conceptualizes a large class of people incapable of both intellectual apprehension and moral self-government. Nothing seems further from a properly socialist theory of human potential.

LOCAL ORGANIZATION

There is in Das's thought on productive organization one final noteworthy cluster of issues: the scale and orientation of production. On several occasions, Das makes clear his preference for small-scale production targeted largely away from private consumer goods. These thoughts may reflect Gandhian influence. They appear as slightly alien elements grafted onto the trunk of Das's thought. At the same time, however, Das's explanations reveal his basic sympathy not only with Gandhi but also with other thinkers examined here.

Like Vivekananda, Das often contrasts the greedy materialist indi-vidualism of the modern West with the lofty spiritual socialism of an-cient India.[93] He sees flaws of Western culture exemplified by large-scale mass production for private consumption. Desire for "ex-clusive possession" of things fuels a "competitive, combative, self-see-king existence," yielding intense exploitation of others and indifference to their well-being. "Successes of the few" and "miseries of the many" are flip sides of the same corrupt coin.[94] Coarsening of taste follows from consumerism, as does misallocation of output toward "luxuries" rather than "necessaries."[95]

Das views both capital-intensive mass production and exaggerated private consumption as parts of a unified syndrome rooted in uncon-trolled desire for "sense-enjoyments." A society so organized dooms it-self to strife and discontent because desire is insatiable and means are scarce. Drives to satisfy desire are self-defeating because enjoyments inflame desire more than they quench it. Meanwhile, the quest for sat-isfaction produces antagonistic struggle over inevitably scarce means of enjoyment.[96]

To Das, it seems that a good society must aim not at satiating but at regulating and transcending material desire. The problem must be addressed in terms of both production techniques and consumption patterns. He favors enjoyments that can go with production over those that come with consumption.

With respect to production, Das accuses existing socialism of per-petuating the drive for capital-intensive technique. Though he does not ignore productive advantages in high-capital technique nor call for its abolition, he does advocate protection and cultivation of low-capital technology. This preserves artistic and craft values, which he sees as higher and more refined than the vulgar consumerism that goes with mass production.[97]

Das repeatedly calls for shifting away from private consumer goods toward public goods. He imagines vast expansion of things like "public parks, museums, children's and youth's playgrounds, reading rooms, libraries, monuments, roads, tanks, wells, places of worship, rest houses, dharma-shalas, saras, almshouses, bathing ghats, hospitals, etc."[98] Enjoyed in common rather than privately, such things enhance society's moral tone. They cultivate an artistic, spiritual sensibility rather than a materialist one.[99] Das stresses that this vision implies conscious restraint in private living standards—a modest but generalized personal asceticism. This liberates minds from domination by sensual desire so that they may focus energy on spiritual growth. He summarizes this vision as "plain living and high thinking," a Wordsworthian phrase also borrowed by Gandhi and others.[100]

Though emphasis on public consumption seems admirable from a socialist perspective, Das envisions private philanthropy as its main engine. "Incentives of public honor" will motivate outpourings of private generosity.[101] Once again, Das misjudges dynamics of private wealth in a capitalist order. Capitalists favor production of consumer goods because their purchase yields profit. Production of public goods yields no profit unless government pays for it in substantial scale. Public goods certainly provide no profit if given away rather than paid for. In capitalist economies, private capital ownership and production for profit intrinsically lean toward predominance of private consumption. Das simply does not perceive the constraints that capitalist ownership places on production of public goods.

Concern with decentralized production and public-oriented consumption lead Das to embrace the Gandhian theme of local autonomy in government and production. Conventional capitalism and socialism, he argues, both foster centralized exploitation and domination by metropolitan elites over non-elite and especially rural people and interests.[102] His remedy is to promote strong autonomous local governments in organizing production and consumption. There is a clear socialist hue to how he frames this. He speaks of such localities as "Communes" where the public, through elected governments or panchayats, controls deployment of productive wealth. He even speaks fleetingly of cooperative community enterprises such as stores and banks.[103]

The problem is that Das relegates these ideas to margins in his overall thought. His treatment of local government and local productive organization appears almost exclusively in one appendix, attached to the third and final volume of *The Science of Social Organization*. Opposition to bureaucratic centralism provides a seemingly obvious thematic link between his advocacy of local autonomy and his interest in guild socialism. Yet he scarcely notices the resonance between local autonomy and guild socialism and he makes no effort to explore it. Local autonomy and guild socialism hang like vestigial limbs from the main body of his thought: anachronistic advocacy of Manu.

In one isolated stab at integrating Manu with local autonomy, Das suggests that village panchayats should comprise representatives of local varna-guilds, while the Central Legislature would comprise country-wide varna-guild representatives selected from lower governments through indirect elections.[104] Unexamined issues abound, similar to those left unresolved in the larger Manu presentation. For example, Das does not clarify management relationships among the following local powers and interests: individual owners, the Vaishya guild of owners, and the public as represented by the panchayat.

Das also fails to examine the function of workers and the Shudra guild in local government and productive management. He suggests that local panchayats should divide their work among committees. He classifies panchayat work into three main functions labelled "Education," "Protection," (which he elsewhere equates with governmental administration) and "Economic and Industrial Ministration." These functions obviously correspond to Brahmins, Kshatriyas and Vaishyas in Manu. Though Das at one point mentions representing the Shudra guild on local panchayats, he conjures no equivalency between Shudras and other guilds. No specific Shudra guild functions receive mention, not even representing worker interests.[105] Here as elsewhere neglect of Shudra issues debases Das's "socialism."

C H A P T E R 3

Aurobindo and Pal: Hegelian Hinduism and Federal Socialism

Zealous bibliophile and yogic visionary, Sri Aurobindo (Aurobindo Ghosh) (1872-1950) began his life at Khulna, East Bengal (now Bangladesh), the son of a surgeon. He schooled in England from 1884-1892 at St. Paul's School, Cambridge and at King's College, Cambridge University. Upon returning to India, he entered the service of the Maharaja of Baroda and taught English and French at Baroda College, later becoming the College's vice-principal.

He launched his career in anti-imperial journalism in 1893 and later became active in anti-imperial political organizations. In 1906, he moved to Calcutta, joined Bipin Chandra Pal in founding the radical newspaper *Bande Mataram*, and succeeded Pal as leader of Bengal's radical Nationalist Party. He was arrested for sedition in 1907, then released, and arrested again in 1908 on charges connected to an attempted assassination of a British official. He remained in prison for a year, enduring several months of solitary confinement. Acquitted of charges in 1909, he founded two weekly journals that same year. He attenuated his activist politics and moved to Pondicherry in 1910. In 1914, he founded the monthly *Arya*, which between 1914 and 1921 published in serialized form his most important works in social philosophy.

Aurobindo began experimenting with yoga and mystical lore as early as 1904 and cultivated these interests throughout the remainder of his active career in journalism and politics. In 1926, he retired fully from his activist career into a life of concentrated meditation, which he pursued until his death. His intellectual life during this period focused on producing works of mystical philosophy.

Scholarly prodigy and ambitious synthesizer, Bipin Chandra Pal (1858-1932) was born to a well-to-do family at Sylhet in present-day Bangladesh. In 1877, while attending Presidency College in Calcutta, he converted to the Brahmo Samaj, a step followed later in life by other significant shifts in religious orientation. He studied comparative theology for a year at England's Oxford University and subsequently toured the lecture circuit in England, France and the United States.

Back in India, Pal began a career in political journalism and became involved in efforts to transform the Indian National Congress toward a mass membership organization with democratic decision-making processes. Along with Aurobindo, he became a principal leader in the radical Bengali faction of the nationalist movement. In 1906, he co-founded with Aurobindo the nationalist journal *Bande Mataram*. He served six months imprisonment in 1908 for refusing to give evidence against Aurobindo in the *Bande Mataram* sedition trial.

Upon release from prison, Pal exiled himself to England until 1911. His imprisonment and self-imposed exile coincided with a marked shift in his political outlook: from "extremist" advocacy of prompt and total Indian independence to an apparently more "moderate" position favoring India's participation in what he imagined as a federation of co-equal nations within a British Imperial Federation. He began to edit an English monthly, *Hindu Review*, emphasizing themes of international cooperation and stressing the dangers of exaggerated nationalism. His emerging concerns, though far from meritless, were markedly out of step with India's rising nationalist consciousness. For the rest of his life, his idiosyncratic development nudged him more or less to the sidelines of political events. He nevertheless continued to speak out publicly on issues of the day and remained active turning out books and articles expressing his religiously-tinged social philosophy. After his early identification with the Brahmo Samaj, Pal's religious orientation continued to evolve, first through an engagement with Advaita, then to the influence of Chaitanya's Vaishnavite (Vishnu-oriented) Bhakti devotionalism.

No one exemplifies India's first radicalism better than Aurobindo and Pal. Together they forged a radical ideology that left India's nationalist movement forever transformed, an ideology of uncompromising anti-colonialism, socialist sympathies and intense religious concern. Like Das, they saw in Hindu culture the prefiguration of socialist society. Unlike Das, however, they declined to interpret classical Hindu social order itself as socialist blueprint. They urged instead a selective recovery of Hindu social values within awareness of historical change. The past could be appropriated not through mere revival but through critical reform and reinterpretation.

It is fitting to study Aurobindo and Pal together, because their careers are both parallel and divergent. In roughly the same time span between 1895 and 1930, both moved from a stage of intense activist involvement in the nationalist movement to a later stage of committed philosophical reflection on the meanings and purposes of social life. In their retirements from activism, both sought to fit their ideas about social action into a larger framework of religious ideas. In both cases, this extended religious reflection emerged from concerns evident even in their early careers. Beginning with similar concerns and comparable outlooks, they evolved orientations grounded in two distinct strands of Hindu tradition: Advaita for Aurobindo and Bhakti for Pal.

Aurobindo and Pal were not only contemporaries and kindred spirits but also friends and collaborators. Together in 1906 they founded *Bande Mataram*, a newspaper that became for a time the ideological flagship of "extremist" nationalism in Bengal.[1] Despite their increasingly divergent Hindu orientations, they resembled each other in many key social ideas. Above all, they converged in a common paradigm of society. Any community, they stressed, is a distinct identity common to its members. Bearing a particular character, genius or personality, it exists in webs of relationships with other communities, just as persons within a society live in similar relational webs. Furthermore, just as it lives within larger communities, it subsumes smaller ones within itself. Those larger and smaller ones also manifest distinct personalities.

Many of Pal's and Aurobindo's leading themes stem from this conception of society. Societies evolve through progressive federalization among distinct groups. Larger and higher societies arise from cooperation for a common good among initially separate lower-level ones. As new societies arise this way, the previously-existing societies are transformed. They ideally retain distinct existences, but also take on new existence as parts of larger wholes. This process of harmonious social evolution through mutual cooperation goes awry only when the distinct existence of some given society is effaced by coercion from an equivalent or higher-level society.

To Pal and Aurobindo, social harmony lies in the willing and reciprocal cooperation of societies in the creation and life of higher societies. Both view historical India as an exemplification of this evolutionary social federalism. They visualize it as a civilization of stable cooperation among the countless distinct communities that variations in geography and culture have thrown up. Harmonious orchestration of potentially chaotic diversity has been India's leading social achievement. If social progress lies in evolutionary federalism, then India's past is the world's future.

Societies impart their distinctive identities to groups and individuals within them. Societies are therefore a ground and source of personal identity. A person's identity forms in the womb of the various groups whose life she shares in various degrees. Any society large or small is therefore a mother to its members, a source of their identities. Since it is fitting to honor one's mother, source of one's identity, Aurobindo and Pal stress service and devotion to one's society or societies. As nationalists, they stress Indian identity as one that has previously been denied her due. The time has come for devotion to Mother India. As Mother, source of identity, India calls her children to honor her with the prayer Aurobindo and Pal popularize: *Bande Mataram* (Revere the Mother). As Pal writes: "This New Nationalism which BANDE-MATARAM reveals is not, therefore, a mere civic or economic or political ideal. It is a religion."[2]

As advocates of the "New Nationalism," so-called "Extremists" like Pal and Aurobindo agitated for a nation-building program designed to hasten Independence by supplanting British rule from within. One key component of that program was *swadeshi* (of one's own country). Swadeshi meant boycotting British-made goods and patronizing Indian goods so as to strengthen India's native economy. Aurobindo and Pal view swadeshi and the whole nationalist program as an effort to fortify India in both material and spiritual dimensions. As Pal writes, swadeshi represents "not a mere economic movement," but one with spiritual significance: cultivation of India's communal consciousness and effort.[3] With such interlocked concern for economics and spiritualities, Aurobindo and Pal fit themselves into our problematic.

SOCIALIST ANTI-IMPERIALISM

Aurobindo begins his public career during the 1890s with journalism calling for India's prompt independence. No aspect of India's well-being, he insists, can be secured without first securing independence. The early nationalist movement exemplified by the Indian National Congress had generally stressed the need for extensive social reform in order to prepare India for self-government. Aurobindo reverses this priority, arguing that no significant social reform can occur under British imperial rule. Political independence must come first:

> Political freedom is the life-breath of a nation; to attempt
> social reform, educational reform, industrial expansion,
> the moral improvement of the race without aiming first
> and foremost at political freedom, is the very height of
> ignorance and futility.[4]

One aspect of the new nationalist program stressed especially by Aurobindo is so-called "passive resistance." This includes non-cooperation with British authority and includes illegal methods, such as non-payment of taxes, in order to subvert and overthrow it. It is worth mentioning some aspects of Aurobindo's views on passive resistance, in order to contrast them later with Gandhi's views.

Passive resistance is not, for Aurobindo, a policy of stringent non-violence requiring practitioners to suffer harm from opponents. Non-violence should be the primary posture of resistance, but only so long as opponents do not resort to force in suppressing resistance, even if such force is "legal." According to Aurobindo, violent suppression can rightfully be met with violence sufficient to repel attack. There is nothing intrinsically wrong with violence, if it responds to violence from authority lacking legitimacy in the first place. At times, Aurobindo seems to repudiate even a presumption in favor of non-violence. Political action, he argues, requires ethics of the "Kshatriya," (warrior) not that of the "priest." Use of violence, as he writes at one point, is "purely a matter of policy and expediency." Violence may be inexpedient, but there is no "moral question." The morality of political action must be judged according to ends pursued and achieved, not means utilized.[5]

In his prolific and brilliant early journalism, Aurobindo emphasizes ways in which British rule has retarded India's development. Imperialism's negative effects are, first, economic. Spokesmen within the Congress had long spoken of the "drain" of Indian resources used to support imperialism's administrative apparatus. Aurobindo focuses instead on the less obvious but far more massive drain he sees stemming from the position of India's entire economy as a field of capitalist exploitation. With the deft irony characteristic of his early work, he writes:

> The huge price India has to pay England for the inestimable privilege of being ruled by Englishmen is a small thing compared with the murderous drain by which we purchase the more exquisite privilege of being exploited by British capital.[6]

To Aurobindo, British rule is in its essence a dominion of capital, incapable of serving India's economic well-being and in fact ensuring "chronic famine" and "impoverishment."[7] India's economic well-being therefore requires an independent national state. "The only possible method of stopping the drain is to establish a popular government which may be relied on to foster and protect Indian commerce and Indian industry…," he writes.[8] Until true independence can be achieved, boycott and swadeshi must be deployed to loosen Britain's hold on India's economy, while strengthening India's own productive capacities.

Aurobindo finds imperialism an obstacle to India's progress not only economically, but also socially and culturally. India must reshape its hierarchical caste society toward a more "democratic" order that Aurobindo calls "socialism." This requires propagating true Vedantic thought, a mission impossible under British rule:

> We must educate every Indian, man, woman and child, in the ideals of our religion and philosophy before we can rationally expect our society to reshape itself in the full and perfect spirit of the Vedantic gospel of equality… And because such education is impossible except through the aid of state-finance…the Nationalist must emphasize the immediate need of political freedom

without which Indians cannot obtain the necessary control over their money.[9]

While stressing the priority of political liberation, Aurobindo insists that Indian nationalism take as its larger goal the radical transformation of Indian society itself. This requires more than merely establishing British-style parliamentary government and political equality as advocated by the Congress. In Marx-like fashion, Aurobindo points out that these achievements would primarily benefit India's "new middle class," which the Congress chiefly represents, in guise of representing India as a whole.[10] He implores the nationalist movement not to recreate in India a British-style capitalist order: political equality combined with sharp social inequality, class divisions, and economic "pauperism" for the lowly. The nationalist movement's focus should be not installation of British-style political institutions, but rather the creation of "democracy and socialism" in the social order. To achieve this, the movement must in socialist fashion stress economic and cultural advancement for India's impoverished millions, "that vast unhappy proletariat," as Aurobindo calls them. Such is the movement's "first and holiest duty."[11]

ADVAITIC SOCIOLOGY

As invocation of "holy duty" indicates, Aurobindo's nationalism is religious, as well as socialist and anti-imperialist. "What is Nationalism?" asks Aurobindo. "Nationalism is not a mere political programme: Nationalism is a religion that has come from God; Nationalism is a creed which you shall have to live."[12] There is a marked Bhakti strand in Aurobindo's early thought on religion and society. He speaks of India, for example, as "the ancient Mother" and as "divinity" and of patriotism as "realization of the Motherhood of God in the country" and as Bhakti.[13] This early Bhakti strand drops away in his mature social thought, supplanted more and more by a different theme: interpretation of religion, society, and morality through Advaita.

Even in his early writings on national religion, Aurobindo deploys an Advaitic moral language reminiscent of Vivekananda:

> …[A]nother name for faith is selflessness. This movement in Bengal, this movement of Nationalism is not guided by any self-interest, not at the heart of it… It is a religion which we are trying to live. It is a religion by which we are trying to realize God in the nation, in our fellow-countrymen. We are trying to realize him in the three hundred millions of our people… This is our religion… the absolute denial of the idea of one's separate self, and the finding of one's higher eternal Self in the three hundred millions of people in whom God himself lives.[14]

Though he seldom again states it so explicitly, Aurobindo organizes his entire social philosophy around this Advaitic theme of sacrificing the illusory private self in order to realize a larger, truer Self which is simultaneously God and society. During roughly the second decade of the twentieth century, Aurobindo authors a massive exposition of his Advaita social philosophy, embodied in a number of works, notably *The Ideal of Human Unity*, *The Human Cycle* and *Foundations of Indian Culture*.

Aurobindo thinks that the life of any person or group within a larger society can be described at least potentially as an activity of simultaneous self-sacrifice and self-realization. This formulation resembles both Vivekananda and such Western thinkers as Hegel and Durkheim.

Spiritual growth, as he thinks, lies in progressive "enlargement of the conception of the self."[15] It entails "asceticism," renunciation of animal-like instinctual or material enjoyments associated with narrow bodily self-hood.[16] It provides, however, a "higher fulfillment," spiritual rather than material, the more so as one's social self-conception grows more universal, hence more distant from one's private material interests.[17] This ascent to higher Selfhoods is ascent from animal life to divine life. It is knowledge of God. It is also the meaning and essence of morality.

This focus on the problem of selfhood provokes Aurobindo to call his social philosophy a "subjective" science. A subjective social science, as he explains, probes the self-understanding of selves, both individual and social. The crucial component of any self is precisely its self-understanding. All persons and groups are selves, or "souls," and display some distinctive self-understanding, some awareness of purpose-being-realized.[18] A "subjective" social science seeks to recognize these self-understandings, yet comprehend them critically within the Advaitic insight of ultimate non-separateness in Selfhood.[19]

Aurobindo contrasts his "subjective" approach to human nature with Western liberalism, which he calls "individualism" or "objectivism."[20] Objectivism views humans in terms of their object-like external separateness. In doing so, it postits artificial problems of freedom and order. The "objectivist" postulate of radical human separateness provokes two opposing anxieties: to protect this separateness in the name of freedom, and to efface it in the name of order. Hence, Aurobindo suggests that objectivism gives rise to opposite exaggerations: "individualism" and "collectivism." Objectivism sees inevitable antagonism between any self and its social existence. This postulated separateness and conflict among selves makes social existence itself hard to explain.

Aurobindo criticizes two liberal responses to this characteristically liberal dilemma, responses he thinks become needful within liberalism's "objectivist" positing of social life as inevitably violent to selfhood. The first, which we may call Hobbesian, envisions social order as an imposition of superior and repressive force upon the separate selves within society. The second, which we may call Kantian, imagines social order emerging from each self's self-imposition of rationality upon itself.[21]

Aurobindo does not say precisely how his own views of the higher self's asceticism and restraint of the lower self differs from Kant's image of the self's self-subordination. It seems that he envisions transcendence of the lower self through communal engagement, while thinking that Kant envisions individuals imposing abstract rationality upon themselves in autonomous isolation from each other.[22]

A stress on subjectivity, he thinks, avoids the dilemmas and errors of liberal theory. Properly conceived, subjective social science can highlight and pay due respect to the inner selfhood of persons and groups while also viewing their social relationships as a species of self-fulfillment. Hence, a subjective theory explains more convincingly than could a liberal theory how individual and communal well-being might coexist harmoniously:

> In this view neither the separate growth of the individual nor the all-absorbing growth of the group can be the ideal, but an equal, simultaneous and, as far as may be, parallel development of both, in which each helps to fulfill the other. Each being has his own truth of independent self-realization and his truth of self-realization in the life of others…[23]

Advaitic science accords proper dignity both to embracing communities and to persons and groups within them, because it recognizes Selfhood manifest equally at all levels of Self.

The right science and practice of relationships in Selfhood Aurobindo calls *dharma* (law, duty, righteousness). Dharma is no fixed moral code, but rather the Self's powerful, though fallible, instinct for true well-being. Because of their inner selfhood, he argues, all persons and groups have their own dharma, *svadharma*, action which comports with their proper well-being. Well-being lies in cultivating both one's own unique localized selfhood and the more transcendent universal Selfhood resident in various social groupings. Dharma is therefore a discipline aimed at proper self-understanding, *moksa* (spiritual liberation). When true dharma reigns, all social restraint appears as voluntary self-restraint, in which proper mutual claims are recognized among various aspects and levels of Selfhood. Like Selfhood, dharma is universal, though each different manifestation of Selfhood has its own svadharma.[24]

Aurobindo's notions of morality and human nature echo through his views of social evolution. If Vivekananda's Advaita is Kantian, Aurobindo's is Hegelian. Aurobindo interprets society in relentlessly evolutionary terms like Hegel, viewing history as essentially the growth of higher and more complex forms of human community. Aurobindo portrays this evolution as a movement through distinct successive "ages" or "stages" in spiritual and social development: the conventional age, the individualistic age, the subjective age, and so on.[25] Emergence of wider communities from smaller partial ones may display varying mixtures of coercion and cooperation, and the moral quality of the wider community depends on preponderance of cooperation over coercion in its internal life. Aurobindo's ideal community is one of close and intense cooperation among free and equal participants. He finds this ideal best exemplified by the participatory democracy of small-scale ancient states:

> The tendency to a democratic freedom in which every man had a natural part in the civic life as well as in the cultural institutions of the State, an equal voice in the determination of law and policy and as much share in their execution as could be assured to him — by his right as a citizen and his capacity as an individual — this democratic tendency was inborn in the spirit and inherent in the form of the city-state... As in the political and civic, so in the social life. A certain democratic equality is almost inevitable in a small community... [I]t was the complete participation not of a limited class, but of the individual generally in the many-sided life of the community...[26]

Aurobindo takes pains to stress the origins, varieties and vicissitudes of these "ancient republics," emphasizing less their institutional forms than their active, participatory and egalitarian spirit. He also finds participatory self-government a key feature of life in ancient Indian castes and guilds, villages and townships, religious communities and even families. Castes and guilds, he suggests, regulated themselves through participatory communal assembly, *jati-sangha*. Villages and townships, participatory communities "autonomous and self-governing," utilized democratic devices like the assembly and the vote. Aurobindo further stresses participatory and autonomous self-government in ancient religious communities, especially the Buddhist *sangha* (organized community of monks), and claims that even clan families often governed themselves through democratic "communal assembly, *kula-sangha*."[27] In short, ancient India displayed "a strong democratic element" manifest in the power of persons and groups to arrange affairs without "autocratic interference" from hierarchical authority.[28]

These autonomous persons and groups arranged their affairs not around mere self-interest, but rather with an eye always toward the spirit and quality of communities enveloping them. Each constituent entity saw its well-being inextricably linked with well-being of larger wholes. The nature of ancient Indian polity, therefore, was "complex communal freedom," with:

> ...each group unit of the community having its own natural existence and administering its own proper life and business, set off from the rest by a natural demarcation of its field and limits, but connected with the whole by well-understood relations, each a co-partner with the others in the powers and duties of the communal existence, executing with its own laws and rules, administering within its own proper limits, joining with the others in the discussion and the regulation of

matters of a mutual or common interest and represented in some way and to the degree of its importance
in the general assemblies of the kingdom or empire.[29]

"Complex communal freedom" echoes Tocqueville's "communal freedom," describing participatory popular self-government in early America's New England townships. The Tocquevillian flavor of Aurobindo's
"complex communal freedom" may represent direct borrowing.[30]

If the well-being of parts stems from that of the whole, the reverse
is equally true. Social wholes have vitality precisely to the extent they
preserve the integrity of smaller units, where the life of participatory
community may thrive. Again, Aurobindo finds a model in ancient Indian civilization. The republican states of ancient India, he argues, fostered autonomy for groups and individuals within them. Meanwhile,
the integrity and autonomy of the republican states themselves was preserved within confederations of states formed for purposes of defense,
trade and cultural exchange. Reflecting on India's republican age and
similar periods elsewhere, Aurobindo concludes:

> [T]he interesting periods of human life, the scenes in
> which it has been most richly lived and has left behind
> it the most precious fruits, were precisely those ages and
> countries in which humanity was able to organize itself
> in little independent centres acting intimately upon
> each other but not fused into a single unity.[31]

The idea presented here contains Aurobindo's essential paradigm of social progress. It lies in the free and equal participation of individuals in
groups and of groups in larger communities, where each participating
entity retains its distinctive integrity and retains an atmosphere of free
and equal participation within itself. Because free and equal participation thrives best in small-scale community, the task is to preserve small

egalitarian communities while developing larger, more inclusive ones: "In the unification of human aggregates, this then is the problem, how the component units shall be subordinated to a new unity without their death and disappearance."[32]

It is difficult to achieve this. Creating and maintaining small egalitarian communities tends to conflict with the existence or creation of larger communities. The historical pattern has been for larger communities to consolidate themselves by stifling the integrity of smaller communities, adopting centralized and hierarchical arrangements at odds with the life of participatory community. Actual social evolution, thinks Aurobindo, tends to rest not on free and equal co-operation but instead upon subjugation and hierarchical exploitation.[33]

Though this snuffing out of smaller communities may seem unfortunate, Aurobindo sees it as dialectically necessary. For all their virtues, small-scale democracies also display certain defects that bespeak their small size. One is that, despite considerable equality, those democracies also display much economic and gender inequality. Such disparity cannot be removed within limits of small-scale social organization. Their remedy can emerge only in a "complex and cumbrous fashion," through achievement of more powerful forms of social organization. This achievement occurs through the expensive dialectical process of expanded hierarchy, centralization, and exploitation.[34] A second defect of small communities lies in the perpetual warfare among them. This defect demands that more inclusive communities develop, even at the cost of stifling the vitality and character of smaller ones.[35]

This effacement of lesser communities, though dialectically necessary, is far from ideal. Much better would be preservation or restoration of vital small communities within larger, more embracing ones.[36] Such lesser communities enhance the well-being both of the individuals within them and of the wider communities embracing them. Between any social "totality" and the individual persons that are its "constituent units," there should stand "intermediary unities" without which "there can be no full development either of the totality or of the units."[37] Individuals require the tangible self-fulfillment of intimate community, not just the more transcendent self-fulfillment found in wider communities. Communities meanwhile, require not only the raw energy of individuals but also the concentrated and magnified energy of various subcommunities.[38] Aurobindo's discussion of these "intermediary unities" recalls discussions of "secondary groups" and "voluntary associations" in Western thinkers like Tocqueville, Durkheim, and Laski.

Aurobindo finds in history at best only flawed approximations of his social ideal. The ideal itself stands as some as-yet-unrealized harmony among three distinguishable social levels:

> The social evolution of the human race is necessarily a development of the relations between three constant factors, individuals, communities of various sorts and mankind. Each seeks its own fulfillment, but each is compelled to develop them not independently but in relation to the others.[39]

Because the dominant pattern of social evolution has been eclipse of lesser communities within construction of higher ones, Aurobindo sees danger as well as promise in humanity's movement toward wider forms of community. He urges that future moves toward wider community combine consciously with dialectical recovery of past principles of community: active, intimate and participatory life patterns. He speaks, for example, of need to "re-create village organization" in India. Village communities, he argues, have been steamrolled by British rule, but this destruction could pave the way for recreation on a higher plane.[40] Aurobindo therefore speaks of recreated "village communities" not solely as ends in themselves, but also as bases and models for the achievement of active "democratic" community in India at large:

> The organization of our villages is an indispensable
> work to which we must immediately set our hands, but
> we must be careful so to organize them as to make them
> feel that they are imperfect parts of a single national
> unity, and dependent at every turn on the co-operation
> first of the district, secondly, of the province, and finally
> of the nation.[41]

A notion of dialectical recovery seems to lie also behind Aurobindo's scattered pronouncements on caste. Like Vivekananda and Das, Aurobindo defends ancient caste as a "socialistic institution" with a "spiritual object" and a "moral basis," in which there was fundamentally "no inequality."[42] The value of caste lay in its application of "complex communal freedom" to the division of labor. Aurobindo writes of internally democratic and autonomous castes co-operating with each other on free and roughly equal footing in overall social governance.[43] In another positive feature, caste subordinates the "material" considerations of members to a "spiritual and moral" emphasis on the "common good."[44] With time, caste has unfortunately degenerated into anti-socialist and anti-democratic hierarchy. Aurobindo therefore calls for its "transformation" in the true spirit of Hinduism and socialism, so as "to fulfill its essential and permanent object under the changed conditions of modern times." Beyond alluding to the "pliable self-adapting democratic distribution of function," he provides no detail as to what this transformation of caste might be.[45]

RECONCILING PRODUCTION AND PARTICIPATORY COMMUNITY

Aurobindo finds modern Western society lacking when measured against his "subjective" view of human nature and his ideal of participatory community. He first attacks capitalist democracy, which he portrays as the hierarchical social dominance of economic elites, despite egalitarian formalities of democratic politics. Capitalist democracy is less a community of free and equal participants than a veiled order of exploitation.[46] An asocial egoism dominates life, checked only by the "ordered conflict" of the market. The market is irrational, thinks Aurobindo, even on economic grounds. It engenders wasteful production and fails to abolish poverty, tending instead to engender long-run depression and stagnation.[47] He deplores the tendency of capital to consolidate in ever more concentrated form.[48]

According to Aurobindo, socialism promises to abolish the "curse of Capitalism" and its consequent exploitation, waste, poverty and stagnation. It will do this through state ownership and control of the economy, a step forward in both equity and rationality.[49] He praises the early Soviet Revolution for its "astonishing" achievements, laying the "initial basis of a new type of society," in the midst of grave internal and external challenges.[50] In the consolidation of state power, however, he sees a threat to freedom and diversity. The asocial egoism and anarchy of capitalism yields to a repugnant collectivist uniformity.[51] The life of active individuality in participatory community finds no home there, though barriers of economic hierarchy are levelled. Socialism constructs its own power hierarchy, embodied in a centralized state hostile to all lesser centers of power and activity. Aurobindo admits the possible emergence of guild socialism or other forms of democratic socialism that would protect freedom and diversity by dispersing power broadly through society.[52] Far more likely, he insists, is that socialism will mean triumph of the bureaucratic central state.[53]

Conventional Western socialism, thinks Aurobindo, suffers from the same "objective" view of human nature that poisons capitalist democracy. It understands humans only in their outward, material aspect, not in their inward "subjective" or spiritual one. This engenders a bias toward conceiving human well-being in terms of institutional arrangements and economic mechanisms.[54] State socialism, though it achieves a higher rationality in these respects and even perhaps because it does so, embodies only a skewed version of human well-being.[55] It modifies but cannot replace or transcend the culture it inherits from capitalism, a culture of "economism," that imagines human well-being as the more and more rationalized satisfaction of material desire.[56]

Aurobindo sees an alternative to Western socialism in the "resurgence of Asia," representing "the emergence of a new and as yet unforeseen principle."[57] Asian culture and India in particular, he argues, begins to incubate a "spiritualized democracy." This seems to mean evangelizing throughout society the "spiritual and inner" achievements of gnostic elites, turning elite insight into an active social force.[58] Defeat of capitalism and imperialism may lie in alliance between this spiritualized democracy and Western socialism. Beyond this, alliance may become synthesis, ushering in a regime higher than socialism.[59] Aurobindo's conception of Indian spirituality as imminent and redemptive world-historical force typifies modern Indian thought.

Aurobindo believes that recovery of active individuality and participatory community will depend on developing a post-socialist "subjective" sensibility, in which various aspects of Selfhood recognize and seek their well-being in the well-being of others. That sensibility will allow movement toward a stateless anarchy akin to Marxist notions of the "withering away of the state." Anarchy will transcend socialism by recovering the freedom and diversity that socialism excludes, while consolidating socialism's equality, unity and economic rationality. The result will be a "free equality founded upon spontaneous co-operation."[60] Aurobindo explains the evolution he envisions by way of the French Revolutionary slogan: liberty, equality, fraternity. If liberty lies with capitalism and equality with socialism, fraternity lies with anarchism. Fraternity transcends the apparent antinomy between liberty and equality and reconciles the two in a principle of active free collaboration among equals toward a shared well-being.[61] Fraternity is the principle of participatory community. Aurobindo envisions post-socialist anarchy as the dialectical recovery and universalization of participatory community.

There is nothing startling in Aurobindo's suspicion of state-centered socialism, nor in his alternative vision of a regime embodying a universalized principle of "free agreement and cooperation."[62] The vision resembles Marx's vision of communism, ushered in by the perfection of institutions under socialism. It is often noted that Marx, though comprehensive in analyzing capitalist production, offers scant discussion of productive arrangements in the post-capitalist future. Marx finds such speculation pointless and trusts that once capitalism disappears through socialization of productive property, details of appropriate arrangements will emerge in light of various unforeseeable contingencies.

There may seem to be some wisdom in refusing to build castles in the air while history is unfolding and pressing tasks lie at hand. But it is hard to see how transformative social action can long or wisely proceed without some reasonable theories of workable institutional forms to pursue. By dreaming of the communist revolution as an all-encompassing salvational moment while by-passing discussion of post-capitalist productive arrangements, Marxism ironically makes itself a form of religion pursuing a version of pure religious ideology. Revolution represents humanity's spiritual redemption. We needn't worry about details of actual productive arrangements. They will emerge from redemptive insight once the revolution triumphs.

On this count, Aurobindo offers no more than Marx and perhaps somewhat less. There is one dense passage in *The Human Cycle*, however, in which he attempts to discuss production in the anarchist regime. The anarchist ideal, he writes, could imply either of two productive systems, which he calls "Stateless Communism" and "communalism." Stateless Communism means a highly-developed productive system operating on "the large and complex scale necessitated by modern life." As in Marx, Stateless Communism is a "free co-operative communism" in which all of production and society exist as "a unified life where the labor and property of all is there for the benefit of all." By communalism, Aurobindo seems to mean a low-productivity economy, centered around independent owner-producers, each contributing the "surplus of his labour and acquisitions…without demur for the benefit of all." This contribution occurs freely and spontaneously, each person exercising the "just freedom of his individuality."[63]

Neither Stateless Communism nor communalism, writes Aurobindo, can be regarded as realistic. Stateless Communism is unrealistic because no complex highly-developed system can operate without "governmental force." Hence, the anarchist ideal cannot lie in a unified high-productivity system. It might then be thought that anarchist "free agreement and co-operation" might lie in a low-productivity system of spontaneous sharing: a radical altruism renouncing the advantages of high productivity. Aurobindo contends, however, that such a vision posits an "impossible self-abnegation." No worthwhile system, he indicates, can be based on overly severe self-abnegation. Though he endorses asceticism, Aurobindo cautions against making it too rigorous. That would risk sapping the bodily vigor animating all activity.[64]

Hence Aurobindo rejects two views on how to embody the anarchist principle of "free agreement and co-operation." The trouble is that he offers no alternative. The anarchist regime, he insists, requires a "deeper brotherhood," a "yet unfound law of love," but he does not clarify how the regime will *produce*.[65]

Much of Aurobindo's thought turns on notions that not only society but human nature itself is involved in a vast process of evolution. The human spirit evolves in history from animal to divine, just as individual persons may so evolve in their private spiritual journeys. The anarchist regime, he suggests, awaits the "future evolution of the race," in which humanity's animal aspects will give way to a "new form of life nearer to the divine." Aurobindo hints that such highly-evolved creatures will find no need to produce at all because they will somehow live lives of spontaneous abundance, dialectically recovering early life form capacities in a sort of spiritual photosynthesis. He makes this hint explicit not in his social philosophy but elsewhere, in a scenario of humanity's future evolution:

> There would have to be a change in the operative processes of the material organs themselves and, it may well be, in their very constitution and their importance; they could not be allowed to impose their limitations imperatively on the new physical life. The will might control the organs that deal with food, safeguard automatically the health…substitute subtler processes or draw in strength and substance from the universal life-force so that the body could maintain for a long time its own strength and substance without loss or waste, remaining thus with no need of substance by material aliments, and yet continue a strenuous action with no fatigue or pause for sleep or repose… Conceivably, one might rediscover and re-establish at the summit of the evolution of life the phenomenon we see at its base, the power to draw from all around it the means of sustenance and self-renewal.[66]

Aurobindo imagines bodily needs transcended not through asceticism but through evolution. As indicated by *The Life Divine*, his late-career work of mystical philosophy, he seems to take such projections of transhuman existence rather seriously. They are not much help in solving problems of actual human beings. In certain moments, he carefully stipulates that humanity should be secured in its "material existence," in order for a worthwhile regime to emerge.[67] Moreover, his discussions of capitalism, socialism, and anarchism imply that modes of production are key to possibilities for a better society.

Elsewhere, however, productive organization seems only marginally relevant. It is far from clear what connection, if any, Aurobindo sees between forming the anarchist regime and developing any particular system for production. Far more critical than production, he insists, is to create a "spiritual comradeship which is the expression of an inner realization of oneness."[68] Just when he shifts from analysis to prescription, Aurobindo abandons all focus on production and retreats to pure religious ideology. For anyone skeptical of transcending needs for production, finding a system compatible with "free agreement and cooperation" will continue to be a crucial issue, one on which Aurobindo offers little help.

RELIGION OF HUMANITY

Aurobindo's overall religious views can be seen as an extrapolation from his nationalist religious views. Just as the nation represents Selfhood, realized through Advaitic insight and self-sacrifice, humanity at large represents Selfhood on a still more universal level. Aurobindo imagines an evolutionary trajectory from lesser to greater religious universality, in which lesser universalities are subsumed and transcended but not destroyed or devalued. Nationalist religion must, therefore, ultimately find and take its proper place within a wider "religion of humanity."

Aurobindo posits a "religion of humanity" as glue of a world community under the anarchist principle of "free agreement and cooperation." This religion of humanity is already afoot in the world, he thinks, rooted in eighteenth century rationalism and formulated dogmatically in Positivism. (He does not mention Comte, though that is probably his reference.) It finds expression in diverse modern ideas and movements. Many progressive developments stem from this religion, which has "encouraged everywhere the desire of freedom, put a curb on oppression and greatly minimised its more brutal expressions."[69] This religion, however, so far looks nowhere nearly powerful enough to eradicate oppression. Further progress requires that it become "more explicit, insistent and categorically imperative."[70]

The task of this religion of humanity is to eradicate "human egoism," both the "egoism of the individual" and the "egoism of class and nation." Individual wrongdoing and social oppression both exemplify the same fundamental ill, egoism, and require the same remedy, a religion of humanity. Can prevailing forms of that religion measure up to the task? Prevailing forms of the religion of humanity, Aurobindo argues, suffer from their overly outward nature. They appeal to shallower "intellectual" and "sentimental" aspects of human being, not to its "centre," which is "Spirit."[71] Because intellect and sentiment are only "instruments" of humanity's spiritual center, a profound religion of humanity must press beyond them into that center.[72] In other words, the religion of humanity's orientation has been too "objective" and needs to become more "subjective." It must de-emphasize "institutions" and the "external machinery of society" and stress realizing the "secret Spirit."[73]

This "spiritual religion of humanity," cannot mean a religion in the usual sense: "a system, a thing of creed and intellectual belief and dogma and outward rite."[74] It must instead mean a "growing realization that there is a…divine Reality, in which we are all one…a real and an inner sense of unity and equality and a common life."[75] In a word, the true religion of humanity, according to Aurobindo, is Advaitic insight on the non-duality of Selfhood. He sketches out the practice of such a religion only vaguely:

> There must be too a discipline and a way of salvation
> in accordance with this religion, that is to say, a means
> by which it can be developed by each man within him-
> self, so that it may be developed in the life of the race.[76]

Aurobindo seems to envision a personal religious practice of cultivating Advaitic insight. Other than calling it a "discipline," he does not specify what this would be: deep meditation perhaps. He makes no mention whatever of communal practices, whether "practical" or "religious" that might stimulate or reinforce Advaitic insight.

Aurobindo struggles to demonstrate social relevance in the new Advaitic religion. He responds to suspicion that a new religion might seem an outworn approach to alleviating social ills.[77] Advaitic insight and religious knowledge generally, he admits, have been unduly confined to "the life of the individual only," never properly applied to "society itself."[78] As applied to society, on the other hand, religion has forever been distorted by outward and mechanical elements like "Church," "priesthood," "ceremonies," "creeds," and "dogmas." Aurobindo concludes that "this false socialisation of religion has always been the chief cause of its failure to regenerate mankind."[79]

Less clear than what Aurobindo would not do is precisely what he *would* do. He criticizes Advaita as insufficiently social, yet criticizes society-oriented religions as insufficiently subjective. The task, apparently, is to develop a religion simultaneously subjective and social. Aurobindo's thoughts on how to do this, however, provoke only puzzlement.

Humanity's new religion should not encrust itself in any system of practice or organization. Its proximate aim should be establishing what Aurobindo calls a "true inner theocracy," to evangelize society but not to dominate it. This "theocracy" is a kind of religious order or sangha, an elite consisting at first of a "limited number of individuals" with superior spirituality. This new sangha will teach and lead the rest of humanity toward higher spiritual life. Aurobindo does not spell out how the sangha shall do this. Because he repudiates any organizational system, he does not even clarify how members of the sangha will or should operate together.

Like Lenin's vanguard of the proletariat, Aurobindo's vanguard of the spirit seeks to make the masses responsive to the superior vision of an elite. Aurobindo bemoans the "unpreparedness, the unfitness of the society or of the common mind of man which is always the chief stumbling-block" to progress.[81] Elite spiritual action will ensure triumph of "subjective" sensibility in human affairs. Then will come application of "subjective principles" to social, political, and economic questions.

Though he acknowledges such questions as critical to creating a better society, he cannot specify what "subjective principles" might actually say about them.[82]

With his notion of participatory community, Aurobindo conveys a vision of human well-being lived out in the spiritual atmosphere of collaborative activity. Unfortunately, however, he gives us scant picture what sorts of collaborative activity we might seek.

FEDERAL EMPIRE AND HINDUISM

Alongside his early compatriot Aurobindo, Pal first reaches public prominence during the 1890s as radical critic of Congress policies. He characterizes the Congress approach as one of "reform" and finds it lacking in two key respects: 1) failure to press for prompt independence from British rule, and 2) failure to visualize and pursue India's transformation into a non-oppressive social order.

Like Aurobindo, Pal in his early career portrays imperial rule as a "despotism" of exploitation directly antagonistic to India's economic interests:

> Our economic interests are in perpetual conflict, under existing conditions, with the economic interests of the British nation and the British Government. And our loss economically is England's gain; our gain economically is England's loss.[83]

We will examine below in detail how Pal analyzes India's economic predicament. Pal likewise worries about imperialism's cultural influence, oriented toward consolidating British rule, destroying Indian practices and values, putting nothing worthwhile in their place.[84]

India's progress requires "complete autonomy": overthrow of imperial rule.[85] Pal criticizes Indian reformers in a paradoxical vein reminiscent of Vivekananda. Reformers, he writes, "can never be true lovers of their country," because they dwell on native ills of Indian life and glorify Britain as prototype of the good society.[86] Reformers think India's well-being requires British tutelage. Like Vivekananda, Pal rebukes such "reform" for a more radical spirit, affirming rather than denying India's greatness. The first demand of this "New Spirit" is political freedom. Freedom cannot come through slavish acquiescence to and imitation of British institutions. It is only through "struggle for freedom itself," Pal writes, that freedom can be learned.[87]

As Pal sees it, this radical affirmation of India, so contrary to reformist spirit, will unleash patriotic energy spurring changes more sweeping than those visualized by the Congress establishment. In contrast to Congress agitations for government reforms, competitive service exams and the like, Pal summons a new agenda, a "new synthesis": abolition of all hierarchical social dominance. This requires a complex forward-looking affirmation of India's own genius, which Pal hopes to provide.

In view of his early radical anti-imperialism, it is striking to find Pal just a few years later advocating continued Indian participation in the British Empire. The shift, though not so contradictory as it may sound at first, marks transition in concern away from nationalist activism toward philosophical reflection on larger principles of sound social order resembling what overtakes Aurobindo.

From around 1910 onward, Pal's writings show increasing fascination with the phenomenon of imperialism as "unification of humanity to an extent and upon a measure that is impossible under any known form of human organisation or association."[88] He outlines a vision for reformulated Empire, wherein India and other dominions enjoy national freedom in "Federal Constitution," equal with Britain.[89] "Federal imperialism," he writes, is the "highest and the most practical Ideal for the Indian Nationalists." It is an idea whose time has come, though this got missed "in the earlier years of our Nationalist agitation." To have advocated continued association with Britain in 1905-1908 would have been "suicidal."[90]

Pal distinguishes between two imperialisms. One, exemplified by then-prevailing British rule, is political "domination" by "central suzerain authority" over subjugated dominions. The other "true empire-idea" is "co-operative partnership" among equals. This true empire-idea is not political, but essentially social. Its value lies in offering:

> ...the largest formula of human fellowship, so far discovered by our social movements and speculation, and that it is, therefore, the largest vehicle and instrument of that Universal Humanity towards which social evolution is always moving as its ultimate ideal end.[91]

Like Aurobindo, Pal visualizes society evolving through progressive federalization toward ever-more-inclusive community. Like Aurobindo and seemingly Hegel—he assigns moral value to this.

Human communities, he writes, embody "moral relations" with "an element of freedom at their very root." Morality and community emerge through self-restraint practiced by individuals and groups so as to create wider associations. Human well-being expands through dialectical sacrifice of narrower freedoms and interests, gaining higher freedoms and well-being through "wider fields of human fellowship." As Pal writes, "Each succeeding state is reached also by simultaneously restricting and expanding the freedom enjoyed by the social units in the preceding stage."[92] Though Pal uses Advaitic idioms far less frequently than Aurobindo, he sometimes equates realization of morality, freedom and well-being with Advaitic self-discovery. "Every new human association, thus, actually expands our self," he writes. "This sense expands itself always through the cultivation of what may be called the sense of ownness."[93]

Values of association, Pal stipulates, diminish with degrees of coercion. Free self-restraint, not coercion, is the crux of morality and community. "Freedom," he writes, "is the very soul and essence of all human fellowship and co-operation." It is the free quality of association that gives "real moral value." Rousseau-like, Pal concludes that the moral quality of community resides in participatory democracy: "self-government in the administration of the common affairs." [94] He echoes Rousseau's notion that freedom lies in living by self-imposed laws through democratic participation in making them. Freedom is "submitting yourselves to the laws that you helped make and submitting yourselves to the regulation that you helped to impose upon yourselves and upon the community at large."[95] Again like Rousseau, Pal finds essential antagonism between "autocracy" and "public spirit." Despotism kills all public life and "civic enthusiasm," driving community members into selfish private life, "sordid" and "parochial."[96]

To embody freedom, association must represent "real community of interests," not forceful imposition of some upon others. India's participation in Empire must therefore transform into that of "co-partner," "equal among equals." India must become a "self-governing unit" before it can participate in "commonwealth."[97] This is what he thinks sometimes at least. Strange in light of his ardent nationalism, he meanwhile verges on positing that British conquest of India has been dialectically necessary, opening possibilities for new and higher association. It is not always clear that he thinks total independence as first step is the only way forward. [98]

How can conflicts of interest between India and Britain transform themselves toward community, especially since conflicts at stake are recalcitrantly material and economic? At times, Pal resolves the conflict with Hegelian metaphysical flourish. Some "reconciliation of opposing interests" must be possible because every "synthesis" is the fruit of some "antecedent antithesis."[99] Force of the moral idea will resolve material conflicts, he suggests. At other times he sticks to material analysis, suggesting that "pure, even vulgar, self-interest" will soon move Britain toward a cooperative, non-exploitative posture. He does not coherently identify what "self-interest" might move Britain this way. The solution to this puzzle, if there is one in his thought, emerges only in detailed economic analyses examined below.

Like Aurobindo, Pal visualizes the good society as federated association and differentiated unity. In this regard, Hindu religion and society are prototypes in several ways of the world's ideal future. Hindu religion, for example, is no unitary dogma or creed but federation of "diverse theologies and dogmas and disciplines and rituals and worships, all moved, however, by one common spirit and pursuing one common ideal." Hindu social economy is similarly federal, with autonomous caste groups cooperating interdependently. Likewise, Hindu polity is "federal type" with communal villages organized into larger confederacies while preserving "all local autonomies."[100]

Federalism is not the only way Hindu culture represents the world's future. Hindu experience and values incubate democratic community. Pal praises democratic habits and procedures in India's ancient states.[101] An even larger theme is Hindu genius for disciplining passion. A democratic community requires disciplined passion so that people find it possible to place a common good ahead of private satisfactions. Pal coins the term "Divine Democracy" to indicate an "essentially modern" democracy holding true to Indian spirituality and culture.[102] He interprets Hindu ascetic discipline as "moral education" in material self-restraint.[103] Like Vivekananda, he interprets Hindu freedom as what Kant could applaud: freedom from slavery to passions, not freedom to satisfy them.[104]

BHAKTI SOCIOLOGY

Though their views converge in many ways, Aurobindo and Pal diverge sharply in theological preference. As Aurobindo leans increasingly toward Advaita, Pal leans increasingly toward Bhakti.

To be sure, Pal sometimes writes in the idiom of Advaita. His non-Advaitic approach emerges, however, in his general philosophy of religion, which rivals Aurobindo's in scope and ambition. The history of religion, Pal writes, lies in human attempts to grapple with the "not-me," that which is strange and external to the self in nature and in society. Self and not-self relate through three persisting modalities—knowledge, emotion, and will—each requiring subject and object. This dualistic scheme removes Pal from Advaitic non-duality.[105]

Pal offers several further reasons for preferring theistic formulations over Advaitic ones. Like Aurobindo, he portrays the activity of ultimate reality, Brahman, in Hegelian language. Brahman moves from unconscious simple unity through diversity to self-differentiated conscious unity. For both Aurobindo and Pal as for Hegel, social evolution manifests and reflects this process. As Pal explains it, however, Hindu thought contains two basic schools that view Brahman's cosmic action differently from each other. The Advaitic or "Samskara" school emphasizes Brahman as simple, undifferentiated unity while the Vaishnavite school sees Brahman as "self-differentiated unity."[106] The Vaishnavite conception as differentiated unity corresponds more closely than does the Advaitic conception to Pal's notion of society:

> The Ultimate Reality does not exist in himself as undifferentiated unity or consciousness but as self-differentiated congeries of relations there in his own being... As we are domestic and social beings here, realising ourselves in organised society so stands the Lord, an organised spiritual society of His own, composed of the endless multiplied forms of his *Prakriti*.[107]

Ultimate Reality is not only society, according to Pal, but society perfected. All social relationships have two aspects, the progressively realising and the eternally realised. In this world, they exist as progressively realising, moving from less to more perfect, but in God's absolute being they exist in a perfect and eternally realized state. God is human society idealized: perfectly harmonious differentiated unity.[108]

In Pal's interpretation, Vaishnava theology portrays God not only as perfect society but also as perfect personality. This is no surprise because Pal, like Aurobindo, sees all societies imbued with distinctive "personalities."[109] As Divine Personality, God resembles the social nature of human beings. Humans grow and realize themselves as personalities only through intercourse with other personalities. Without plural personalities, there can be no personality at all. As Personality, God too needs other personalities in order to grow and attain self-knowledge. This explains God's eternal self-differentiation into multiple human personalities with whom to have relationships.[110] This implies the divine nature of all humans who stem from God's ongoing process of self-differentiation. Vaishnava theology pushes the analogy between human and divine still further by conceiving the Absolute, in the form of Krishna, as "Perfected Man."[111] In sum, Vaishnava theology sets up for Pal complex equivalents among God, society, and human personality. This equivalency emerges once again in his discussion of Mother Worship, a theme explored below.

In still another argument, Pal sees Vaishnavism, allowing for differentiation in unity, as less world-negating than Advaita. Advaita portrays both senses and normal human relations as distractions from undifferentiated insight into reality. It therefore lays exaggerated stress on suppressing sensations and human relations. Vaishnavism, by contrast, seeks not to expunge but to regulate sensual appetite, which it sees as an aspect of Godhead, not merely illusory distraction. Senses are neither indulged nor repudiated, but regulated and consecrated. Normal social relations are not devalued but transvalued as relationships with God.[112]

On another issue also, Pal praises Vaishnavism over Advaita. In Advaita, he argues, the Ultimate is approached solely through insight, while Vaishnava Bhakti approaches God also through passionate emotion and willing activity. This passion and will Pal finds more humanly engaging than mere insight.[113]

Pal praises Vaishnavism not only as theology but also as social movement. The spirit of Krishna (incarnation of Vishnu) Bhakti is democratic because it delivers a "new social message," the Divine presence in all persons and society. Vaishnavism provides ideology for "mass movement" against caste hierarchy. In Bengal, according to Pal, medieval Vaishnavism sought lower-caste emancipation from social and religious disability so as to create a "new and reformed community" with a "new set of Vaishnavic laws" targeted toward equality. Regrettably, this transformative project proved short-lived and ineffectual, with Vaishnavism captured by high-caste Hindus steeped in the old attitudes.[114] Nevertheless, the early spirit of Bengal Vaishnavism foreshadows and partly embodies the transformative spirit Pal praises for modern times.

VARNASHRAMADHARMA AND SANNYASA:
RECONCILING SOCIAL ENGAGEMENT AND MORAL AUTONOMY

Though Pal defends Vaishnavite Bhakti in particular, he also extolls other aspects of Hindu religion and society. Sometimes his comprehensive praise makes him hard to interpret. Pronouncements on caste, for example, manifest ambivalence. His Vaishnavite sympathies reveal distaste for hierarchical dimensions. Pal lays little or no stress, however, on caste as system of economic exploitation. Moreover, he perceives certain virtues. First, as mentioned, he praises the caste system as a social economy composed of autonomous but federated communities, combining virtues of freedom and cooperation. Second, within any particular caste he finds "essentially democratic institutions," though he fails to elaborate.[115]

Pal also urges that criticism of caste often misses the mark. First, caste divisions contradict equality and fraternity no more than social divisions elsewhere, such as class divisions in Europe. Caste should not be singled out for condemnation when shortcoming is universal.[116] Second, Pal finds much of modern Indian anti-caste sentiment ill-motivated. Indians who repudiate caste do so primarily because it irksomely restrains eating and sexual appetites, not because they hold lofty aspirations for human fraternity. To abolish caste restrictions for the sake of free appetite satisfaction is for Pal—because he believes that appetite restraint undergirds all true community—a negative step, especially if, as is likely, caste divisions may quickly be replaced by class divisions.[117]

Despite these qualified defenses of caste, Pal shows little sympathy with caste as system of hierarchy. He sometimes suggests that the outward hierarchy of caste was not in the Hindu past consciously experienced in terms of superiority and inferiority. The spiritual detachment cultivated by traditional Hindu culture blocked any such sense of superiority or inferiority. Pal explains this spiritual detachment in terms of traditional embeddedness of caste in the varnashrama system. The varnashrama system softened outward inequalities by submitting practitioners from all castes to the equalizing inward spiritual disciplines of the four sequential life stages: student, householder, mendicant and renouncer. This system of life stages, thinks Pal, promoted a sense of "spiritual democracy" among all ranks. He seems unaware of or untroubled by low-caste exclusion from Sanskritic culture in which the ashramadharma of sequential life stages was normatively practiced. What counts is the ideal, perhaps imperfectly realized, of inward spiritual discipline and democracy cutting across merely outward divisions of caste.[118]

Pal defends ashramadharma not only as spiritual equalizer of caste, but also on another ground, as odd in its way as the first. The strict social discipline of the ashrama system has as its paradoxical purpose liberation of each individual as sannyasin in the final renouncer life phase. As Pal notes in many contexts, higher forms of freedom require restraints upon lower forms of action. "*Through* subjection *to* freedom," he writes, is precisely the "key-note of Hindu culture."[119] He describes the sannyasin as having been cured of the "natural conceit of self" by the "rigid laws and disciplines" of his early-life "social obligations." The future sannyasin, through the practice of these disciplines, renders himself devoid of "self-regarding" desires, "his will freed from all individualistic impulses." Kantian overtones lie in Pal's description of the sannyasin as a "law unto himself," willing the "Universal," with "his intellect established in the verities of Reason." Self-subsistently moral, the sannyasin stands free of all social ties. He is, Pal suggests, "super-social,"meaning "beyond social." [120]

This conception of the sannyasin is commonplace. More surprising is that Pal himself should endorse this vision of an asocial state as supreme moral achievement. How does this fit with his view that human morality and freedom thrive best through communal engagement and commitment? Only paragraphs after explaining his Kantian sannyasin, Pal writes that human personality "realizes and perfects itself, not through individualistic isolation but through increasingly larger "associations."[121] Pal's criticism of "individualistic isolation," though directed at Western individualism, seems relevant also to the Kantian sannyasin he seems to applaud. The paradox partly dissolves by recognizing that Pal's Kantian sannyasin and his socially moralized person resemble one another in selfless orientation, cultivated self-discipline and transcendence of narrow appetite. A striking difference remains: the sannyasin is moral and free *after* and *separate from* his associative life, while the socially embedded person is moral and free *during* and *within* social experience.

Pal does not seem to notice or address this paradox, much less resolve it. We can perhaps resolve it for him, however, if we take as the crux of his vision the moral life of social engagement and work from there.

In this light, Pal's social ideal might be an order in which two 'moments'—the life of social engagement and restraint over here, the life of autonomous moral fulfillment over there—become more closely and subtly harmonized. The traditional Hindu scheme of ashramadharma plus sannyasins could be thought a crude first approximation of Pal's ideal. In the classical progression through ashramadharma toward sannyasa, social restraint and autonomous moral fulfillment fall into distinct and separate life phases, rather than harmonizing and intertwining. Just as 'moments' of restraint and autonomy are segregated, so are the 'geographies' of those experiencing them. Sannyasins live as isolated "supersocial" beings while everyone yet to reach sannyasa lives in webs of social engagement. In both time and space the ashrama/sannyasin scheme combines social engagement and moral autonomy more crudely than an order in which moral autonomy exemplifies itself all along through social engagement.

Pal might well applaud the ashrama/sannyasin scheme and yet concede its crudeness, preferring a subtler scheme harmonizing the two moments and geographies—social engagement and moral autonomy—that the classical scheme separates.

This interpretation is borne out by Pal's essay on Tolstoy called "Civic Freedom and Individual Perfection." It rebukes Tolstoy for a vision of moral transformation Pal finds excessively "individualist." By this, he means that Tolstoy imagines moral and spiritual life as private spiritual endeavor, divorced from "social and civic" effort. This fails to recognize "organic unity between the individual and the social organism." Personal character and social institutions "act and re-act" together. Individual and social transformation require each other.

Pal accuses Tolstoy of an aspect of what I call "pure religious ideology": artificial separation of "spiritual" issues from "material" ones. Pal ridicules this, calling it "medieval." In both Europe and India, he argues, medieval thought visualizes private self-realization as distinctly "spiritual," separate from the "material" life of social action. His critique of this medieval tendency seems to bespeak dethronement of the sannyasin ideal. His praise is for the mythically democratic life of ancient India, when the "Hindu" lived as "free citizen" seeking the "highest self-realization not through the denial and negation of social and civic rights and responsibilities but through a due discharge of these."[122]

CIVIL RELIGION AND THE MOTHER

To heal the medieval split between spirituality and social engagement is a task of civil religion. Like Aurobindo, Pal pictures India's rising nationalism as "religion." Indian nationalism, he argues, should exist as an "organised *cult*" with "patriotic rites" and "sacraments of our civic life." This will alleviate the artificial medieval split between "cult of patriotism" and "religion specifically so-called." Though conceding that India's civil religion should not lie with any particular religion,[123] Pal sees ways in which Hinduism already represents a veiled but powerful form of civil religion.

Pal takes pains to interpret what he calls the "Cult of the Mother" in radical Indian nationalism. The rhetoric concerning Mother India, though surely patriotic, goes beyond the "mere civic sentiment" of European "secular patriotism." The Cult of the Mother is a truly religious devotion, through which Indians actually worship their own society. The Mother worshipped, writes Pal, is "the idealisation and spiritualisation of the collective life and functions of our society." Durkheim applauds.

The symbolism of Motherhood, Pal explains, is appropriate because "society" provides its members with the "mental and spiritual nourishment" they need to thrive as humans. In sustaining life and providing nurture, society resembles both God and actual human mothers. Around Motherhood Pal organizes a religious conception of dependence and devotion simultaneously theological and sociological.

For Pal as for Aurobindo, it is not just the nation that stands as an object of worship. "The Cult of the Mother" links to what Pal calls the "Cult of Humanity." Humanity itself stands as God and mother to all human beings. All human beings and collectives exist as equal manifestations of the Divine. Human society represents and embodies the differentiated unity of the Divine.[124] The Cult of the Mother is therefore a sort of federal religion in which the Divine can be worshipped at various levels from the most particular to the most universal, no focus of worship excluding others. There is, in particular, no contradiction between worship of God in her transcendent dimension and devotion to society as immanent manifestation. As Pal argues, Hinduism denotes both Humanity and Divinity by the same word, Narayana. "Humanity and Divinity are, indeed, one," he writes.[125]

By the same token, there is no contradiction between devotion to one's particular society and devotion to humanity at large. One's particular society, valuable in its own right, finds meaning and fulfillment beyond itself as contributor to humanity at large. As Pal tirelessly repeats, the life of any social entity completes and fulfills itself through service to larger totalities in which it participates.

Hinduism, to Pal, bears special affinity to the sociological religion he has sketched out. First, as a federal religion Hinduism lends itself to the complex orientations that sociological religion implies. It provides an appropriate basis not only for Indian national religion but for a religion of humanity. It has been "the purpose of God in India," he thinks, to develop the "federal idea" and to "lead humanity" into a religiously-bonded "universal Federation."[126]

There is a second respect also in which Hinduism fits perfectly in simultaneous roles as Indian national religion and universal religion. Forms of religion, Pal argues, typically evolve through stages: ethnic, creedal, and universal. Hinduism is distinctive because it has no creed and therefore skips the creedal stage, developing directly into a universal religion without losing its ethnic dimension. Hinduism exists as religion "both national and universal," aptly suited as sociological religion of both Indian nationalism and wider human universalism where nationalism fulfills its destiny.[127]

As Pal explains, the Cult of the Mother in Hinduism has prominently served as India's civil religion. "Our history is the sacred biography of the Mother," he writes.[128] The Divine Mother has been worshipped in various forms. Different names and forms of the Goddess represent different stages and aspects of India's national life. Jagaddhatri, for example, stands for primitive struggle with nature, while Durga represents conscious national unification. Lakshmi stands for economic life, Sarasvati for intellectual life, Karttikeya for military life, and so on. In short, Goddess worship represents an elaborate civil religion. Different incarnations of the Goddess have "deeper meaning" as "different manifestations of Mother India."[129]

Pal's sociological religion bespeaks influence from Durkheim. It recalls Durkheim's notion of "organic solidarity" when Pal speaks of society as "organic unity," cemented by "solidarity."[130] Like Durkheim, Pal visualizes society as organism, functioning through interdependent subparts making distinct contributions to the whole. Pal equates "organic unity" with "federal organisation," meaning "freedom of the parts in the unity of the whole." In society, this means that separate sub-parts and individuals should enjoy "legitimate freedom" but pursue well-being through "larger collective ends."

Pal contrasts his social vision with European liberal individualism where people pursue only their "natural instincts and appetites" in "perpetual antagonism" to fellow humans. Pal links liberal individualism to capitalism, speaking of "the doctrine of the survival of the fittest" and "conflicts of economic competition." This "individualistic social philosophy" must yield to an organic conception that Pal calls "socialism."[131]

Pal stipulates that the socialism he favors should not be confused with what he calls "pagan socialism." Pagan socialism stifles individual freedom and self-fulfillment so as to achieve collective ends. This stifling, perhaps Durkheim's primitive "mechanical solidarity" returning as communist zombie, is as faulty as exaggerated liberal individualism in the modern West. Socialism should "reconcile individuality with social unity, freedom with subjection."[132]

FRAGMENTS OF A HINDU SOCIAL ECONOMY

Close scrutiny of his detailed economic analyses confers some credit on Pal but also highlights shortfall at the end of the day. India's native social economy, writes Pal, based itself on "co-operation" and "socialism," not competitive and exploitative Western principles. Meanwhile, India's attitude toward material life has been one of "renunciation," not "appropriation" as in the West.[133] Habits of co-operation and renunciation are, of course, precisely what Pal deems necessary for constructing a satisfactory socialist order. Such views are of a familiar stripe by now. Hinduism is good values and socialism, while the West is bad values and capitalism.

Pal differs from thinkers examined so far, however, in the degree to which he grasps capitalism as an economic system, not mere moral perversity. His taste and aptitude for economic analysis bring him close to discussing socialism too as an economic system, not merely as correct moral outlook. In the end, however, he fails to engender more than vague germs of socialist theory for India.

Pal's 1920 publication, *The New Economic Menace to India*, sets out a sustained discussion of India's predicament. Pal attempts to formulate an economic philosophy and strategy for India. The core of India's economic predicament has been and remains subjugation to imperial British capital.

Like Aurobindo, Pal insists it is not imperialism's administrative drain but British capital itself that most threatens Indian wealth.[134] This occurs in several ways.

First, once-thriving native industries such as textiles have been destroyed by policies designed to maintain India as Britain's captive market for manufactures. Devastating consequences of this de-industrialization include massive dis-employment, poverty, population pressure and permanent agrarian crisis. Meanwhile, Indian wealth drains abroad to pay for manufactured imports.

Second, new industries on Indian soil are foreign-owned such that drained-off profits are unavailable for domestic investment and development.

Third, Indian natural resources are exploited for foreign purposes rather than those of India's own development.

Fourth, labor laws have been enacted ensuring plentiful cheap work forces for British enterprise.

Pal's analysis, though hardly exhaustive, paints a general picture of retarded, distorted development and rising poverty due to foreign control. Exploitation is one of Britain's avowed goals in India, Pal argues, quoting a remark he attributes to Lord Curzon that "exploitation and administration" were unified parts of Britain's "duty" in India.[135]

India requires independence, as Pal contends at this point in his career, so that its government may follow policies conducive to India's own economic well-being rather than that of British capital. A free national government could regain domestic ownership of land and resources, drive tougher bargains with foreign capital on matters of wages and other economic benefits, and enact a protective tariff to foster domestic industrialization. Such a government could also borrow foreign capital, paying interest and retaining a share of profits from effective investment, rather than losing all profit abroad.[136]

India's short-term prognosis, Pal writes, is not bright. British capital has moved into a new phase. Formerly, the British state, though favorable to capital, was not engaged with it in outright collaboration. As capital has grown more massive, however, a new era emerges in which British state policy and the interests of big capital fuse together. The British state, including the government of India, will initiate direct wealth transfer to big capital, through tax-financed research and revenue subsidies, forcible land acquisitions and so on. The state may also enter profit-sharing monopoly enterprises with capital. It may even launch profit-making enterprise in its own right. All in all, Pal foresees emergence of higher symbioses between state and big capital that some call "late capitalism." Pal calls it "State Socialism," with "capitalistic spirit."[137] We will call it "state capitalism" to conform with our discussion of Das and distinguish it from "state socialism" understood as a system of state-centered public ownership.

Pal imagines British state capitalism transforming both India and Britain. India faces a more unified and aggressive imperial capitalist program under which Indian markets, labor and resources will lie ever more savagely exploited.[138] The ensuing enrichment will help British capital transform the situation at home, where militant labor has begun to agitate for transfer of the economy into public hands. New infusions of wealth from the colonies may allow British capital to take the steam out of this militancy, bribing labor with higher wages and benefits, thus siphoning off mounting pressure for public ownership. In fact socialist unrest at home is prime driver for newly aggressive state capitalism in the empire. Capitalism's ruthlessness at home, having provoked labor's militancy, must be reined in, but also replaced by heavier ruthlessness abroad.[139]

India's only hope is to forge alliance with Britain's socialism against its capitalism. The combined power of such an alliance will secure the true interests of both British labor and Indian development in a unified anti-capitalist strategy. British labor cannot long rest in any "deal" with imperial capital for higher living standards. Modern capital is mobile so as to flow always to fields of highest profit. British capital will flow away from home so long as Indian labor remains ill-paid, un-unionized and devoid of rights. Formerly British jobs will flow into India while wealth will flow increasingly in reverse from India to British capital. With fewer jobs available, British labor's bargaining power and living standards will decline. India will meanwhile become more and more a mere workforce for foreign owners.

British labor's best strategy is not junior partnership with British capital in colonial exploitation. It lies rather in promoting India's independence and a unionized Indian workforce pressing for parity with British labor's living standards. According to Pal, this would secure British labor's own living standards against threat of capital mobility induced by the lure of cheap Indian labor. If conscious enough of these considerations, British labor could push policy in helpful directions: independence for India and unionization of its workforce.[140] If not, all is lost.

Pal's keen sense of capitalism as international system matches up with his sense of socialism as a force for international cooperation.[141]

It is here, if anywhere, that Pal solves the puzzle of transforming the British-Indian relationship from exploitation to cooperation. British capital is a "particularistic" interest, holding captive the true interests of both Britain and India. An alliance of the subjugated could transform the Empire from a structure of dominance toward a co-operative federation. Pal seems to imagine abolishing capitalism as part of this transformation, establishing a co-operative socialist federal empire.

After analyzing India's imperial predicament, Pal tries to outline a vision of India's post-independence economy. "Socialism," he writes, "represents the most advanced thoughts and speculations of modern economics."[142] Though Pal clearly intends his vision to be progressive and socialist, his suggestions are too random and scattered to provide a unified socialist viewpoint. He never comes squarely to grips with what patterns of ownership and productive organization India should adopt.

At some moments, expanded industrialization seems to be key. India must become "not only an agricultural but a manufacturing nation also," Pal writes.[143] Much of his displeasure with Britain's rule, as we have seen, is that it stifles India's industrial development. In various passages, he offers strategies such as tariffs, capital imports, and national industrial research aimed at fostering rapid development.[144] Moreover, Pal often seems to imagine India's industrialization occurring within a largely capitalist framework. The national industrialization strategy will provide Indian capitalism with needed opportunities for growth.[145] The well-being of the masses, meanwhile, lies in stiff taxation on capital's "Excess-Profits" in order to finance social spending for benefit of the poor.[146] Pal does not speak explicitly of a publicly-owned Indian economy, though he is well aware that public ownership is on the agenda for British socialism.

The strands in Pal's thought just mentioned seem to contemplate India's economy not as true socialism but as a sort of nationalist industrial capitalism, combined with a progressive social welfare state. There are other strands in his thought, however, quite at odds with such a vision. Over and over, he criticizes both capitalism and large-scale industrialization, which he equates too simplistically with each other. "Capitalist industrialism" for India, he suggests, is simultaneously impossible, unwise and immoral.

First, large-scale capitalist production requires imperially-captive markets, such as India has provided for Britain, in order to sell mass-produced commodities at a profit. Because it does not command such captive markets, India cannot effectively rely on large-scale capitalist production. Second, overly capital-intensive industrialization will displace workers, exacerbating India's already massive problems of unemployment and overpressure on agrarian land. Third, capitalist industrialization will degrade the moral tenor of Indian life, replacing it with the "corroding evils" of capitalist culture.[147]

Pal's critique of capitalist industrialism, though not erroneous, suffers from failure to articulate a non-capitalist model of industrialization that might alleviate the ills he points out. Pal fails to distinguish capitalism from industrialism and shows no familiarity with theories of how socialism, through investment according to priority needs rather than profit, might achieve industrialization without market imperialism or mass unemployment. His critique of capitalist industrialization therefore verges on a backward-looking and romantic anti-industrialism.

Pal's rejection of "capitalist industrialism" integrates poorly with his image of an industrializing capitalist welfare state. Perhaps he sees the capitalist welfare state as a transition to something beyond capitalism or envisions capitalist enterprise as a limited component of a larger socialist economy. He specifies no position. His rejection of "capitalist industrialism" implies that he would perhaps tolerate a "socialist industrialism," but he provides only meager hints of what a socialist industrialism might look like.

Tension between Pal's advocacy of industrialization and rejection of large-scale "capitalist" industrialism can perhaps best be construed as sympathy for light decentralized industry. We might infer that Pal envisions continuity with what he calls the "communistic" organization characteristic of traditional Indian craft-style production, prior to imperial depredations. In that system, according to Pal, craft workers typically owned land to ensure their subsistence and organized themselves on a "co-operative" worker-ownership basis with no wage labor class of subservient non-owning workers.[148] This may be something of what Pal imagines for India's future. India's industrial development, Pal writes, "will have to follow the lead of her own genius" in accord with her "past historic evolution."[149] Pal does not, however, outline what modern industrial forms India's past might prefigure.

Pal recognizes overpopulation on land as India's most massive problem, with its consequent underemployment and poverty. Industrialization must seek to relieve this by soaking up excess agrarian labor, not exacerbate it by displacing still more non-agrarian workers, forcing them to seek subsistence on the land.[150] To absorb surplus agrarian labor, India's best bet might be a scheme of light and labor-intensive village industry, perhaps along principles of co-operative ownership.

Pal sets out to reconstruct India's villages as autonomous democratic communities. Even prior to independence, he argues, villages can organize themselves to function in relative autonomy from the imperial structure, introducing a grass-roots germ of Indian independence and democracy. Through collaborative self-organization and self-taxation, villages can improve themselves in medicine, education, safety and sanitation. Into this scenario Pal dribbles hints of socialized production, suggesting that villages "combine" for purposes of "industrial advancement" and that public works be constructed and operated through "co-operative labour of the villages."[151]

In the past, writes Pal, village communities existed as "isolated units, without any wide outlook or outside concern." Pal envisions that "history will...work itself back" to an Indian regime based on democratic village communities. In such a dialectical recovery, not unlike what Aurobindo imagines, villages will not be isolated but integrated into larger federal associations.[152] Pal offers little to nothing by way of detail.

Pal also fails to offer actual strategy for ameliorating hierarchy and neglect of the downtrodden. He speaks of a "new synthesis" to abolish hierarchy and praises Vaishnavism for its "massive movement" and socially transformative dimensions. No suggestion emerges, however, as to how India's social and economic hierarchies might actually be dissolved.

Pal's work, in short, contains only tentative hints of how to build a worthwhile Indian social economy. By imagining resolutions of paradoxes in his thought and extrapolating from hints, we can piece together vague but plausible scenes of decentralized and labor-intensive, worker-owned industrial production, closely coordinated with agrarian life. Possible roles for larger-scale production, capitalist ownership, national planning, and social welfare policy receive hazy mention while methods of transformation remain unexplored. This disjointed quality in Pal's strategy disappoints because he musters serious competence in economic thinking. His aptitude applies better in criticizing what he dislikes than in explaining what he favors. In the end, he is less interested in describing strategies and arrangements for modern Indian socialism than in contemplating the "socialist" spirit in traditional Hindu order.

CHAPTER 4

Ambedkar: (A)-Political Buddhism and State Socialism

Well-launched Untouchable and relentless achiever, Bhimrao Ramji Ambedkar (1891-1956) met the world at Mhow in Central India, youngest child of a military officer. Despite financial and social adversity due to untouchable status, Ambedkar attained impressive achievements in his early life. He took his B.A. in 1913 from Bombay's Elphinstone College. By 1923, he had earned his M.A. and Ph.D. from Columbia University in the United States and his M.Sc. and D.Sc. from the University of London, all with theses on Indian economic issues. He had also read law at Gray's Inn and qualified as barrister in 1920.

Back in India, Ambedkar pursued a varied career in academics, law, and journalism, gaining prominence as political leader on behalf of Untouchables. Among his activities was organization of non-violent civil disobedience (satyagraha) aimed at securing rights of Hindu temple-entry for Untouchables. In 1947, he became chair of the drafting committee for independent India's Constitution. He decisively influenced that document. Also in 1947, he became Minister of Law in independent India's first cabinet, but he resigned in 1951 to protest Nehru government policy on Kashmir, foreign relations and programs for Untouchables. Thereafter, he continued until his death to pursue a public career, which increasingly included participation in Buddhist organizations.

The first two chapters of this Part explored two distinguishable attitudes toward the Hindu religious tradition. Das attempts to fashion society according to Manu's detailed socio-religious doctrines. Aurobindo and Pal attempt to extract from Hindu tradition less detailed, more general precepts of sound social order. They adopt a critical or selective posture toward the tradition, a willingness to recognize limitations and shortcomings. In his work, Ambedkar offers still a third attitude toward Hindu tradition, an attitude of unrelenting rejection and rebuke. Where Das, Aurobindo, and Pal see freedom, harmony, and cooperation, Ambedkar sees oppression, strife, and struggle. Far from urging modern India and the world to school themselves on the genius of Hinduism, Ambedkar calls for its extermination.

DEMOCRACY: "ENDOSMOSIS" VERSUS CAPITALISM AND CASTE

Ambedkar greatly concerns himself with issues of democracy. Democracy to Ambedkar is "not merely a form of government," the framework of institutions he calls "political democracy" or "parliamentary democracy."[1] There is also what he calls "social and economic democracy," or sometimes simply "social democracy."[2] This involves two related but distinguishable strands, one of them basically spiritual, the other economic. In exploring them we can see how Ambedkar situates himself within our problematic.

Ambedkar describes the spiritual component in various ways. It is, first, the "principle of fraternity," a sense of "common brotherhood," "unity and solidarity" in social life.[3] Fraternity, he writes, "is only another name for democracy." It is "primarily a mode of associated living, of conjoint communicated experience." He equates fraternity with what he calls "social endosmosis," described as follows:

> An ideal society should be mobile, should be full of channels for conveying a change taking place in one part to other parts. In an ideal society there should be many interests consciously communicated and shared. There should be varied and free points of contact with other modes of association.[4]

For Ambedkar, democracy—as fraternity and social endosmosis—implies the sharing of experience in social life. Endosmosis is the precise opposite of endogamy, caste.

A second spiritual aspect Ambedkar labels the "functioning of moral order in society."[5] Because democracy is a regime of freedom, vast aspects of social life are left unregulated by law. This means that citizens must sense and practice a "moral order." This moral order is really just the principle of fraternity from a different angle, because "fraternity" and "morality" are the same.[6] Key to moral order is what Ambedkar calls "public conscience," a conscience agitated at every wrong, no matter who the sufferer may be. It means that everyone, whether suffering that particular wrong or not, is willing to join the sufferer in seeking relief.[7] Public conscience implies the sharing of suffering, an aspect of "endosmosis" or the general sharing of experience.

The economic component of democracy, thinks Ambedkar, lies in equality. There must not be "a class which has got all the privileges and a class which has got all the burdens to carry."[8] Class cleavage threatens democratic stability by provoking violent unrest. It threatens the fundamental idea of democracy, which is "one man, one value." The idea of "one man, one value" is captured only partially by the egalitarian political practice of "one man, one vote." It must be completed by egalitarian economic structures.[9]

Ambedkar's conception of democracy as fraternal spirit and egalitarian economy animates his condemnations of both caste and capitalism. "The two enemies are Brahminism and capitalism," he writes. Both caste and capitalism represent systems of social division that are also systems of economic exploitation. There is Marxist hue to his conclusion that caste and capitalism are but two manifestations of the same ubiquitous ill: division of societies into classes.[11]

Ambedkar equates capitalism with inequalities of wealth as well as with poor living standards and working conditions.[12] He also finds capitalism incompatible with democracy. Private capital exercises self-interested control over social life and workplaces, compelling the economically weak to suffer "dictatorship of the private employer."[13]

Ambedkar rejects naïve analyses of capitalism, of which he finds Gandhi especially culpable. His criticism of Gandhi applies in varying degrees to thinkers discussed above who confuse capitalism with either industrialism or with mere selfishness. The evils of capitalism, Ambedkar argues, should not be blamed on "machinery and modern civilization." Industrialism and modernity hold out a promise of liberating humanity from brutish existence and making possible for all a life of leisure, culture and socio-economic equality. He calls for "more machinery and more civilization."

If anti-industrialism is no solution, neither is "moral rearmament" of the "propertied classes," which is how Ambedkar describes the Gandhian notion of capitalist "trusteeship." As Chapter 5 will explore, Gandhi's doctrine on "trusteeship" envisions large property-holders devoting their wealth primarily to common well-being. The notion that "moneyed classes" would "hold their properties in trust for the poor" Ambedkar calls "ridiculous." Both the anti-industrial approach and the capitalist-as-trustee approach miss the central nature of capitalism, which is "wrong social organization:" "private property" in production.[14] It is capitalism that must disappear.

Ambedkar disputes the notion that the Indian National Congress represents the common interest of the whole Indian nation. Though the Congress includes in its membership the lowly and modestly comfortable as well as the fabulously rich, it nevertheless sits under the sway of "wealthy people" and "big business" and will basically serve as "protector of the capitalists." Ambedkar concludes that a self-conscious working-class party must emerge to protect the downtrodden. In 1936, he helped organize the Independent Labor Party to oppose the Congress in Legislative Assembly elections under the 1935 Government of India Act. The Party's purpose, he declared, was "to fight for the interest of the untouchables, the working classes, the poor and deprived people."[15] Ambedkar's formation of the ILP, though perhaps a good idea in itself, arguably typified his tendency to overemphasize electoral and parliamentary action as principal means of fighting entrenched power. We shall return to this theme.

Much of Ambedkar's thought centers around critical analysis of caste. Caste he sees as India's peculiar variant of class divisions characterizing all societies up to the present. Caste and class, he thinks, are "next door neighbours," distinct yet close. A class system has permeable boundaries allowing a degree of social mobility and intermarriage. A caste system, however, sets up rigid boundaries stemming from endogamy, so that castes are walled off from each other. "A caste is an enclosed class," Ambedkar writes.[16] Though caste and class both violate social endosmosis, caste does so more aggressively and rigidly.

Like most social ills, caste proceeds most fully from higher social echelons. Caste exclusivity is practiced most fully among Brahmins. In fact, Ambedkar argues, caste originated with exclusionary practices of Brahmins, then was imitated in decreasingly exact fashion by progressively lower classes. The atmosphere of exclusivity sets up a "fissiparous" logic resulting in multiplication of castes.[17]

Caste inflicts damage both spiritual and economic. Spiritually, caste constricts the morality and public conscience of Hindu society, leading people to practice morality and respond to suffering only within caste-bound limitations. Economically, caste relationships largely correspond to property. Ambedkar analyzes low-caste Shudras and Untouchables from a Marx-like viewpoint as classes of propertyless labor.[18]

The chief predicament faced by thinkers wishing to portray Hindu culture as socially progressive is what to do about caste. We have seen above how the problem of interpreting caste provokes Hindu-oriented thinkers into fits of ambivalence. Ambedkar avoids this because his first concern is to criticize caste. Opposition to caste animates his entire rejection of Hindu religion and society. To combat caste, one must combat the "religion of Caste." "To ask people to give up Caste is to ask them to go contrary to their fundamental religious notions," he concedes.[19]

Ambedkar accuses Hinduism of lacking precisely what Aurobindo and Pal find it rich in: mutual solidarity and communal consciousness. Where those thinkers portray caste at least partly as an expression of solidaristic spirit, Ambedkar insists that "anti-social spirit" is its "worst aspect." He argues in loosely Durkheimian fashion that, insofar as Hindu society lacks a "unified life and a consciousness of its own being," it is not truly a "society" at all. A society truly exists only to the extent that its members share activities such that common emotions are aroused in them. For society to exist as a coherent whole, its members must "possess things in common with one another." This implies both religious and economic components.

With respect to religion, Ambedkar mentions common celebration of festivals as an index of social bondedness. Hindu castes, he argues, celebrate festivals largely in separation from one another, thus obstructing emergence of a common life transcending caste. Economically, to "possess things in common" implies common ownership in production, so that success and failure in "associated activity" are shared.[20] Hence, in his mind, a society must be socialist in the Marxist sense before it can truly be a "society" in the Durkheimian sense, with the sharing of social experience Ambedkar calls "endosmosis." It is not, of course, only Hinduism that he finds lacking in this respect.

To Ambedkar, caste is India's paramount social problem. Political democracy cannot flourish without the social and religious revolution needed to eradicate it. Though himself a socialist, he rejects the

Marx-like viewpoint that "equalization of property" is India's paramount social task. Especially in India, the Marxist view that property relationships determine all others fails to convince. Religious attitudes weigh more heavily than economic structures in determining Indian hierarchies. Because of this, no meaningful movement toward economic equality can occur in India without prior spiritual transformation replacing caste with a "spirit of equality and fraternity."[21]

DEMOCRATIC RELIGION:
ATTACK ON HINDUISM, EMBRACE OF BUDDHISM

Ambedkar's twin focus on spiritual and economic transformation places him squarely within our problematic. Though he addresses economic dimensions more thoroughly than thinkers examined above, Ambedkar departs from materialist socialism by giving priority to spiritual over economic change.

Though the problem of caste is religious, its solution cannot be sought in mere abolition of religion. Such might be the Marxist solution, but Ambedkar declines to applaud. Unlike Marx, Ambedkar sees religion as crucial to any social order. He approves Burke's claim that "True religion is the foundation of society" and lays out a Durkheimian position that social morality requires religion.[22] It is not the case, however, that all religions are equally true or adequate, as the negative example of Hinduism proves. Ambedkar insists that religion should comport with reason and science and should offer relief to the downtrodden.[23]

Ambedkar distinguishes between a religion of "rules" and one of "principles." Rules prescribe action externally to the actor, rendering it unconscious, habitual and servile. Principles, by contrast, act as guidelines for judgment, facilitating independent choice and action. Conscious responsible choice in light of principles makes up true religious life. Religion, he writes, "must mainly be a matter of principles only." As he continues, "The moment it degenerates into rules it ceases to be religion, as it kills responsibility which is the essence of a truly religious act."

Hinduism, Ambedkar thinks, lies far from a religion of principles. So rule-bound as scarcely to deserve the name "Religion," it is "nothing but a mass of sacrificial, social, political and sanitary rules and regulations...nothing but a multitude of commands and prohibition." It is, moreover, a system of "legalized class-ethics...iniquitous in that they are not the same for one class as for another." What Ambedkar calls "true Religion" teaches spiritual principles equally applicable to all, guiding adherents toward a conscious life of moral responsibility.[24]

What Indian society needs then is not abolition but transformation in religion. Ambedkar ultimately concludes that Hinduism should be replaced by Buddhism. Before getting there, however, he toys with other possible avenues. In 1936, Ambedkar suggests reforming Hinduism itself by eliminating its caste aspect, which he calls "Brahminism." This would require repudiating Brahminical texts, which he characterizes as political class lies.[25] As he puts it:

> ...[Y]ou have got to apply the dynamite to the Vedas and the Shastras, which deny any part to reason, to Vedas and Shastras, which deny any part to morality. You must destroy the Religion of the Shrutis and the Smritis. Nothing else will avail.[26]

Ambedkar's suggestions for Hindu reform verge upon the fantastic. First, there should be a standardized "book of Hindu religion" accepted and recognized by all Hindus. Preaching of other sacred texts should be penalized by law. Second, the Brahmin priesthood should be abolished or regulated by the state. In sum, Ambedkar proposes reconstruction of Hinduism into a new and official civil religion "in consonance with Liberty, Equality and Fraternity, in short, with Democracy." He cannot say how this new religion would be recognizable as Hinduism, except to suggest it should draw on principles from the Upanishads.[27]

Amdekar searches widely for a religion compatible with democratic values. In the same year that he endorses radical transformation of Hinduism, he admonishes fellow Untouchables to convert away from it:

> If you want to organize yourself, change your religion.
> If you want to gain self-respect, change your religion.
> If you want to create a society which ensures co-operation, and brotherhood change your religion. If you want to achieve power, change your religion. If you want equality, change your religion. If you want independence, change your religion.[28]

To high-caste audiences, Ambedkar stresses democratic reform of Hinduism. To low-caste audiences, he stresses conversion to some alternate faith. When he first formulates the latter suggestion, he remains unclear what direction to take it in. Which other religion? Should an entirely new religion be founded? Suggestions focus on Islam, Christianity, and Sikhism, all protected by special minority rights under the Government of India Act. Meanwhile, however, Ambedkar sermonizes his audience with Buddhist messages of spiritual self-reliance.[29]

It is not until 20 years later in 1956 that Ambedkar announces conversion to Buddhism and launches his campaign of Buddhist conversion among Untouchables. His embrace of Buddhism turns substantially on doctrinal appeal. Beyond this, however, he finds value in the fact that Buddhism is Indian, not Western. If an alternative to Hinduism must be found, better that it be Buddhism with its indigenous heritage, rather than be imported like Christianity, Islam, and to a lesser extent Sikhism.

Like Hindu-oriented thinkers, Ambedkar seeks to ground an ideology of India's and the world's future in India's religious past. He partly endorses the notion that ancient India excelled in democracy. He associates it with Buddhism, noting both Buddha's purported approval of democratically-governed communities and the democratic procedures practiced within the sangha itself. Ambedkar suggests that the Indian history of democracy links closely with the history of Buddhism.

Buddhism and democracy align not only historically but also ideologically. They link through their common foundation in "morality," true religion. Morality distinguishes Buddhism from Hinduism. Hinduism, is "not founded on morality." Morality is not "integral" to it, at best only secondary. In Buddhism, morality is the core. "The religion of the Buddha is morality," Ambedkar writes. "Buddhist religion is nothing if not morality...What God is to other religions morality is to Buddhism."[30] It is in Buddhism that he finds "True Religion," a Religion of Principles.

Ambedkar sometimes seems unsure whether Buddhism should be classified as religion at all. Though he speaks of "Buddhist religion" and though it corresponds to "True Religion," he partly wants to place Buddhism in a category of its own. In Buddhism, calling it "Dhamma" (alternate word for "dharma"), morality is all: "Morality is Dhamma and Dhamma is morality," while in religion, morality is "not the root," but only secondary. Despite distraction over how to classify Buddhism, Ambedkar's consistent concern is with religion in a Durkheimian sense: exaltation of morality to the status of "sacred" in society.[31] Buddhism turns morality itself into religion.

If Ambedkar links Buddhism to Durkheimian concerns, he also links it to Marxist ones. Though the purpose of religion is to interpret the world, the purpose of Buddhism is to change it, he explains, borrowing from Marx's Eleventh Thesis on Feuerbach: "The philosophers have only *interpreted* the world in various ways; the point, however, is to *change* it."[32] His adaptation of Marx's aphorism distinguishes Buddhism from religion and may imply that Buddhism represents the Marx-like abolition of religion or that it changes the world through morality in ways that worn-out "religions" never could.

Ambedkar wants to draw toward Buddhism sympathies that might otherwise go to Marxism. In courting those sympathies, he stresses sometimes similarities and sometimes differences he sees between Buddhism and Marxism. Both Buddhism and Marxism begin with problems of worldly suffering. He suggests that Buddhist doctrine on *dukkha*, suffering, represents an early version of Marxist doctrine on exploitation. Buddhism and Marxism jointly repudiate "supernatural" concerns, concentrating instead upon removal of worldly injustice. The Buddha's conception of dukkha is "material," writes Ambedkar, focused largely around the problem of poverty. Buddhism and Marxism also take similar positions on property ownership, he explains. Just as Marxism banishes private ownership of productive property, the Buddhist sangha bans private property among its members. Moreover, Buddhism generally fosters an attitude of propertylessness among its adherents.[33] In fact, he concludes, more than a trifle simplistically, Marxism adds nothing of substance to Buddhism.[34]

Despite his socialism and Marxist interpretations of Buddhism, Ambedkar vehemently denounces communism, which he associates with violent change and repressive rule. He claims that Buddhism provides superior means of achieving goals it shares with communism. One of these is "reformation of the mind," spiritual transformation required to actualize a higher social life. Another is a "democratic and republican form of government," as in the early sangha.[35] It remains to be seen how Ambedkar finds Buddhism superior in attaining goals shared with communism.

DEFEAT OF DEMOCRATIC BUDDHISM
BY HIERARCHICAL HINDUISM

The mixture of Ambedkar's Buddhist and Marxist notions finds expression in two book-length studies of Indian history: *Who Were the Shudras?* and *The Untouchables*. These works illustrate Ambedkar's proclivity to think simultaneously in terms of religious struggle and class struggle. He interprets Indian history as a set of religious and class struggles resulting in prolonged entombment of democracy.

In *Who Were the Shudras?*, Ambedkar inquires how there came to be a subjugated varna, the Shudras, in Hindu society. Present-day Shudras, he argues, are not the original ones. They are a motley collection of tribes and groups subordinated and degraded by a powerful Hindu culture. They are called Shudras because, while subjugating them, Hindu culture pushed them into the lowest and most degraded varna. Little remains of the group that originally occupied the Shudra varna, but present-day Shudras are propertyless, like the original ones also became after a prolonged religious class war.[36]

Who then were the original Shudras? The original Indo-Aryan society, Ambedkar argues, comprised only the three high-born varnas: Brahmin, Kshatriya, and Vaishya. The Shudras were a wealthy and powerful group within the "Kshatriya class." Ambedkar sees evidence in the Vedas that at an early stage there were two different Aryan groups that later merged into one. These came with two distinct ideologies, embodied mainly in their creation myths. One supported the varna system and the other opposed it. Shudras belonged to the anti-varna group, which practiced a republican form of society rather than a hierarchical one.[37]

Though republican in ideology and former practice, the original Shudras came to occupy the second varna rank as a distinct group of Kshatriyas (warrior/governors) in Indo-Aryan society. There they engaged in a sort of see-saw class struggle with Brahmins, in which Shudra kings at some moments subjected Brahmins to "tyrannies and oppressions and indignities" while Brahmins at other times subjected Shudras to the Brahmin "pretension to social superiority" and "claim for special privileges," which Ambedkar describes as "outrageous" and "unbearable."

In this early class struggle, Brahmins eventually gained the upper hand. This occurred as Brahmins developed a keen "class consciousness" of their "class interests." They may even have begun transforming themselves from "class" to "caste," presumably through endogamous exclusivity. As religious specialists, moreover, Brahmins held the ultimate upper hand. In order to defeat their antagonists once and for all, they began refusing to perform for Shudras the sacred string rite of *upanayana*, which qualifies initiates to participate fully in Hindu religious life. Denied the religious status conferred by upanayana, the Shudras also lost their rights to education and property. Combination of these disabilities led to subjugation as the fourth varna. Motley subordinated groups and tribes subsequently wound up in that propertyless fourth varna, while the original Shudras largely vanished over time.[38]

Several features of Ambedkar's account warrant emphasis. First, he portrays the modern caste system as the outcome of class struggle waged through the vehicle of religion: denial of upanayana to Shudras. Second, he identifies religious degradation with economic exploitation. Loss of upanayana for the original Shudras means a descent into propertylessness. It is a typical Ambedkar departure from materialist Marxism to portray a religious factor determining the economic, rather than the reverse. Third, Ambedkar portrays the struggle as pitting a more democratically-minded group, Shudras, against a more hierarchically-minded group, Brahmins. Variants of these themes emerge in Ambedkar's other historical study.

The Untouchables sets out Ambedkar's thesis on the origins of untouchability. In Ambedkar's account, the groups that later became Untouchables were conquered tribal groups forced to settle on the perimeters of conqueror settlements. Vanquished groups were propertyless "paupers," economically dependent on the "wealthy community" to which they were subject. Ambedkar calls these groups "Broken Men."

At some point, the Broken Men became Buddhist, along with most of Indian society. The Broken Men then became the peculiar victims of a momentous religious class struggle between Buddhism and Brahminism. Buddhism was the religion of the majority, the masses, the anti-hierarchical "leftists," while Brahminism was the religion of hierarchical "rightists." For a while, Buddhism dominated the subcontinent and put Brahmin supremacy on the defensive, but Brahminism eventually triumphed in a victory for caste hierarchy.[39] It caused the wane of Buddhism throughout India, while visiting the peculiar new harm of untouchability on the Broken Men.

Ambedkar argues that the class struggle between Brahminism and Buddhism played out through the religious symbolism of diet and practices with respect to cows. In early times, he argues, all of Indian society had practiced the eating of meat, including beef. Moreover, cow sacrifice was a crucial component of Brahminical religion. Ambedkar argues that Brahmins abandoned cow sacrifice and became vegetarians in order to defend and enhance their religious prestige against competition from Buddhism. His analysis is complex and somewhat hard to follow.

The Buddhist masses objected to Brahmin cow sacrifice, he contends, on both religious and economic grounds. With respect to religion, cow sacrifice violated Buddhist non-violence. With respect to economics, it offended the sense of utility in a mainly agrarian population valuing multiple uses of cows other than for eating. Buddhist monks, meanwhile, acquired religious prestige by eating meat only if slaughtered for some reason other than to feed them. In order to seize the upper hand in religious symbolism, Brahminism took two strategic steps: it adopted vegetarianism and abandoned cow sacrifice. Cow worship replaced cow sacrifice, with consequent prohibition on cow-slaughter and special abhorrence of beef-eating.[40] These moves helped Brahiminism defeat Buddhism and incidentally inflicted disastrous secondary effects upon society's lowliest, the Broken Men.

Because of the cow's new sacred status, profane treatment of cows took on the character of sacrilege. This applied to any eating or handling of cows living or dead. Broken Men, however, had no choice but to eat beef and handle dead cows. The division of wealth in settlements had always been such that the well-to-do would eat fresh-slaughtered beef while their dispossessed underlings would eat only carrion beef from already-dead cattle. As prohibition on cow-slaughter gained allegiance, the wealthy stopped eating even slaughtered beef. Due to economic plight, however, Broken Men could not afford to stop eating carrion, "their principle sustenance." By eating cow meat, the Broken Men committed sacrilege, rendering them untouchable to higher castes. Moreover, their lowly status left them in occupations handling dead cow materials, as in the leather trade. This made them even more untouchable. It did not, however, violate either Buddhist non-violence (*ahisma*) or Brahminical cow-protection for untouchables to consume carrion beef. Hence, carrion beef eating continued, despite being sacrilegious from the viewpoint of orthodox Brahminism.[41] Buddhist religion allowed lowly Broken Men to eat what economic exploitation forced upon them. Hindu religion, meanwhile, worked actively against them, foisting upon them the degraded status of Untouchable, thus rendering them even more vulnerable to economic exploitation.

In *The Untouchables*, as in *Who Were the Shudras?*, Ambedkar explains how present caste inequalities stem from past class struggles waged through religious symbolism. He tells also of symbiosis between religious degradation and economic exploitation, and of triumph of hierarchy over democracy.

BUDDHISM REINVENTED:
MARXISM OR PURE RELIGIOUS IDEOLOGY?

In 1956, Ambedkar announced his personal conversion to Buddhism and launched his campaign of mass Buddhist conversion among Untouchables. Revival of Buddhism, he hoped, would reverse the verdict of Indian history by eradicating hierarchy, religious degradation and economic exploitation. Untouchables would gain most of all from Buddhism's resurgence.

A crucial task for propagating Buddhism, Ambedkar thinks, is "[t]o produce a Buddhist Bible."[42] He sets out to do just that and launches a work called *The Buddha and His Dhamma*. The book looks and reads like a Bible, with chapters and short numbered verses, along with doses of myth-like poetical language. Siddhartha is born miraculously, with the 32 marks signifying greatness.[43] Passages on the young Siddhartha's sensual temptations are racier than the Song of Solomon. Women press upon Siddhartha "with their full, firm bosoms in gentle collisions" and beseech him to "Perform thy rites of adoration here."[44]

There is not just myth and titillation but also political instruction in Ambedkar's retelling. The account soon departs from tradition and pursues a political agenda. In place of the Sorrowful Sights—which in the traditional story launch Siddhartha's search for the roots of suffering—Ambedkar substitutes Siddhartha's early insight into the nature of economic exploitation:

5. Once he went to his father's farm with some of his friends and saw the laborers ploughing the land, raising bunds, cutting trees, etc., dressed in scanty clothes under hot burning sun.

6. He was greatly moved by the sight.

7. He said to his friends, can it be right that one man should exploit another? How can it be right that the laborer should toil and the master should live on the fruits of his labor?[45]

If such is Siddhartha's insight, what could Marx possibly add? Later on, Siddhartha discovers that "the conflict between classes is constant and perpetual." As he further reflects: "It is this which is the root of all sorrow and suffering in the world."[46] The resolution of suffering, according to Ambedkar's Siddhartha, must be found in a new social doctrine, which is Dhamma.[47]

The social insights ascribed to Siddhartha dovetail with Ambedkar's notion of Buddhism as anti-exploitational, anti-hierarchical religion. "Dhamma is social," which implies "right relations between man and man in all spheres of life." One might therefore expect that Ambedkar's exposition of Buddhist principles would emphasize socially transformative action as key to Buddhist life. Such is not the case, however. Nowhere does Ambedkar articulate how Buddhism applies to transforming social institutions. Ambedkar's Buddhism, though linked with a "Social Message" of fraternity and social morality,[48] contains scarcely any theory of collaborative social action or vision of ideal institutional arrangements. This is strange because collaborative action aimed at rectifying injustice and building communities seems to capture some of what Ambedkar means by "endosmosis," the sharing of social experience.

Ambedkar takes care to spell out certain specific principles of Buddhist conduct. Noteworthy about these principles, however, is that they focus exclusively on cultivating personal virtue. He summarizes the "Buddhist Way of Life" with admonitions like "Do good...Commit not sin...Cherish no anger...Win your enemies by love." He describes "Righteous conduct" in terms of the five traditional Buddhist proscriptions: non-killing, non-theft, sobriety, continence and truthfulness. He suggests that "man's inequity to man" can best be solved through cultivating "good disposition."[49]

In consonance with other thinkers examined here, Ambedkar stresses the role of religion in restraining material appetite. Buddhism urges neither indulgence nor asceticism, but moderation in material satisfaction. All suffering stems from the quenchless greed of passion. "Nibbana," (alternate word for "nirvana") or salvation, means "control of passions." It is odd that Ambedkar stresses this traditional doctrine that all suffering stems from passion, since he argues equally emphatically that all suffering stems from economic exploitation. He finesses this ambiguity between traditional and Marxist Buddhism by suggesting vaguely that "uncontrolled acquisitive instinct" is the "correct analysis of class struggle." He articulates no Buddhist solution to "uncontrolled acquisitive instinct," however, except for mere cultivation of personal virtue.[50] No collaborative or institutional approach emerges.

It is striking that Ambedkar takes pain retelling the Siddhartha story so as to link Buddhism with critique of economic exploitation only to retreat into pure religious ideology when outlining tenets of actual Buddhist observance. His only attempt to connect Buddhism with institutional community life comes in portraying the sangha as practical embodiment of Buddhist principle:

> 11. But the Blessed Lord also knew that merely preaching the Dhamma to the common men would not result in the creation of that ideal society based on righteousness.
> 12. An ideal must be practical and must be shown to be practicable. Then and then only people strive after it and try to realize it.
> 13. To create this striving it is necessary to have a picture of a society working on the basis of the ideal and thereby proving to the common man that the ideal was not impracticable but on the other hand realizable.
> 14. The sangh is a model of a society realizing the Dhamma...[51]

Ambedkar notes with approval certain features of life in the sangha. The monks (*bhikkus*) do not live unto themselves but always as part of their community, the sangha. They do not obey superiors, but only Dhamma in a regime of free thought. There is mutuality in cultivating character and virtue. Bhikkus are propertyless.[52] All these features may be taken to represent ideals of egalitarian community for Ambedkar.

In portraying the sangha as practical community organized around Buddhist principles, Ambedkar almost pushes his Buddhism beyond confines of pure religious ideology. He does not, however, probe sangha organizational details, nor explain how they or facsimiles might be reproduced in the outside world. He takes no notice that the sangha has no production problem to solve, since it relies on material support from the wider society. Ambedkar should notice serious problems in showing how the sangha, with no production problem, represents a model for society at large, which does have production problems. Failure to explain how the sangha might be a model for a society with production requirements is especially strange in a thinker normally keen in appreciating economic issues.

Not only the collective sangha, but individual bhikkus have social tasks, according to Ambedkar. The bhikku's role is not merely to practice self-culture, but also to act as "social servant devoting his life to service of the People..."[53] But no mention emerges of how bhikkus should serve the people other than by propagating Dhamma.[54] If Ambedkar imagines bhikkus as agents of institutional social change, he does not say so.

CONSTITUTIONAL SOCIALISM, BUDDHIST VIRTUE

It is not in his Buddhist thought but in his constitutional thought that Ambedkar spells out his concrete social and economic ideas. Ambedkar chaired independent India's constitutional Drafting Committee, earning esteem as chief architect of the Constitution with the ironic appellation of "modern Manu."[55] During the constitutional drafting, he argued for embedding state-centered socialism within the Constitution itself. Though he did not succeed in this, he did help secure endorsement of socialism in the Constitution's preamble and also secured in the Directive Principles of State Policy a constitutional agenda for what he calls "economic democracy."[56]

Despite Ambedkar's oft-voiced opposition to communism, he favors a highly-centralized public economy that he calls "State Socialism." He portrays state socialism as crucial to India's rapid industrialization. Private capitalism, he argues, cannot carry out the industrialization task for India and certainly cannot accomplish it without producing vast wealth disparities. Though some private enterprise should be tolerated, key industries should be state-owned and operated, with lesser industries also state-owned but operated perhaps by quasi-independent state corporations. Insurance should be nationalized and compulsory. Agriculture should become a state industry, the government acquiring all farmland and establishing a system of "collective farms." Capital should be disbursed to industries and enterprises by the state.[57] In short, Ambedkar proposes a highly centralized socialism, with public ownership and planning articulated mainly at the level of the national state.

As indicated, Ambedkar fought hard to secure such socialist arrangements within a framework of "Constitutional Law." Why? A constitution that merely secures political freedoms may leave citizens open to tyrannies of wealth. It is a higher form of constitutionalism that secures against economic as well as political tyranny. This would help to place socialism beyond legislative suspension or disruption at the hands of temporary anti-socialist majorities. Seeking to protect against parliamentary anti-socialism, Ambedkar favors securing socialism within a fixed and non-suspendable constitution. The only alternative lies in protecting socialism with lawless "Dictatorship," which might suspend parliamentary democracy altogether if it threatens socialism. Keen to protect both socialism and parliamentary democracy, he can only conclude that parliamentary democracy should be bound within a fixed and unalterable socialist constitution.[58]

This line of thought reveals much. To Ambedkar, socialism emerges simply as a structure of ownership and organization imposed upon the economy by the state. Its implementation of socialism is a purely material and economic task, without direct linkage to spiritual or moral transformation in social relations. Socialism is less a social movement than an institutional framework, which can be created whole-cloth by the Constitution and implemented by the state.

What this view of socialism lacks is a theory of collaborative social action and community-building. Ambedkar does not ask what sorts of communities will characterize the socialist order. His theory of socialism contains no comment on transforming everyday attitudes, habits and practices in actual social life so as to create egalitarian communities. Of course, he insists that there is a spiritual dimension to social transformation. This he assigns to Buddhism. As indicated above, however, his portrayal of Buddhist practice makes it a species of pure religious ideology: social transformation through the cultivation of private personal virtue. Here too, Ambedkar lacks a theory of collaborative social action and community-building.

More than any other thinker examined here so far, Ambedkar comprehends socialism as a productive system organized around public ownership. At the same time, he thinks ambitiously about the religious dimensions of oppression and liberation. The oddity is that though he explores in detail both sides of our problematic—religion and economics—he fails to synthesize them. He oddly seems to fall for pure religious ideology and materialist socialism at the same time.

As shown above, Ambedkar believes that social democracy requires two components that go beyond parliamentary political democracy. There is the spiritual component: fraternity, morality, endosmosis. There is also the economic component: equality and non-exploitation. In Ambedkar's vision, Buddhism provides the spiritual component, state socialism the economic. They may both be necessary, but little common ground connects them. To Ambedkar, Buddhism is simply the practice of personal moral virtue, while socialism is simply the practice of public productive ownership and economic planning by the national state. A Buddhist and a socialist, Ambedkar is neither a socialist Buddhist nor a Buddhist socialist. The spiritual problem and the productive problem find resolution at entirely different levels with entirely separate methods and techniques.

Ambedkar's Buddhism and his socialism fail to synchronize precisely because he confines his Buddhism to the personal sphere and his socialism to the state sphere. But it is in an intermediate sphere, the sphere of collaborative action and community-building, where practice of spiritual virtue and implementation of socialism might bear mutual relevance. They might coalesce in creating and operating common local institutions, including those concerning production. In his activist career, Ambedkar was no stranger to community-building. He was in fact an exceedingly active organizer, especially of institutions aimed at educating Untouchables.[59] It is odd that neither his Buddhist ideas nor his socialist ideas get expressed in terms of collaborative organization and community-building.

METHODS OF CHANGE:
THE BLIND SPOT IN CONSTITUTIONALISM

The split between Buddhist personal virtue and state socialism finds an echo in Ambedkar's insistence on mind change and democratic government as the only acceptable alternatives to violent revolution. In each case, Ambedkar sees the virtuous individual and the progressive state as adequate forces of social transformation. Ignored in each case is the force of collaborative social action, independent of the state. It is especially striking that Ambedkar repudiates satyagraha—organized nonviolent and often illegal resistance to authority—as an alternative to revolutionary violence. Democratic government, he argues:

> …means that we must abandon the method of civil disobedience, non-cooperation and satyagraha. When there was no way left for constitutional methods for achieving economic and social objectives, there was some justification for unconstitutional methods for achieving economic and social objectives. But where constitutional methods are open there can be no justification for these unconstitutional methods. These methods are nothing but the Grammar of Anarchy and the sooner they are abandoned the better for us.[60]

Several things are strange about Ambedkar's repudiation of non-violent satyagraha. First, Ambedkar had himself once been an organizer of satyagraha aimed at securing temple entry and drinking water rights for Untouchables.[61] Second, Ambedkar ignores the spiritual role of satyagraha in fostering exactly the kind of fraternity, solidarity, and "endosmosis" he sees as crucial to successful change and a worthwhile social order. Third, he seems not to notice that non-violent direct action is arguably quite compatible with Buddhism and with one of its main values: ahimsa. Fourth, his insistence on "constitutional methods" relies on a surprising degree of trust in institutions of "political democracy." This fourth point requires elaboration.

Ambedkar finds political democracy empty without social democracy, but insists that social democracy must be pursued exclusively through political democracy. Political democracy is a "form and method of government whereby revolutionary changes in the economic and social life of the people are brought about without blood-shed…"[62] This surely overstates political democracy's power to subvert entrenched social and economic structures.

Ambedkar seems both sufficiently and insufficiently aware of how a politically democratic state can be ensnared by entrenched social and economic power. He clearly recognizes that a politically democratic state may easily be captured by a socio-economic "ruling class," as long as social and economic inequality persists.[63] Yet he regards the democratic state, once established, as the sole legitimate means for fighting the very structures of social and economic power that subvert true democracy.[64]

Ambedkar sidesteps the obvious problem that elites dominating a politically democratic state may prevent it from attacking socio-economic structures undergirding their power. Focus on this dilemma might drive him to conclude that extra-parliamentary methods may be justified and even necessary in attacking socio-economic hierarchies, even under political democracy.

Too much the constitutionalist, Ambedkar hastily disallows extra-parliamentary methods of change in a democracy. We shall see that Gandhi's position is different and more satisfactory. To be sure, Ambedkar's view raises points to ponder. Under democracy, social change efforts should indeed be channeled heavily through lawful petitions upon government. Moreover, the meaning of satyagraha under democracy can become hazy. By whom and against what can it legitimately and effectively be directed? These are valid concerns, but Ambedkar's adamant stance still disappoints. His life comes to its end just as widespread civil disobedience against racial caste rises in the U.S. Had he lived longer, might this have pushed him to think further on satyagraha?

Though Ambedkar understands better than Gandhi what capitalism is, Gandhi sees better than Ambedkar what should be done to transcend it. Ambedkar's attempt to constitutionalize socialism, securing it against temporary anti-socialist majorities, reflects his fear of elite state capture. Paradoxical then is his misplaced confidence that proper constitutional organization of the state itself can prevent it. If his fears are well founded, the confidence cannot be.

Ambedkar can be praised for willingness to wield state power against inegalitarian social structures. He ducks too easily, however, the problem that elite power may dominate the state itself and prevent it from being so wielded. For example, there is no strong reason to believe as Ambedkar does that an anti-socialist legislature could effectively be checked by the mere presence of a socialist constitution. Moreover, even progressive laws passed by a pro-socialist legislature would stand in danger of subverted implementation by elites. In short, even within a nominally progressive democratic state, there is good reason to countenance extra-parliamentary forms of non-violent direct action against the state and other institutions. This helps ensure that movement toward social and economic justice does not falter. In the long run, socialism can secure itself against subversion only through a citizenry mobilized toward action and participation in affairs. Ambedkar slights this dimension by excluding satyagraha in his enthusiasm for implementing socialism through a proper technical structure of government.[64]

ECONOMIC VISION:
IMPLICATIONS OF A NON-COMMUNAL FOCUS

Characteristic strengths and weaknesses of Ambedkar's thought can be discerned in his approach to India's most monumental economic problem: rural poverty, unemployment and backwardness. Ambedkar warrants praise for examining the economics of rural backwardness more adequately than any other thinker examined here so far. He warrants criticism, however, for trusting too heavily in statist economic structures, without attention to nuances of community-building.

It is precisely in the rural villages that many modern Indian thinkers see opportunities for non-statist community-building. They develop an ideology of village community as foundation for a reconstructed society. Some germs of this ideology can be found in thinkers already examined. One problem with this ideology lies in exaggerating the communal character of villages, downplaying structures of division and exploitation within them. Strongly vigilant against this tendency, Ambedkar emphatically repudiates the entire ideology of village community. He refers to villages as India's "ruination," calling them "sinks" of social evil.[65] It is certainly fair to repudiate glorification of Indian village life. His contempt for the villages, however, goes beyond realistic skepticism. It reflects inability to contend with issues of small-scale community and an ill-founded bias favoring statist solutions.

Despite Ambedkar's emphasis on fraternity and "endosmosis," a powerful strain of liberal individualism permeates his thought. Individuals and states are far more real in his mind than are communities. To those critics of the Constitution he drafted as overly statist and insufficiently attentive to village communities, Ambedkar retorts that he prefers a constitution based on individuals, not communities.[66] He insists that a socialist constitution should protect individuals from oppression not fuse them into vibrant communities.[67]

Ambedkar's statist bias emerges in specific rural policy proposals. Fundamental to India's rural crisis is drastic population pressure on land, with consequent small and divided land holdings, inefficient production, and underemployment. Ambedkar identifies deindustrialization, largely via British colonialism, as root of the problem. As a remedy, he proposes an industrialization strategy that would redeploy redundant low-productivity agrarian labor into higher-productivity industrial work capable of generating surpluses. Surpluses could then be invested to increase capitalization of agriculture, increasing its efficiency through larger holdings and lower labor-intensivity.[68]

Ambedkar's industrialization strategy overlooks key problems. An industrialization strategy requires proper balance if it is effectively to absorb redundant labor. For maximum employment, success could lie with light, labor-intensive industry, not capital-intensive industry. It should perhaps concentrate on producing goods useful to an agrarian economy so that adequate markets exist, without unduly displacing existing modes of producing such goods. All of this urges that industrialization be synchronized with wise development of agrarian communities.

Industrial strategies that overlook integration of industry with agrarian communities could easily worsen matters, not improve them. It makes sense in a land like India to stress light agrarian-linked industry as a priority and as a prerequisite to heavier industrialization. Moreover, heavy industry tends to confer great power on huge enterprise, generating disparities and elites antithetical to social democracy. This seems true even for enterprises under public ownership of an ostensibly democratic state.

Ambedkar contemplates public ownership of industry resting chiefly in the hands of the national state, rather than with smaller communities. This renders links between industrialization and community-building hard to sustain. In short, Ambedkar overlooks much when proposing that India alleviate its agrarian crises through industrialization.

Another dimension of India's rural crisis is gross inequality in land holdings, which concentrates misery amongst those who own least. In characteristic fashion, Ambedkar views this phenomenon simultaneously in terms of caste and class, religion and economics. It is Untouchables who suffer worst. Untouchables and caste Hindus, divided from each other by religion, also constitute two distinct economic classes. Each village is a tiny system of class exploitation, reinforced by religious oppression. Caste Hindus own all productive property, including land, while Untouchables own nothing and therefore subsist as landless labor, impoverished and exploited.[69] To Ambedkar, such a situation cries out for action by the state.

Ambedkar argues first of all for radical reform in land ownership, through creation of Soviet-style state-owned collective farms.[70] He rejects more moderate socialist proposals for land redistribution yielding egalitarian private ownership.[71] It is not clear why. He might be offended by retention of private property or by the small, inefficient size of contemplated holdings, or by the prospect of continued low capitalization in the agrarian sector. All these are valid concerns, but Ambedkar misses possibilities for addressing them through cooperative farming and marketing, profit-sharing, common ownership of tools and machinery, and other forms of structured collaboration. These could profit from state aid, but would also require and foster solidarity, flexibility and creativity. Ambedkar fails to notice morale and productivity problems typical of Soviet-style collective farms, which seem to discourage any sense of local power, responsibility or incentive.

Ambedkar proposes a state plan of constructing separate villages for Untouchables, providing them sure escape from caste Hindu exploitation. The state would commandeer uncultivated waste land as well as private landholdings for this purpose.[72] It is characteristic of Ambedkar to imagine abolishing caste oppression through a single state initiative: separate villages. Progressive social action comes from the state, with the downtrodden its mere beneficiaries. Ambedkar does not explore how Untouchables might organize themselves for struggle against oppressive arrangements. No doubt such struggle is challenging within a highly decentralized and entrenched village order. State initiative is surely necessary to assist low-caste efforts. Indeed, the separate-village proposal could be precisely the sort of state initiative needed to help Untouchables organize themselves. Still, it is disappointing that Ambedkar comments so little on organizational initiatives Untouchables might take themselves. Such initiatives could help support new village arrangements. Ambedkar offers no commentary on how his proposed Untouchable villages should operate. Are they separate state-owned collective farms?

When it comes to what Untouchables can collectively do for themselves, Ambedkar offers little except religious conversion. Conversion will remove the stigma of untouchability, which blocks economic progress, he thinks. Does he really imagine that conversion will remove stigma in high-caste attitudes or that it could by itself remove economic roadblocks? He mentions little to nothing on conversion entailing new arrangements. New arrangements come from the state.

We have explored Ambedkar's rural policy ideas in some detail, to illustrate implications of an overly statist socialism, combined with religious notions insufficiently linked to social change effort. Ambedkar's willingness to wield state-socialist power against oppressive structures is praiseworthy, but he misses the need for and inherent value of non-statist forms of transformation.

More than any other thinker yet examined here, Ambedkar weaves together religious perspectives on oppression and liberation with socialist ones. He explores spiritual and economic aspects of democracy, develops a Marxist critique of Hinduism and a religious critique of materialist socialism. He seems within reach of a socialist Buddhism or Buddhist socialism. In the end, however, he fails to press Buddhism beyond pure religious ideology and he settles for a statist socialism clumsily biased toward simplistic solutions. It is perhaps right-minded criticisms of village and caste that prompt him to emphasize the state rather than lesser spheres of community. Much is lost, however, in such an emphasis. Only in notions about the sangha does he link Buddhism with community-building. Even there, he fails to articulate a Buddhist agenda for transformation. Instead, he assigns social transformation to the state, which wields power but does not cultivate the spirit.

PART III

PROBLEMATIC UNLOCKED

CHAPTER 5

Gandhi: The Social Logic of Ahimsa

Jain-willed and born lawyer, Mahatma Gandhi (Mohandas G. Gandhi) (1869-1948) began life at Porbandar in present-day Gujarat, son of a man who served as prime minister of several small princely states in that region. In 1888, he departed for England to complete his education and in 1891 he was called to the bar. After a brief return to India, Gandhi migrated to South Africa in 1893, where he took up the practice of law and soon became a leader in campaigns to reform racist laws adverse to South Africa's Indian population. During his two-decade career in South Africa, he began his lifelong experiments in building utopian communities and also developed the techniques and philosophy of satyagraha, confrontational non-violent resistance to authority, as a method of pursuing progressive social change.

In 1915, Gandhi returned to India, where he soon became closely engaged in the nationalist movement and a variety of other political and social campaigns. He launched the campaign of Non-cooperation with British authority in 1920 but called for its suspension as violence broke out in 1922. Sentenced to a six-year prison term in 1920, he gained release in 1924 for reasons of ill health. In 1930, the Indian National

Congress resumed its campaign of Non-cooperation. Gandhi subsequently led the famous "salt satyagraha," defying British law on the manufacture, sale and taxation of salt. He served time again for his role in that campaign.

In 1931, Gandhi nevertheless negotiated a pact with Britain's Lord Irwin. In return for suspension of civil disobedience, Britain agreed to recognize India's prerogative of constitutional self-government. Through the late 30s, Gandhi urged that the Congress maintain focus on total independence from Britain, but did not oppose its adoption of socialism as its post-independence goal.

Under the complex political pressures of World War II, Gandhi helped launch the anti-British "Quit India" campaign, beginning in 1942. He was consequently arrested and he remained in detention until 1944. Between the war's end in 1945 and the achievement of Indian independence in 1947, he strove energetically to prevent the split-off of Pakistan and to diminish Hindu-Muslim antagonisms, antagonisms that many blamed on Gandhi's own Hindu loyalties and political misjudgments. His assassination at the hands of a Hindu partisan came at a time when he might well have felt a sense of enormous failure: his dream of a united independent India dashed, his non-violent principles eclipsed by a bloodbath of savage Hindu-Muslim violence.

We have so far traced out several vicissitudes of a problematic: how to juxtapose Indian religious ideas and socialist ideas in a relevant Indian social ideology. Several approaches have been explored and certain inadequacies identified. We will now explore Gandhi's thought within the context of this problematic. It is scarcely possible to examine here Gandhi's vast volume of writing on religion and society. It is possible only to sketch out some themes, along with their related problems and promise.

RELIGION AS AHIMSA

Gandhi's religious thought centers around two key concepts. The first is *satya*, or Truth. The word satya stems from sat, meaning "pure being" and is therefore an appropriate name for God. "Truth is God," proclaims Gandhi.[1] Gandhi's other chief religious concept is *ahimsa*: love or non-violence. Ahimsa is not God, but rather the practice of religion, that is, the quest for God. Gandhi writes: "(W)ithout Ahimsa it is not possible to seek and find Truth. Ahimsa and Truth are so intertwined that it is practically nearly impossible to disentangle and separate them. Nevertheless, Ahimsa is the means; Truth is the end."[2]

Human nature has two contending aspects, one spiritual or divine the other bodily or animal. Ahimsa characterizes spirit or soul, while *himsa*, violence, characterizes the animal body. "Man as animal is violent, but as Spirit is non-violent," Gandhi writes.[3] As a property of the soul, ahimsa is a virtue that people can cultivate. It is also a property of society. All social life expresses at least partially the attribute of ahimsa. "All society is held together by non-violence," Gandhi writes. Ahimsa is harmony and co-operation, while himsa is coercion and exploitation. It is possible through conscious social action to expand the proportion of ahimsa in the world.[4] To Gandhi, religious life is the practice of ahimsa. The practice is one of both personal self-cultivation and social action. The enlargement of ahimsa both personal and social is humanity's way to realize God and is God's progressive incarnation in the world.

Ahimsa and himsa, spirit and matter, live in perpetual antagonism. The practice of ahimsa is spirit's struggle to subdue matter. At the personal level, this means the soul's attempt to subdue and master the body. Like thinkers examined above, Gandhi sees the religious life as one of exercising restraint upon bodily and material passions. Ahimsa is "self-denial" and "self-restraint."[5] In the social sphere also, ahimsa is the struggle of spirit against matter. In particular, it is sometimes the struggle to spiritualize or moralize the life of material production. Individual ahimsa, material self-restraint, makes social ahimsa, spiritualized productive relations, easier to achieve.

AHIMSA IN GANDHI'S SOCIAL VISION

Gandhi finds Western society lacking in virtues of material restraint. He joins several thinkers examined above in condemning Western industrialism as immoral or at least detrimental, while praising Indian culture for its high spiritual and moral tenor. When he pens *Hind Swaraj or Indian Home Rule* in 1908, Gandhi condemns Western industrialism on three main counts. First, through British imperialism, it has specifically impoverished India by destroying her handicraft production. Second, it fuels rather than restrains material greed. Third, it exploits and coerces the downtrodden. In light of these evils, Gandhi hopes industrial civilization will disappear.[6]

Though Gandhi maintains this early suspicion of industrialism throughout his career, his views grow more nuanced with time. He continues to advocate a low-industry social order but comes to acknowledge a social usefulness for industry, appropriately organized. Moreover, he increasingly sees not industrialism itself but capitalism as source of the ills he condemns. He looks more and more for an industrial order shorn of capitalist features.

Gandhi's three early criticisms of industrialism manifest themselves in various ways in all his thoughts on socio-economic organization.

On the first count, de-industrialization, Gandhi partly misidentifies the problem. Had Indian handicrafts been destroyed by native Indian industry, loss of employment and consequent impoverishment and land crowding could have been less severe. It is perhaps the fact that Indian handicrafts were wiped out by *British* industry that made the crisis so drastic. Displaced handicraft workers cannot be absorbed by industry located in another land. Though Gandhi partly misconstrues the problem, he worries that heavy industrialization may do little to alleviate India's rural poverty. For that, close attention to problems of rural production is needful.

Gandhi's latter two counts against industrialism, material greed and exploitation, reveal Gandhi's conception of ahimsa. Material greed contradicts ahimsa in that it is impelled by body, not soul. Exploitation contradicts ahimsa in that it entails coercion and oppression. Gandhi therefore looks for a social order that will embody ahimsa. It would be one of both material self-restraint and non-exploitation, in contrast with the greed and exploitation he attributes to industrialism in his early career, more to capitalism as time goes on.

Gandhi's concerns about rural poverty and desire to create an ahimsa society come together in his thought about reconstruction of India's villages. Among thinkers examined above, two main attitudes towards India's villages may be found: a concern over rural poverty and a myth of model community. Gandhi puts the concern and the myth together in his programs for reconstruction. In doing so, he attends to both spiritual and production problems.

Ahimsa implies non-coercion. The society of ahimsa must therefore be democratic. Conversely, true democracy requires ahimsa. Because states are essentially violent, perfect ahimsa would imply stateless anarchy. Gandhi's emphasis on statelessness and anarchy echo Aurobindo. Short of anarchy, democratic government is the closest possible approach to ahimsa, because in democracy coercion is collectively self-imposed by the people and is therefore coercive in only the most minimal sense. All centralization frustrates ahimsa by placing coercive power in the hands of the few. Democracy is therefore best if decentralized rather than state-centered. These considerations taken together lead Gandhi to conclude that ahimsa is maximized by a system of decentralized village self-government.[7] His notions for such a regime come to be designated as *panchayat raj*.

In panchayat raj, he writes, every village is a "republic," with maximum power to regulate its own affairs. Ahimsa is maximized because, with each person joining closely in regulation of affairs, coercion diminishes. Panchayat raj is a regime of personal as well as social ahimsa. Members of the democratic regime must practice material self-denial and moral self-restraint so as to minimize possibilities for conflict, himsa. Gandhi designates moral self-restraint with the term *swaraj* ("self-rule"), which is a synonym for democracy.[8] Swaraj, like ahimsa itself, is both personal and social. Non-violence, self-restraint, and democracy imply one another.

Gandhi joins the chorus of those who find in India's past a paradigm for ideal community. He suggests, in particular, that India's ancient villages followed principles of ahimsa.[9] His work, however, goes beyond invoking communal spirit and the past that mythically embodies it. His distinctive contribution is to fix attention on the sorts of material organization that would foster such spirit today. He writes copiously about the material life of reconstructed villages, including such matters as improved water supply, sanitation, housing, health, and farming techniques. Typical is his advocacy of manure composting in order to promote sanitation and provide fertilizer.[10] Moreover, he refers, though vaguely, to cooperative ownership of land, animals and tools, to cooperative farming and dairying, and to cooperative credit institutions. These gain his favor both for their productive superiority and for their value in fostering moral growth.[11]

Gandhi deploys the term *sarvodaya* ("welfare of all") to refer to village reconstruction. Central to sarvodaya, he holds, is the village social worker who exemplifies ahimsa in his person and activity. It is, for Gandhi, part of ahimsa to identify with and share the experience of society's most downtrodden. Gandhi's socialist sympathies stem from this same conviction. To succeed, the sarvodaya worker must as far as possible become a villager, sharing village poverty and problems while working to relieve them.[12]

Gandhi insists that village reconstruction is far more crucial to progressive social change than is political control over the state. Late in his career, he proposes that the Congress, banner organization of Indian nation-building, disband itself as a party seeking and wielding state power. Instead, it should reorganize as a *Lok Sevak Sangh* ("society for service to the people"), focusing mass organized effort into progressive village work.[13] His proposal falls on stony ground.

Another dimension Gandhi stresses is village industrial production. He envisions a network of light, labor-intensive, farm-linked industries connected to every village. He outlines advantages to such a decentralized productive scheme. First, it puts underemployed rural labor to work, counteracting some of the damage done by de-industrialization. Second, it avoids the concentration of economic power that goes with heavy industry, thus ensuring that villages can regulate their own affairs in consonance with ahimsa.[14] Gandhi imagines maximizing each village's autonomy by making it self-reliant in terms of basic necessities.[15] He hints at an insight later developed by J.P. Narayan: that decentralized democracy makes no sense if determinative economic decisions and events take place beyond the scope of the village. Third, decentralized industry avoids radical disparities of wealth that Gandhi thinks go with heavy industry.[16]

Though Gandhi envisions basic adequacy in village material wealth, he repudiates affluence. He advocates instead "voluntary poverty," which implies equality, lack of material greed, and a communal spirit of mutual dependence and service. In the tradition of Vivekananda, he adopts and transvalues Hindu admiration for the renouncer. He interprets renunciation or "voluntary poverty" as a religious virtue for the many, not just for the few. The true renouncer or sannyasin is one who devotes himself to selfless social service.[17]

With his notions of panchayat raj and sarvodaya, Gandhi begins to paint a picture of the reconstructed village as a democratic cooperative production community. Such a village community represents to Gandhi the incarnation of ahimsa.[18] It could be called "socialist anarchy," to contrast it with what we have called "state socialism." Its realization lies in the interdependent development of spiritual virtue and proper productive organization.

Gandhi's socialism stems from profound fundamental sympathy for economic equality. There are, to be sure, many passages in Gandhi's work where he disavows allegiance to radical economic equality or where he doubts the possibility of it. Nevertheless, the logic of ahimsa makes it impossible for Gandhi to suppress a yearning for equality. At one point, he voices that yearning in an analysis of wealth that combines a Marx-like labor theory of value with a concern for minimizing himsa, coercion. Wealth, he argues, is power to command people's labor so as to furnish oneself with goods and services. This implies power to turn the labor of others to one's own use. This is coercion and therefore violates ahimsa.[19]

Though Gandhi thinks wealth disparity intrinsically at odds with ahimsa, this does not lead him to uncritical endorsement of socialism. One trouble with most socialism, he thinks, is its separation from religion. Socialism typically repudiates religion, he argues, but in fact requires religion—ahimsa—in order to thrive. He suggests that socialism is implied in the first verse of the *Isopanishad*, advising spiritual growth through renunciation of wealth.[20] Socialism is therefore more a matter of personal conversion than of institutional transformation. To be sure, Gandhi explores problems of institutional transformation. Nevertheless, the spiritual dimension he sees in socialism means most to him.[21]

This spiritual emphasis prompts Gandhi to criticize conventional socialism, the sole aim of which is "material progress."[22] Orthodox socialism's materialist outlook pushes it toward violence, which is related to over-emphasis on the state. He links his own socialism with material restraint, ahimsa and the village community, in contrast to the materialism, violence and statism he associates with conventional socialism.

AHIMSA AND SATYAGRAHA

It is not for Gandhi enough to establish a picture of ahimsa realized in socialism. To him, the proper method of pursuing ahimsa is more important than any institutional embodiment of it. The ahimsa method Gandhi finds most powerful he calls "satyagraha," organized non-violent action against injustice. Its most dramatic and obvious manifestations are strikes and mass public disobedience. It can also, however, include the social action of committed individuals like sarvodaya social workers. "Satyagraha" can be translated as "cleaving to Truth." It captures the connection in Gandhi's mind between God (Truth) and non-violence. One cleaves to God/Truth by practicing non-violent social action. God is both approached and made manifest through ahimsa and satyagraha.

Ganhdi insistently claims that the purpose of true satyagraha can never be to coerce an antagonist. On the contrary, the point must be "to convert the wrongdoer."[23] This contrasts with Aurobindo's view, explored above, of "passive resistance" as merely the least violent way to coerce an adversary into stopping his wrongdoing. Gandhi's satyagraha aims, in theory, to move the soul of the adversary, not the body. To coerce the opponent materially is himsa, violence, but to move the opponent's soul or sense of justice is ahimsa.

Gandhi's claims as to the non-coercive nature of satyagraha lie open to serious question. One form of satyagraha, for example, is a non-violent labor strike, such as the one Gandhi helped organize in 1918 among Ahmedabad textile workers. It is seldom true in a successful strike that the employer accedes to strike demands from a sense of sympathy and justice. Success in a strike generally comes when the employer feels a coercive economic pinch sufficient to impel accession to worker demands. In this light, Gandhi's insistence that success be defined entirely in terms of converting the adversary's sympathy seems disingenuous. In the Ahmedabad strike, to take one example, it was Gandhi's own 'fast unto death,' not sudden insight into the "justice" of the worker demands, that impelled the mill owners to relent. This case was itself atypical due to Gandhi's public stature and his personal friendship with the mill owners. In the usual case, an employer relents at the point when a strike grows overly threatening to profits. Hence, the strike acts upon the employer primarily through material considerations and is therefore coercive. Similar considerations often apply in situations of civil disobedience to authority, such as non-payment of taxes.

No one would quarrel with Gandhi's position that converting an adversary is better than coercing him. It would be helpful to acknowledge, however, that there are gradations of conversion and coercion, rather than ironclad contrast between them. In this light, satyagraha can be viewed as a preference for moral conversion and for least coercive transformation. In short, satyagraha seeks minimum violence. The achievement of minimum violence, however, may entail complex case-specific judgments as to degrees of violence and coercion embodied in social institutions before and after transformation, as well as the degree of violence and coercion embodied in various transformative methods. This is a point Gandhi does not express but often seems to practice.

A conception of satyagraha as minimum rather than absolute non-violence comports with other notions Gandhi holds about ahimsa. For Gandhi, bodily life itself represents departure from ahimsa, since bodily life involves matter and himsa, while only the soul is ahimsa. Gandhi does not carry this deeply Jain perspective to its ultimate Jain solution of self-starvation unto death in order to avoid all himsa. (Gandhi does, of course, practice fasts-unto-death as satyagraha on particular issues.) Instead, Gandhi concludes that bodily life implicitly requires compromise on issues of ahimsa. The body, vehicle of violence, must be cared for but indulged as little as possible.[24] Because bodily life intrinsically represents departure from pure ahimsa, one arguably cannot expect satyagraha to adhere to absolute non-coercion. Rather, satyagraha succeeds if it conduces to minimum overall violence, though it may entail elements of coercion. Again, this interpretation seems compatible with Gandhian practice, if not with Gandhi's explicit theory of satyagraha as pure non-coercion.

In Gandhi's mind, satyagraha refers to more than non-violent action against injustice. It refers also to the practitioner's spiritual self-cultivation. Satyagraha depends on faith in God.[25] The activist practitioner must cultivate inner ahimsa or love even for the adversary and must also cultivate capacity to bear suffering in pursuit of worthy goals.[26] Capacity to take suffering upon oneself helps minimize the suffering imposed on adversaries by the desired transformation. Inner ahimsa therefore reinforces outward ahimsa. Because satyagraha is cultivation of inner ahimsa, it can never fail. Even if it falls short of its outward objective, satyagraha inevitably expands ahimsa in the world by expanding the practitioner's inner non-violence. As Gandhi writes: "Satisfaction lies in the effort, not in the attainment. Full effort is full victory."[27] In satyagraha, the "minimum is also the maximum" where the only possible movement is advance.[28] Here again, Gandhi's views differ from Aurobindo's on evaluating non-violent resistance. To Aurobindo, the value of passive resistance lies exclusively in the outward social change it achieves or fails to achieve.

With all this before us, a caveat requires mention. Gandhi emphatically cautions against viewing satyagraha as some straight-off-the-shelf panacea. It is a severe discipline, first of all, and is not appropriate for all situations of injustice. (Post-Gandhi literature on satyagraha is surprisingly thin. For the best review, explication and synthesis I have found see *Strategic Nonviolent Power: The Science of Satyagraha* by Mark A. Maitaini.)

Gandhi establishes two social corollaries of ahimsa: panchayat raj/sarvodaya on the one hand, satyagraha on the other. Though these corollaries stem directly from Gandhi's central religious sensibility, they each transcend the boundaries of pure religious ideology and bear directly on organized social action. Because of this, creative Indian socialists have found themselves able to assimilate these Gandhian notions, and in doing so they have made contact with the religious sensibility lying behind them.

Not all of Gandhi's notions, however, are so fertile. Gandhi's religious sensibilities sometimes lead him astray. This is especially true of one of his leading ideas, so-called "trusteeship." By exploring certain vicissitudes and ramifications of "trusteeship," we can uncover problems in how Gandhi traces out the social logic of ahimsa. We can also see how Gandhi finally transcends, if only partly, those problems.

TRUSTEESHIP AND EVOLVING SOCIALISM

The notion of "trusteeship" arises in Gandhi's thought from a simple dilemma in ahimsa. On the one hand, Gandhi favors a non-exploitative order where wealth is used for common rather than for private good. On the other hand, he opposes wealth expropriation from private owners, because this amounts to coercion. What he fears most is violent revolution.[29] He therefore seeks a non-violent means to reach the non-violent end. The ahimsa social economy cannot be sought, he suggests, through means that are themselves violent, such as coerced wealth redistribution. What he proposes instead is that owners should regard themselves as "trustees" of their wealth for the common good. In this way, a non-exploitative economy can arise voluntarily rather than through coercive expropriation.[30]

One can easily stumble over substantial ambiguity in Gandhi's frequent pronouncements on trusteeship, related issues of private and public ownership, and use of legislation and satyagraha to redistribute wealth. Gandhi wavers almost ceaselessly between aversion to massive private wealth and aversion to state power. No satisfactory interpretation of his shifting pronouncements can be reached without paying close attention to the evolution of his ideas through his career.

In its simple early form, trusteeship is a recipe for altruistic capitalism. In Gandhi's vision of trusteeship, capitalists retain private ownership, but deploy their capital in the "public interest."[31] They come to do so under the impact of moral conversion, perhaps resulting from campaigns designed to provoke such conversion. The object, Gandhi claims, is "not to destroy the capitalist," but to "destroy capitalism."[32] The destruction of capitalism sounds radical, but Gandhi errs in thinking that this can be accomplished through conversion of capitalists to the spirit of public interest. Gandhi's reasons for preferring trusteeship over state ownership are revealing. The capitalist, he argues, has a "soul" and is therefore presumably capable of ahimsa, while the state is "soulless" and therefore inextricably violent.[33] In couching things this way, Gandhi overlooks the "soullessness" of the market which, more than personal moral outlook, determines capitalist behavior.

As indicated above, in order to maintain capitalist status in a competitive regime, capitalists must deploy their capital with a fundamental eye toward profit accumulation. To place the "public interest" ahead of profit-making is to lose out in profit competition and jeopardize one's capacity to maintain capitalist status. Precisely contrary to Gandhi's formulation, voluntary trusteeship is a formula not for destroying capitalism but for destroying as capitalists its most ardent practitioners. In attempting to follow out the social logic of ahimsa, Gandhi fails to grasp the social logic of capitalism.

With this image of trusteeship, Gandhi succumbs to pure religious ideology, imagining social transformation through private spiritual conversion—in this case, conversion of individual capitalists to more benevolent dispositions. Capitalist benevolence does indeed occur, but largely within constraints set by profit imperatives. It is little wonder that trusteeship manages to win few, if any, true converts. Sometimes it is unclear whether Gandhi even cares about this. Trusteeship is valuable "even if only one man lives up to it," he writes.[34] This implies that trusteeship is valuable more for the capitalist's personal moral redemption than for relief of the downtrodden. Gandhi's concern for personal virtue seems to overshadow concern for social justice.

Gandhi's trusteeship doctrine fails to comprehend capitalism as a system. Gandhi is more acute when it comes to grasping imperialism as a system. Resistance to the British, he insists, must not attribute the evil of imperialism to particular persons or to the British people as a whole. Imperialism is evil as a system and it is the system that "must be destroyed."[35] Gandhi argues that imperialism cannot be destroyed through conversion of individual imperialists, but must disappear as a system: hence the importance of satyagraha designed to cripple it. Why then does Gandhi not conclude that capitalism too must be abolished as a system, a task to which efforts at personal conversion are by and large irrelevant?

Gandhi goes through contortions to avoid admitting the inconsistency between attacking imperialism as a system, while attacking capitalism only through conversion.[36] He makes two mistakes that prevent him from noticing this contradiction. The first, criticized above, is to imagine that trusteeship actually does attack capitalism as a "system," thereby failing to grasp how the profit-driven logic of capitalist decision-making inherently limits altruistic motivation. A second mistake is to insist that satyagraha succeeds only by conversion, not coercion, so that anti-imperialist satyagraha and trusteeship can be seen as parallel non-coercive approaches. Despite Gandhi's claims, it is difficult to interpret anti-imperialist satyagraha, such as mass non-payment of the salt tax, as coercion-free. It deprives the government of revenue while raising fears of lost control. As argued above, Gandhi fails to reconcile his conceptualization of satyagraha as absolute non-violence with its practice, which frequently entails aspects of coercion. As a result, he fails to see the contradiction between utilizing satyagraha in a systematic and coercive attack on imperialism, while repudiating it for attack on capitalism in favor of personal conversion. Only in his late career does he begin to resolve this contradiction, revising his early ideas on trusteeship and suggesting satyagraha to dissolve wealth disparities.

Gandhi's notions about trusteeship evolve during the course of his career, along with his views on socialism. The stress in Gandhi's socialist thought remains throughout on the village production community.

Despite persistent anti-industrialism, however, Gandhi does not—after his very early career—deny need for some large-scale industry. In the 1920s and 1930s, he generally takes the position that limited large-scale industry should exist and remain under capitalist ownership, tempered by trusteeship.[37] During this period, Gandhi sees violent revolution with its coercive expropriation as the sole alternative to voluntary trusteeship.[38] Over time, however, he begins to distrust his own vision of altruistic capitalism and starts to think increasingly in terms of institutional rather than personal transformation.

Gandhi reads Marx's *Capital* in 1942, while jailed for his role in the Quit India Movement. Though Gandhi praises Marx's "acumen" and describes his experience reading Marx as an "opportunity and privilege," it is difficult to say what he absorbed or what effect his study may have had.[39] It might, however, have deepened a view of capitalist production as a system of exploitation and an order of ongoing—though camouflaged—violence. Perhaps Gandhi began to view capitalist wealth as an accumulation of congealed violence or himsa in the same way Marx views capital as the accumulation of congealed exploited labor. If Gandhi indeed comes to see things this way, it might strike him that ahimsa would demand efforts to dissolve the congealed but camouflaged violence embodied in private capital. If so, expropriation might suggest itself because it could re-deploy existing capital in ways conducive to diminishing himsa. In any case, during the 1940s Gandhi endorses increasingly recognizable socialist positions, and also begins to imagine battling entrenched wealth with weapons beyond the tepid persuasion and conversion emphasized earlier.

Gandhi gropes during this period toward the idea of worker-owned firms. His movement in this direction begins at an earlier career stage with exhortations admonishing workers to take responsibility for the firms where they work, "as if they were part owners." This mirrors his exhortations with employers to act as trustees, "as if" the wealth belonged to all. Gandhi hopes to abolish labor-capital conflict and replace it with non-violent harmony. Through most of his career, he sticks to this picture of trusteeship and worker-ownership as states of mind and moral attitude. Owners should "convert" to trusteeship and "regard" their workers as fellow-owners, while workers should "regard" firms as their own and "realize" common cause with owners. There is nothing legally binding, however, about either owner responsibilities as "trustees" or worker "rights" as part owners.[40] Trusteeship and imaginary worker-ownership could be called "subjunctive socialism," captured in the phrase "as if." Owners and workers both pretend to create through their moral attitudes a system of common ownership that does not exist in actual fact.

With time, Gandhi begins to take the idea of worker-owned firms more seriously as an actual legal arrangement. Throughout his career, he stresses labor organization as a method of constraining the power of wealth within tolerable limits. In his late career, he begins toying with the idea that worker organizations could operate as firms, borrowing capital and hiring salaried managers, but controlling management for their own purposes, sharing profits amongst worker-owners.[41]

In another direction, Gandhi moves toward imagining trusteeship as a statutory arrangement, with trustee prerogatives and responsibilities legally stipulated and state-regulated, not left to whims of owner conscience. Just as worker-ownership evolves from the subjunctive to a legal arrangement, so with the trustee as public officer. Gandhi even begins to imagine trustees as state-salaried managers. To be sure, it is mainly owners who qualify for the office. Nevertheless, Gandhi more and more suggests that ownership and use of wealth should be regulated through legislation. Private wealth is hence socialized, depending on stringency or laxity of regulation.[42]

Gandhi's move toward statutory trusteeship reflects a growing, though wary, tolerance for state socialism. He never entirely abandons suspicion that state socialism contradicts ahimsa. Even in his early career, however, Gandhi begins to recognize a role for state ownership in large-scale production. He never attempts to reconcile this position with continued defense of capitalist trusteeship. In his late career, however, his pronouncements in favor of state ownership grow more decisive. Capital accumulation under public ownership, he argues, comports with ahimsa, while private capital accumulation does not. "I would have state ownership," Gandhi writes, "where a large number of people have to work together" and adds that "ownership of the products of their labor, will vest in them through the state."[43]

SATYAGRAHA AND THE PURSUIT OF SOCIALISM

Gandhi remains troubled, however, over how to negotiate transition from private to public ownership. He has trouble specifically in deciding whether ahimsa permits confiscation in order to convert private wealth to public wealth or simply redistribute wealth from the rich to the poor. In scattered comments, he endorses confiscation "where necessary," though he worries there is "an element of coercion in it."[44] He does not specify what "where necessary" means and does not analyze how the coercion involved fits or fails to fit with ahimsa.

It is difficult to say, from comments on confiscation alone, whether Gandhi grows more comfortable with it over time. His growing endorsement of statutory trusteeship, however, does indicate increasing willingness to wield state power against concentrated wealth. It is not far-fetched to assume that this applies also to wealth expropriation. Gandhi seems to associate ahimsa more and more with an image of the democratic state and seems increasingly to see ineradicable himsa in the soulless market.

His acceptance of the state is grudging at best, however. Gandhi increasingly begins to seek some intermediate position between voluntary trusteeship on the one hand, coerced expropriation or violent revolution on the other. He finds it in satyagraha. In his late career, Gandhi speaks more and more of wielding satyagraha not only against imperialism but also against capitalism and other forms of dominance by wealth. Satyagraha, he concludes, is the truest means of bringing socialism to pass.[45] He thus erases contradiction between his treatment of imperialism and his treatment of severe wealth disparity.

Gandhi lays out little theory or program for deploying satyagraha so as to ameliorate wealth disparity or achieve socialism. Strikes and civil disobedience are part of what he has in mind.[46] Otherwise, goals, targets, strategies, methods, organization and scale remain vague. At maximum ambition, satyagraha might involve mass movement civil disobedience pressuring the state to pursue socialist agendas. This would pose anomaly for Gandhi, however, who so often portrays state action as coercive. Satyagraha makes little sense as an alternative to state action if aimed precisely to secure it.

When focusing on society at large, Gandhi sees big contrast between the state—government action—and satyagraha—citizen action. This contrast disappears at the village level where, in Gandhi's ideal, the local government or panchayat could be made to function as direct agent of the organized citizenry. The panchayat could legislate redistribution of local wealth and ownership and also, if necessary, organize satyagraha to ensure that recalcitrant owners comply with wealth redistribution.[47] Obscuring the question whether this would work when confronting property rights, Gandhi envisions village satyagraha as a decentralized wealth-transferring device, combining virtues of democracy and ahimsa. The panchayat that organizes both satyagraha and actual wealth redistribution also organizes other aspects of village cooperation. Various corollaries of ahimsa—decentralization, democracy, socialism, cooperative production and satyagraha—coalesce in a unified vision of egalitarian community-building.

THE PROBLEM OF CASTE

Discussion so far has not stressed Gandhi's particular identification with Hinduism. Gandhi sees his personal theology, centered on Truth and Ahimsa, as consistent with various religions. All religions, he thinks, grasp Truth in some fashion worthy of study and respect. He nevertheless identifies as an orthodox Hindu.[48] Hinduism is his own religion, and he feels it best to adhere to one's own. Just as a good husband may be blind neither to faults in his wife nor to virtues in other women and is nevertheless faithful, so with loyalty to one's religion.[49]

As self-styled Hindu and socialist, Gandhi runs afoul of caste. Because caste is so obviously central in Hinduism, it must somehow be reconciled with egalitarian aspiration. Gandhi's treatment is as convoluted as that of Hindu thinkers examined above. A brief sketch will illustrate its family resemblance to views found in Vivekananda, Das, Aurobindo and Pal.

Like those others, Gandhi distinguishes the decadent and hierarchical present-day caste system from the original four-varna social system he attributes to ancient scripture and society. Hierarchy, the "idea of superiority or inferiority" was "wholly repugnant" to the original varna order, which was a system of egalitarian functional division and mutual selfless service.[50] Varna observances, Gandhi indicates, encourage material self-restraint, crucial to moral strength. Limits on inter-dining and intermarriage put healthy restriction on appetite satisfaction.[51] By the same token, the practice of hereditary occupations puts restraint on using one's work life to pursue material ambition. This restraint liberates energy for spiritual endeavor.[52]

Just as Gandhi's views on trusteeship and socialism migrate during his career, so do his views on caste. Over time, Gandhi's pronouncements on caste display a higher quotient of criticism and a lower quotient of apology. To take but one example, Gandhi in 1921 endorses caste restrictions of interdining and intermarriage, but by 1935 he emphatically repudiates them.[53]

There is, moreover, one respect in which Gandhi hits especially hard against caste practice: his campaign against untouchability. Though he may defend caste as an idealized varna scheme, he cannot square untouchability with ahimsa. Efforts to help Untouchables and eradicate untouchability customs become central to his public persona. His fight against untouchability arises from the same egalitarian sympathies and concern for the downtrodden propelling him toward increasingly strenuous socialism.

Gandhi does not fail to hold Hinduism accountable for untouchability, which he characterizes as an "excrescence" upon Hinduism.[54] He wants Hinduism to redeem itself by repudiating untouchability. He can nevertheless be criticized for downplaying the centrality in Hinduism of hierarchical social attitudes and practices, including those of untouchability. His own commitment to the social logic of ahimsa makes it difficult for him to fathom or recognize the social logic of caste in Hinduism.

GANDHI'S CONTRIBUTION

Serious ambiguities and weaknesses arise in Gandhi's socialist thought. Nevertheless, Gandhi forges a more consistent and fertile synthesis of religious and socialist ideas than does any thinker examined above. He traces out the implications of ahimsa and discovers forms of social practice exemplifying it. He links his central religious conception both to organization of social change—satyagraha—and to organization of production—panchayat raj and sarvodaya. Gandhi's work and advocacy with respect to satyagraha and village reconstruction strongly influence his Marxist compatriots in the nationalist movement. They rethink their socialism not only in light of these Gandhian organizational ideas, but also in light of the religious sensibility behind them. It is through Gandhi that Indian Marxists learn to consider religion.

Meanwhile, despite his insistence on primacy of the spiritual in socialism, Gandhi moves almost in spite of himself toward increasing insight into socialism's real institutional prerequisites. Gandhi's relevance for Indian Marxists is reinforced by his late-career adoption of increasingly institutional socialist positions, exemplified in his changing views on trusteeship, public ownership and satyagraha. It is partly Gandhi's own convergence on socialism that fosters socialism's convergence on Gandhi.

PART IV

PARTIAL GANDHIAN SOCIALISM

CHAPTER 6

Asoka Mehta: Gandhi as Utopian Socialist

Open-minded, disciplined scholar and activist, Asoka Mehta (1911-
1989) was born at Bhavnagar, Gujarat and educated at Wilson College,
Bombay, and at the Bombay University School of Economics. After
imprisonment by the British for his role in the 1932 Civil Disobedience Movement, Mehta helped found the Congress Socialist Party
in 1934, then served as editor of the Congress Socialist Weekly from
1935 until 1939.

Mehta served time again for participating in the 1941 Individual
Satyagraha Movement and then again for the 1942 Quit India campaign. He later became Chair of the Praja Socialist Party (P.S.P.),
formed in 1952 by merger between the Socialist Party, heir to the Congress Socialist Party, and the Kisan Mazdoor Praja Party ("Kisan"
means "farmer"; "Mazdoor" means "worker"; "Praja" can mean "citizen"). Later in the decade, he feuded with other P.S.P. leaders, especially Lohia, over Mehta's view that the P.S.P. should cooperate
extensively with Nehru's quasi-socialist Congress government.

Mehta served in the Lok Sabha, powerful lower house of Parliament, in the years 1954-57, 1958-61, and 1967-70. He was Deputy

Chair of the Indian Planning Commission from 1963 until 1966; Minister of Planning, 1966-67; and Minister of Petroleum, Chemicals and Social Welfare, 1967-68. Though he had been a minister in Mrs. Gandhi's government, he later split from her faction of the Congress and became president of the oppositional Congress (O) Party. He was detained under Mrs. Gandhi's Emergency decree in 1975 and released in 1976. He played a key role in putting together the Janata Party coalition that temporarily toppled Mrs. Gandhi from power in 1977.

Among Indian socialists, Mehta is perhaps the greatest scholar of socialist thought. He articulates his own changing socialist positions through commentary on different schools in socialism. In the course of his career, his socialist views change considerably and so does his assessment of Gandhi.

CRITIQUE OF GANDHISM

In 1935, Mehta's first publication, *Gandhism and Socialism*, explores various intellectual responses to industrial capitalism. One of these responses Mehta dubs "Romantic reaction." This response erroneously blames industrialism itself for ills in capitalism and seeks return to an idealized pre-industrial world. Romantic reaction stresses a "revival of religion and mysticism" as antidote to the exploitational ethos of industrial capitalism. Mehta identifies Gandhi as an exponent of Romantic reaction, which Mehta calls "regressive."

Gandhism, writes Mehta, envisions an impossible return to pre-industrial life. It naturally flourishes in India due to devastating deindustrialization under British imperial capitalism. Gandhism also advocates material renunciation as a religious value. Though Mehta scorns capitalism's unceasing inflammation of appetite, he finds Gandhian renunciation over-severe and advocates instead an intermediate "vital standard" of appetite-satisfaction.[1] In his later career, he develops more intricate quasi-Gandhian views on the socialist relevance of material abstemiousness.

Progress, argues Mehta in 1935, lies not in Gandhian reaction against industrialism but rather in socialism, an industrial order shorn of capitalist features such as exploitation, unemployment and periodic depression. Two features of Mehta's early socialism require emphasis. First, he advocates what we have called state socialism—an emphasis on large-scale industry under direct state ownership and control. Second, he praises Marxist "scientific" socialism over pre-Marxist "utopian" socialism. Though he does not say so, state socialism and scientific socialism seem linked in his mind.

Mehta endorses the common Marxist or "scientific" socialist critique of utopian socialists such as Proudhon, Fourier, and Owen. The utopians, on this view, are essentially moralists without grasp of economic reality. They spend their time imagining or trying to build ideal production communities, failing to understand that their efforts are not generalizable so long as capitalist economic evolution is still taking place. Socialist community-building is premature and indeed impossible within the constraints of that evolving capitalist order. Hence, community-building is far less relevant to constructing socialism than is revolution-making. Rather than fantasizing about ideal communities, socialists should study the "laws of capitalist production," which define actual reality and reveal how and when capitalism might break down and be supplanted.[2] Once the state owns the economy, detailed problems of socialist organization can be worked out realistically.

Expanded productive scale and centralization are key to capitalist evolution and industrial progress, Mehta argues. For this reason, the socialist productive regime will be a centralized one, characterized by large-scale production along with state ownership and control. Visions of decentralization fly in the face of economic science. Small-scale production under socialism will be a matter of art and enjoyment, but not of meeting basic needs.[3]

GANDHI AND UTOPIAN SOCIALISM

To the early Mehta, both scientific socialism and state socialism seem to reflect hard-headed economic analysis, while utopianism reflects valid but misdirected moral ambition. Gandhi, meanwhile, represents a backward-looking romanticism inapplicable to current realities. By 1959, however, when Mehta publishes *Studies in Socialism* (also published as *Studies in Asian Socialism*), his views of both utopianism and Gandhi have changed drastically. By this time, he not only applauds both Gandhi and utopian socialism, he equates them with each other. He calls for an "upsurge of utopianism" and, contrary to his early view of Gandhi as a "reactionary," praises Gandhi as the "highest watermark" of utopian socialism.[4]

The essence of utopianism, Mehta argues, is "community-building." Contrary to his early views, Mehta now criticizes Marx, who has "no patience with community-building."[5] Emphasis on community-building, thinks Mehta, follows from Gandhian insight into the "organic relatedness" between means and ends. Ends cannot be achieved except through means consistent with them. Means that partially embody their end cannot fail, since the end is at least partially realized in the means itself. Utopian community-building exemplifies this means-ends relationship. If the purpose of revolution is ultimately to foster community, community-building must itself be part of transformative effort. It cannot be left to emerge as by-product of revolution pursued through other means. Mehta writes that "we must create here and now the space *now* possible for the thing for which we are striving, so that it may come to fulfillment *then*... A *post*-revolutionary utopia...can emerge only through a *pre*-revolutionary utopianism."[6]

Mehta praises Gandhi's agenda for combining community-building—sarvodaya—with direct pressure—satyagraha—against oppressive structures. The Gandhian agenda hence avoids the possible Marxist error of over-emphasis on revolutionary activity, while also avoiding a possible utopian overemphasis on community-building to the neglect of direct efforts to replace the old order.[7]

Utopian socialism's focus on community-building implies de-emphasis on the state. Mehta therefore increasingly abandons his early-career allegiance to state socialism. Statist socialism, he suggests, is as much the enemy of community as is capitalism.[8] Like several thinkers examined above, he stresses the importance of voluntary associations and intermediate communities standing between individuals and the state. He endorses a socialism of communities "small in scale and dense in structure," coordinated by federalized association, not by a centralized state.[9]

Utopian community-building strikes Mehta as primarily a moral and spiritual endeavor. Utopian socialism's key contribution is cultivating an "ethos" or "spirit" of "community solidarity."[10] This ethos or spirit, however, requires appropriate institutions in order to thrive. Mehta applauds Gandhi's vision of village communes, featuring coordinated and community-owned networks of light industrial and agrarian production. Such a system, he urges, provides what "alone can be the locus of healthy men and rich community."[11] The village commune, as he explains in Gandhian language, maximizes swaraj, self-government, in both its senses: democracy and personal spiritual discipline.[12]

The Gandhian village vision is, for Mehta, the core of utopian socialism. It demands, if not common ownership, at least equal ownership with a hope that cooperative methods and common ownership may evolve. Mehta insists that landlordism and landless labor be abolished.[13]

Mehta's reassessments of Gandhi and utopianism prompt his growing appreciation for religion. Though Mehta develops no deep religious sensibility, he begins to speak of religion's positive dimensions. The early Mehta had shunned the "religion and mysticism" he then associated with Gandhian "reaction."[14] The later Mehta, however, acknowledges an inevitable "streak of mysticism" in the utopian socialism he comes to embrace.[15] Religion, a spiritual bond among humans, is the ultimate goal of socialism, he suggests. It should not be that religion restrict itself to spiritual concerns and socialism to material ones. In utopian socialism, he thinks, a true synthesis of religion and socialism can be found.[16]

DEVELOPMENT AND SOLIDARITY-IN-AUSTERITY

Prior to full-blown embrace of Gandhi and utopian socialism, Mehta drifts through a transitional period characterized by disillusionment with his earlier state-centered and "scientific" socialism. In his 1951 book, *Democratic Socialism*, he expresses reservations about industrial socialism, provoked by growing disenchantment with the Soviet Union, the "Moscow Road" he once had praised. He worries that perhaps not only capitalism but industrialism itself "enriches economically, but vulgarizes and impoverishes spiritually."[17] Moreover, he cities the Soviet Union as an example of how socialist overemphasis on industrial development leads to exploitation of the peasantry.

In the Soviet development strategy, Mehta argues, peasants are herded into state collective farms where they are forced to produce more, while their consumption is held down coercively. This generates surpluses needed to finance rapid industrialization. Light industry, helpful for agrarian needs, is neglected in favor of heavy industry. Mehta sees no advantage in this kind of socialist development, where the state squeezes investment surplus out of the peasant class, over capitalist development, where surplus is squeezed out of non-owning industrial workers by capital owners. He repudiates Soviet socialism as ruthless, centralized, totalitarian.[18]

Mehta's repudiation of Soviet development later pushes him toward Gandhi and utopian socialism, which emphasize agrarian well-being, not rapid industrialization. He indicates that this makes particular sense for India, with its massive agrarian problems.

In another direction, meanwhile, Mehta grows preoccupied with the specific problem of generating investment surpluses for development. Development requires that society's level of production exceed its level of consumption, so that investment surplus exists. Mehta seeks a surplus-generating method different from both capitalist labor exploitation and Soviet agrarian exploitation. He proposes generating socialist surplus non-exploitatively through collectively and democratically self-imposed restrictions on consumption levels.

This road, which Mehta calls "democratic socialism," cannot succeed without radical economic equality, so that consumption restrictions rest evenly and voluntarily upon all, not disproportionately and forcibly upon some. As Mehta puts it in later works, democratic socialism requires "equality and austerity." For a time at least, there must be a "low standard of life willingly accepted and *evenly shared*..."[19]

Mehta joins thinkers examined above in criticizing the pointless and insatiable quest for higher living standards he finds in both capitalism and conventional socialism.[20] He is stimulated in this by Gandhi's influence but unimpressed with Gandhi's emphasis on austerity as a spiritual end in itself.[21] He transvalues Gandhian austerity into notions of socialist solidarity. It is not austerity itself that is valuable, he contends. What is valuable is solidarity and equality, which may accompany austerity if proper arrangements prevail. Solidarity-in-austerity can actually be directed toward achieving greater abundance. Abundance itself, however, is no more the goal than is austerity. The point is to maintain solidarity-in-austerity, whatever wealth level is desired or achieved. Mehta's socialist ideal is a moderate abundance, where solidarity-in-austerity provides greater satisfactions than those obtainable from the ceaseless quest for greater abundance.[22]

Because democratic socialism follows principles of solidarity-in-austerity, it can succeed only through cultivation of what Mehta calls a "high moral temperature."[23] This high moral temperature makes democratic socialism as much a spiritual as an economic regime, thus distinguishing it from state socialism. Mehta's concern for solidarity-in-austerity, along with concern over spiritual emptiness he finds in industrial culture, fosters an emerging interest in religion. At first, Mehta cannot bring himself to speak specifically of "religion," but he does speak of "self-culture" and "war against poverty of the spirit" as components of socialist life. Explicit endorsement of "religion" awaits his late-career emphasis on utopian socialism, with its community-building focus.

The revival of utopian socialism strikes Mehta as an Asian and Indian phenomenon.[24] Like thinkers examined above, he sees India as current flag-bearer of the world's most progressive views. He is not, however, entirely uncritical of utopian socialism. The Gandhian vision of village community can be overemphasized, to the neglect of issues concerning larger-scale production.[25] Mehta's own devotion to heavy industry has softened considerably over time, both for the spiritual reasons already indicated and because, as he comes to think, India's labor surplus cannot be put to work by exclusive focus on heavy industry.[26] He nevertheless insists that much large-scale production will remain necessary. Mehta's exploration of these issues is complex and beyond our scope here. It is worth mentioning, however, that his growing anti-statism prompts an interest in forms of non-capitalist economic control other than exclusive state ownership. In this vein, he calls for worker management and for trade union ownership of enterprises. He also recommends limited use of markets, instead of exclusive reliance on state planning, to coordinate the economy. These new concerns point up a marked difference in style between the anti-Gandhi and the pro-Gandhi phases in his career.

As hinted, Mehta could be in the running for top-shelf straight-up socialist thinker among any of the figures considered here. As plausibly as anyone, he tries to think out how Gandhian socialism with its village focus relates to wider realities and priorities. Doing justice to that intellectual endeavor could make for a longish chapter and it would stray from my focus on Gandhian socialism narrowly. This is precisely because, as I think of it, Mehta is a "partial" Gandhian socialist. By no means is that a knock on him or reason not to consider his thinking closely. The shortness of this chapter is more compliment than oversight.

CHAPTER 7

Narendra Deva: Gandhi and Democratic Socialism

Sought-after speaker and lifelong organizer, Narendra Deva (1889-1956) was born at Sitapur, (U.P.), the son of a well-to-do and well-educated lawyer. In his youth he learned Sanskrit, Pali, and Bengali. While acquiring his B.A. at Allahabad, he became an admirer of the Extremist leaders Aurobindo and Pal. Though he received a law degree in Benares in 1915, he had little interest in a legal career. Instead, in the early 1920s he became a lecturer in Benares at the Kashi Vidyapith, founded after Gandhi's noncooperation movement so as to fortify national education. Highly learned, Deva knew a great deal about classical Indian culture. He fervently admired Aurobindo and served under Das at the Kashi Vidyapith, succeeding him as Vice-Chancellor in1926.[1]

In 1934, Deva presided over the founding conference of the Congress Socialist Party. In 1936, he helped found the All-India Kisan Sabha (Peasant Society), designed to function as political instrument on behalf of progressive agrarian development. He twice served as president of that body. Deva served prison terms in the early 1930s and early 1940s for anti-imperial activities and was hand-picked by Gandhi

167

to help organize and lead the Quit India movement. Following the achievement of independence, he redoubled his socialist organizing efforts, despite the cumulative effects of lifelong respiratory ailments. He was chair of the Socialist Party at the time of its 1952 merger with the Kisan Mazdoor Praja Party.

The newly-formed Praja Socialist Party (P.S.P.) was soon torn among the divergent viewpoints of its major leaders. Mehta favored cooperation and possible merger with Nehru's quasi-socialist Congress. Rammanohar Lohia favored militant party-political opposition to the Congress. J.P. Narayan stressed village campaigns aimed at securing bhoodan, voluntary redistribution of agrarian land from rich to poor. Deva died in the course of mediating such struggles in an increasingly splintered socialist movement.

Deva was, from the 1930s until his death in 1956, perhaps India's most prominent socialist spokesman. He served as president in all three major incarnations of the organization that began as the Congress Socialist Party, socialist wing of the Congress, then became the independent Socialist Party, and later, through merger, became the Praja Socialist Party. Unlike Aurobindo, Das and others, Deva never tries to interpret Indian tradition as in any meaningful way "socialist." He is as steeped in Marxism as in classical learning and his loyalties as social thinker lie with the former. Faint traces of Aurobindo appear in his thought, however, along with major influence from Gandhi. These influences help modify his early views of socialism, eventually leading him to notice some loose associations between Indian tradition and socialism.

SOCIALIST MORALITY

Deva displays his early Marxism in his 1934 Presidential Address at the All-India Congress Socialist Conference, which resulted in formation of the Congress Socialist Party. The address stresses large-scale economic issues, including analysis of the worldwide depression and why capitalist remedies must fail. The details cannot detain us, except to note that Deva diagnoses the depression as symptomatic of capitalism's tendency to stagnate under demand shortages caused by artificially low mass purchasing power. Deva argues that only socialism can permanently remove this problem. He contends that the Soviet Union, untouched by the depression and unemployment afflicting capitalism during the 30s, is making rapid progress while capitalism stagnates.[2]

Socialism, as Deva argues in his speech, must strive for revolutionary economic change, not for moral transformation in human nature. He specifically advocates "scientific socialism" as opposed to "utopian socialism." Like the early Mehta, he equates utopian socialism with ineffectual "social reformism." Improvement in "character," humanity's moral stature, can only follow upon abolition of capitalism.[3] Hence, Deva in the 30s exemplifies what I call "materialist socialism." He does not entirely abandon this view of things for many years. As late as 1950, he writes that social change cannot be sought in the "minds of men," but only in "forms of production and exchange." Socialism must stress "economic structure," not "philosophy."[4]

Much different is Deva's viewpoint when he authors a policy statement for the 1955 P.S.P. conference. The statement contains a key chapter on the "Socialist Conception of Morality."[5] The most striking thing about this chapter is that it is there at all. In it, Deva addresses a range of concerns he would previously have viewed as peripheral. Where he had earlier stressed economic transformation as the practice of socialism and prosperity as its objective, he now stresses moral development as something integral both to socialist practice and to its objectives. In contrast with his earlier view that moral development awaits establishment of socialism, Deva now thinks that "conscious human efforts for moral development" must be part of efforts to achieve it. This "moral evolution" requires a "moral attitude," which presupposes "subjective efforts for self-cultivation."[6]

Deva remains Marxist enough in his 1955 statement to stress the limited possibilities for moral transformation within confines of a pre-socialist order. He remains convinced that true human morality can fully emerge only in a society of cooperative work and common ownership of productive property, with no "distinction between owners and producers." Unlike Gandhi, who sees perfection of virtue as prerequisite to full socialism, Deva sees socialism as prerequisite to full virtue. He nevertheless emphasizes a close interdependence between a "psychological" dimension of moral self-transformation, and a "social" dimension of economic transformation. There must be "simultaneous change."[7] A socialist party should pursue the moral aspect of change along with the economic. He urges his party to "cultivate socialist morality and promote socialist culture."[8]

The late-career shift in Deva's viewpoint appears also in his criticisms of the famous 1958 Congress resolution endorsing a "socialistic pattern of society." That resolution struck many as weak, vague, and open to varied interpretation. Many scorned it as a tepid rhetorical compromise with landlord and capitalist elements in the Congress, who might take offense at a more forthright call for "socialism." Deva predictably ridicules the "apologetic tone" of the Congress's brand of socialism. Less predictable is his critique of the Congress resolution as too narrowly focused on mere economism. Deva insists that socialism be understood not merely in reference to the "economic sphere" but also as a "philosophy of life." This is a far cry from his earlier insistence that socialism deal with "economic structure," not "philosophy." The socialist philosophy, to be sure, cannot be seen as "formal doctrine." Still, it must have a "basis in some set of beliefs."[9] Socialism, for Deva, has acquired quasi-religious overtones.

RELIGION: GRUDGING RECONCILIATION

Deva's views on religion itself are not easily sorted out. He delivers denunciations of religion but also makes tentative attempts to reconcile religion with his social concerns. Though he ultimately grows fairly comfortable acknowledging spiritual components in socialism, he insists on separating those components clearly from their original religious contexts.

In his denunciatory mode, Deva assesses religion as a hindrance to human progress, distracting people with other-worldly concerns and attributing divine sanction to oppressive social structures. Religion "defiles and disintegrates human life" and "wants to maintain the status quo." Socialism, he argues, "helps release man from the thraldom of religion" by presenting a "correct perspective." He rebukes Indian religion specifically for encouraging retreat into "mysticism" and for its deeply "pessimistic" outlook on worldly change.[10]

Despite these denunciations, Deva offers in one speech a defense of Indian religion, which he says can "help establish a moral order," crucial to satisfactory human life. A cursory and tentative character to his argument reveals his reservations. Key to Indian religion, he argues, is *moksha*, liberation, attained through personal "meditation" and "introspection." The point of religious practice is to "correct ourselves" and bring about "purity in behavior." Thereby, "the whole society may improve." This, of course, smacks of pure religious ideology and Deva voices this viewpoint wanly and briefly, as if aware that it lacks due attention to conscious institutional transformation.[11]

Deva's strong Marxist sensibility allows him only the most guarded endorsement of religion. His growing concern with "socialist morality," however, prompts at least some critical sympathy with religion. The "basic principles" of socialist morality can be found among past religious figures such as "Rishis, Acharyas and prophets... Saints and Sufis," he suggests. Such "basic principles"—properly segregated from their original backward religious context, especially its "hierarchical character"—can support a "spiritual humanism" underpinning socialist culture.[12] "Spiritual humanism," to Deva, is a sort of socialist religion.

By the time he writes his 1955 policy statement, Deva has arrived at a view that true socialism—true Indian socialism, at least—lies in a "creative synthesis" of Indian and Western spiritual and social insight.[13]

He shares this conclusion, more or less, with all the thinkers examined above. He is more cautious than any of them, however, about linking socialism specifically to "religion."

Aurobindo's influence can be discerned in Deva's thought about socialism's spiritual component. Deva writes that, "It is man's nature to seek self-realization by expanding his self."[14] Aurobindo-like, he imagines humanity poised before its next big evolutionary step. He even takes up Aurobindo's suggestion that this step will be led by a "new race of men who will form the *elite* of society," in their superior spiritual vision and humanitarian instincts.[15] This notion of a spiritual elite stands out strangely, for Deva is convinced that mass action, perhaps by what Marxists call the proletariat, functions as the main agent of social change. For Deva, leadership by the "spiritual vanguard" and by Lenin's "proletarian vanguard" are one and the same. In Deva's mind, Gandhi embodies this confluence of "spiritual" and "proletarian" vanguard. He praises Gandhi for his genius in bringing mass participation into India's national struggles.

GANDHI AS DEMOCRATIC SOCIALIST

Deva credits Gandhi with providing Indian socialism its trans-economic focus on moral and cultural transformation. The essence of socialist morality, Deva writes at one point, is "purity of means," a Gandhian notion. It links to particular practical ideas, most importantly satyagraha and democratic decentralization.[16] Satyagraha and democratic decentralization lie at the core of Deva's brand of socialism, which he labels "democratic socialism."

Deva repeatedly emphasizes that Gandhi envisioned using satyagraha not only to overthrow imperialism, but also to secure social and economic justice in independent India. There is, as he contends, good reason to stress non-violent strikes and civil disobedience as an ongoing Gandhian program. The Congress government, he argues, has done far too little in securing social justice in post-independence India, yet has meanwhile condemned satyagraha as out of place in a democratic national state. More specifically, the Congress government, while paying lip-service to socialism, restricts rights of workers to strike and does little to alleviate capitalist ills. Furthermore, progress towards socialism has been hobbled by the Indian Constitution's guarantee of a fundamental right to property.[17]

Under these conditions, "constitutional parliamentary" democracy, though valuable in a limited sense and certainly not to be ignored or abolished, cannot exhaust the meaning of either democracy or Gandhian ahimsa, thinks Deva. He meanwhile rebukes communism for countenancing violence and for disregarding the real, though limited, value of parliamentary democracy.[18] Stressing Gandhian "purity of means," he argues that "democratic socialism" insists on fundamental moral linkage between methods and outcomes in social struggle. In this respect, he contrasts "democratic socialism" with communism, which he thinks pays no heed to moral methods in pursuing revolutionary aims. He portrays non-violent satyagraha and strikes as simultaneously democratic and revolutionary, representing an alternative between revolutionary violence and mere parliamentary democracy. Because it represents collaborative endeavor aimed at securing economic justice, satyagraha is "democratic socialism" par excellence.

Another key Gandhian legacy, writes Deva, is the notion of "decentralized democracy and economy."[19] He enthusiastically belabors themes of agrarian community-building. The core program lies in cooperative enterprise for production and marketing, he argues. Through resource-pooling, cooperative enterprises will foster improved techniques. Meanwhile experiences of collaborative endeavor will promote fraternal spirit. In short, decentralized agro-industrialism can provide villages with new forms of production, employment and experience.[20]

Popular participation is central to such a regime. Deva endorses Gandhian panchayat raj, which envisions village governments spearheading village reconstruction. He is more realistic than Gandhi, however, in calling for state action to support villagers in pursuing agrarian transformation. Where Gandhi had often disparaged state action and in his late career urged the Congress to transition from parliamentary party into rural reconstruction movement, Deva reminds socialists to pursue "parliamentary work aimed to secure state action" alongside village work. The state must take the lead, first, in land reform, which cannot be entrusted to local popular pressure acting without help against rural elites. The state must act, second, with education and propaganda on habits and skills needed for cooperative and progressive agrarian production.[21]

Deva carefully distinguishes democratic socialism from Soviet socialism. An early admirer of Soviet economic achievements, he remains more hopeful than some that the Soviets will eventually create a nonrepressive political culture. Nevertheless, he finds serious fault with Soviet emphasis on centralized state ownership and economic control, which he thinks yield bureaucracy and repression, scarcely an advance over capitalism.[22]

Democratic socialism, in avoiding Soviet centralism, must not fall into the opposite error of exaggerated decentralization. There must, Deva insists, be national economic planning and an appropriate level of heavy industry, publicly-owned. At the same time, however, there should be maximum popular participation in economic decision-making. To ensure this, stress should lie on what Deva calls "social ownership"—public ownership at levels below that of "state ownership" by the entire society. Workers, meanwhile, should have protected rights and powers in enterprise governance.[23]

Satyagraha and democratic decentralization, key ingredients of "democratic socialism," are also distinguishing aspects of what Deva calls "Indian socialism," the "creative synthesis" of Indian and Western insight.[24] That which makes socialism most Indian—satyagraha and decentralization—also make it most democratic. Unlike thinkers examined above, Deva repeatedly denies that democracy has any roots in traditional Indian culture.[25] To create democracy in India is to conjure something wholly new. Nevertheless, thanks to Gandhi, modern Indian socialism emerges as the world's breaking wave in democracy, thinks Deva. Like socialism itself, democracy carries quasi-religious overtones for him. It is a "creed and a living faith," governing a people's "entire life and behavior."[26] Ahimsa is likewise a "creed."[27] Through its democratic socialism, crystallized in satyagraha and decentralized democracy, India may come to occupy the world's spiritual frontier.

CHAPTER 8

Nehru: The Advaita of Non-Violent Revolution

Privileged by pedigree and ambitiously inquisitive, Jawaharlal Nehru (1889-1964) was born in Allahabad, in a well-to-do Brahmin family. Son of famed lawyer and nationalist leader Motilal Nehru, he graduated from the Harrow School and Cambridge in England, before reading for the bar in London. He returned to India in 1912 and pursued both law and journalism before joining Gandhi's Non-cooperation Movement in 1920. He went to prison in 1921 for anti-imperial activity and was thereafter jailed several more times for such activitiy. He served as General Secretary of the Indian National Congress, 1927-29, and as President of the Congress several times, beginning in 1929.

Alongside Gandhi, Nehru led the major Congress campaigns in resistance to British rule until attainment of Indian independence in 1947. He became independent India's first Prime Minister and served in that post until his death. Nehru's writings and speeches, taken as a whole, exhibit impressive range, erudition and nuance. From a very early career stage, Nehru can articulate and address himself to numerous competing considerations at once, holding them in sophisticated tension. His historical works, *The Discovery of India* and *Glimpses of World History*,

177

suggest Nehru had not only the talent but some of the temperament for ambitious theoretical work

Major themes in Nehru's political outlook appear throughout his career and undergo no startling transformations, no major additions or deletions, no major reversals. There are, to be sure, various modest shifts in emphasis among themes. These shifts, highlighted below, broadly track a pattern observable more markedly with several socialist comrades, familiar from foregoing discussion of Mehta and Deva. It is from early-career "state socialism" or "scientific socialism"—emphasizing central planning, heavy industry, and economic abundance generally—to late-career "Gandhian socialism"—emphasizing shortcomings in state/scientific socialism and stressing alternatives tied to Gandhi-inspired religious themes.

These shifts are undramatic because all Nehru's themes can be found throughout his career. Closer to Gandhi than any of his socialist comrades from early on, he responded to this intimacy in two contrary ways. On the one hand, Gandhi's influence leaves its traces in Nehru's thought from the beginning, distinguishing it from that of socialists less sympathetic to Gandhi. On the other hand, this intimacy impels Nehru to acquire habits of critical distance and perspective on Gandhi's ideas, habits he maintains throughout his career.

For both these reasons, Nehru's intimacy means that he never "discovers" Gandhi so as to induce major transformations in his thought. This makes his outlook seem static compared with the more sensational intellectual journeys of Mehta, Deva, and J.P. Narayan. His thought develops so little because it is from the beginning so broad, nuanced, and anti-dogmatic, powerful skepticism balancing powerful curiosity.

ECONOMIC ANALYSIS

Nehru's socialism is Third World, driven by analysis of the nature and effects of imperialist capitalism. Nehru deems European imperialism an integral manifestation of capitalism.[1] He takes special interest, of course, in implications for India. Rather than reduplicate Nehru's narrative analyses of how British capitalism damaged India, we can instead run down a list of factors mentioned in those analyses:

1) Unlike previous conquerors who inhabited India and ruled from within, Britain ruled from afar for benefit of foreign interests.

2) To keep India effectively subjugated, Britain pursued a deliberate and damaging divide-and-rule policy, fostering antagonisms and interest conflicts among India's distinct subcommunities.

3) Also in furtherance of effective domination, Britain allied itself with and consolidated the power of elite groups, who in reactionary fashion stymied efforts toward progressive change.

4) Gold plundered from India supplied capital needed for England's early industrialism.

5) The British government in India, using debt to buy the British East India Company out of its interests, saddled the subcontinent's population with the taxation burden of defraying the debt.

6) Britain controlled and restricted a once-flourishing import trade of items produced in India, engendering collapse in India's artisan industries.

7) Britain forestalled India's industrial development and, utilizing both market advantages and political control, flooded the subcontinent with British manufactures, further undermining India's artisan production.

8) Stagnation in artisan production threw millions of Indians onto the land for subsistence.

9) Indian agriculture was meanwhile skewed toward the supply of raw materials for British factory production.

10) Britain introduced an intensely oppressive system of private property rural landlordship, which supplanted quasi-communal indigenous land-management traditions.

11) British rule and the economy that grew under it placed native Indian capital in a position of dependent subservience to the interests of foreign capital.

12) Prosperity fueled by exploitation of India raised British working-class living standards, which defanged British labor militancy at home and brought the Labor Party into complicity with empire.

13) Low Indian living standards, exemplifying conditions throughout the capitalist colonies, crimped worldwide demand so severely as to engender industrial stagnation and worldwide depression.[2]

In light of this detailed indictment, it is scarcely surprising Nehru should identify economic concerns as the locomotive force behind Indian nationalism, nor that he should see total independence from Britain as prerequisite to India's progress. Nehru has nothing but scorn for proposals like Pal's that India seek its freedom within boundaries of the British Empire. Pal's abstract concerns about higher forms of international community through federalized empire have little meaning to Nehru.[3]

If the culprit is imperialist capitalism, the remedy must embrace not only nationalism but socialism. Nehru's outlook on capitalism stems not only from its colonial impact but from its stagnation during the Depression. Nehru rehearses the notion of capitalist breakdown in overproduction/underconsumption. According to this theory, the system generates income disparity along with unemployment stemming from galloping mechanization, resulting in artificial but powerful limits on mass purchasing power and effective demand. This puts downward pressure on productive activity, which responds only to hope of profits embodied in effective demand. Stagnation results. Especially in his early career Nehru focuses on obstacles to achieving stable and widespread prosperity within the confines of capitalist arrangements. The problem is not lack of sufficient capital to generate accelerating prosperity. It is that capital cannot flow to its most beneficial uses if responsive only to vagaries in fluctuating profit prospects.[4]

Nehru has difficulty imagining socialism as anything but a highly-industrialized order. The young Nehru admonishes his mentor Gandhi not to blame industrialism itself for ills properly attributable to capitalism.[5] Nehru never wavers in his fundamental conviction that socialism requires a relatively high level of material abundance and that such abundance in turn requires substantial industrialization.[6]

Over time, however, Nehru grows more sympathetic to low-capital production. Even early on, in his 1936 presidential address to the Indian National Congress, Nehru admits a place for *khadi* ("homespun") and village industry in strategies for Indian development. He insists, however, that such industry should play a "subsidiary role" in development and that its contribution will be chiefly transitory. It sometimes seems that he views the Gandhian Congress's infatuation with khadi as sentimental. In his late career, however, he grows less grudging in his assessment of low-capital strategies. On hard-headed economic grounds, he grows more attentive to difficulties in favoring high-capital industry while also seeking rapid alleviation of unemployment. Nehru's ambivalence on this development dilemma finds expression in a 1954 speech to the National Development Council:

> Industrial growth would, no doubt, reduce unemployment, but the capacity of the industrial sector is limited. We will not solve the unemployment problem until we lay the greatest stress on small and cottage and village industries and also attach the greatest importance to heavy industries. It is not a question of giving a secondary place to either of them. Both have to be tackled.[8]

Nehru more and more comes to stress a key role for small-scale industry in alleviating India's unemployment. He credits Gandhi with correcting his own "lop-sided" earlier viewpoint not only on the "economic" issues involved but also on broader moral or "human" issues of small-scale technology.[9]

Nehru never has difficulty seeing rural poverty as India's gravest problem.[10] Axiomatic to any rural development strategy, he insists, is abolition of landlordship and equitable redistribution in land ownership.[11] He also endorses several other basic strategies for enhancing rural prosperity. Attentive to diseconomies in the small-scale, fragmented landholdings that could result from land reform, he posits three options—capitalist farms, cooperatives, and collectives—as alternatives.

Nehru rejects capitalist farming—consolidated land ownership utilizing wage labor—as essentially a revival of landlordism and inequitable ownership.[12] At the same time, he is skeptical of collective ownership and/or state-owned farms, at least in the near term. He associates collectives with productive deficiencies and with bureaucratic effacement of initiative.[13] As an alternative, he endorses cooperative strategies that combine private land ownership with the pooling of labor and resources to achieve scale economies in credit, supply, production, and marketing.[14] Nehru sees both economic and moral advantages in cooperative farming. Like others discussed above, he places local self-government or panchayat raj alongside cooperatives at the center of his rural reconstruction vision.[15] Like others, he also favors small-scale industry to combat unemployment and raise village living standards.[16]

Nehru's ambivalence on controversies within socialism cannot be comprehended without glancing at his views on the Soviet Union. Though Nehru's early admiration for the Soviet Union might be thought romantic, it is doubtful he was at any time uncritical of Soviet ills. Nevertheless, he does call attention to apparent Soviet achievements.

With early Soviet industrial growth seemingly impressive, Nehru admires the system's prowess in sustaining growth while capitalism plunges the rest of the world into Depression.[17] Even during the 30s, however, Nehru acknowledges that Soviet progress has come at what he calls "terrible cost," alluding probably to authoritarian politics, agrarian oppression, and domestic state violence.[18] It is a matter of shifting emphasis, not wholesale re-evaluation, when Nehru during the 50s begins to stress the "autocratic and authoritarian" nature of Soviet rule.[19]

Enamored with socialist industrial growth, Nehru also perceives in Soviet life a decisive advance in democratic political culture. He describes with enthusiasm the Soviet scheme for blanketing the country with participatory policy councils, providing forums for public debate and power. As Nehru portrays it:

> …(S)cores of millions of men and women are constantly taking part in the discussion of public affairs and actually in the administration of the country. There has been no such practical application of the democratic process in history.[20]

Though the incipient democracy perceived by Nehru failed to flourish in Soviet history, it flourishes in his mind as a vision of Indian socialism.

Nehru does not, like Gandhi, deceive himself on the need for socialist expropriation of wealth. He contends that neither equality nor production for the common good can emerge without forced wealth redistribution. Moreover, his Marxist sensibilities leave him unconvinced that wealth expropriations are in any way unjust.[21] Even uncompensated takings pose no injustice if expropriated wealth had been accumulated through exploitation.

Though Nehru does not deem compensation for property expropriation morally necessary, he nevertheless endorses it for practical reasons like maintaining social peace.[22] He insists, however, that compensation be limited and graded, rather than gauged to full economic value. He suggests that large wealth holders be compensated only modestly but that smaller holders receive progressively fuller compensation.

Insofar as taxes to finance compensation for the wealthy fall upon the wealthy, they pay for it themselves. What is the point? If compensation taxes fall instead on the poor, the arrangement becomes self-defeating since the very purpose of expropriation is to benefit the downtrodden. Such considerations impel Nehru's endorsement of limited and graded compensation, equalizing wealth by leaving the rich less compensated, the poor more so. Small holders should either escape expropriation or be compensated fully.[23] Nehru's ideas found their way into the original Article 31 of India's Constitution, providing that compensation be paid for confiscations but authorizing discretion in determining levels.[24]

Especially in his late career but even before, Nehru stands for a "mixed economy," combining public and private ownership so as to avoid vices of both socialist bureaucracy and capitalist neglect of the lowly. He insists repeatedly that for impoverished India, rapid wealth accumulation must be the polestar of socialist strategy.[25] He is not, however, impervious to meditations on the non-material implications of development strategies, as we will see below. He scorns Gandhi's "trusteeship" vision for capitalism-made-gentle.[26] In his early career, he seems to insist on thorough nationalization as India's proper strategy.[27] Later, however, he cautions against seeing nationalization as an "immediate cure" for India's ills and defends a role for private enterprise, so long as its power can be contained so as to prevent dominance.[28] He believes private sector incentives will foster initiative and provide stimulating competition for public enterprises.[29] He hopes vaguely that most private enterprise will eventually operate under co-operative principles, presumably to replace traditional capitalism's reliance on wage labor without ownership rights or management role. He also hopes that habits of cooperative effort may increasingly supplant the profit motive as economic propellant.[30]

DISPASSIONATE RELIGIOUS CURIOSITY

Nehru's basic outlook is secular and he counts this a strength. Nehru's ecumenical curiosity does, however, manifest itself in a lifelong though intermittent interest in religious ideas. In his late career, he somewhat intently begins to weave religious themes into his pronouncements.

In his *Autobiography*, Nehru recounts how an interest in Theosophy came over him in early adolescence. At roughly the same time, his father had notoriously repudiated ritual practices sacrosanct within the Kashmiri Brahmin community.[31] Neither episode was at all decisive in young Nehru's development, but taken together they marked out poles in Nehru's lifelong approach to religion. A characteristic tension emerges in the following passage from Nehru's *Autobiography*:

> The spectacle of what is called religion, or at any rate organised religion, in India and elsewhere has filled me with horror, and I have frequently condemned it and wished to make a clean sweep of it. Almost always it seems to stand for blind belief and reaction, dogma and bigotry, superstition and exploitation, and the preservation of vested interests. And yet I knew well that there was something else in it, something which supplied a deep inner craving of human beings. How else could it have been the tremendous power it has been and brought peace and comfort to innumerable tortured souls? Was that peace merely the shelter of blind belief and absence of questioning, the calm that comes from being safe in harbour, protected from the storms of the open sea, or was it something more? In some cases certainly it was something more.[32]

Nehru repudiates religious domination in social affairs and does not hesitate to denounce its pernicious effects. He nevertheless maintains openness to religious ideas. Toward India's religious traditions, Nehru holds a balanced and dispassionate stance. Though not without admiration for some traditional elements, he debunks popular notions found in thinkers discussed above on the superior "spirituality" of India compared with the rest of the world. He calls such notions delusional.[33] Much of Nehru's religious commentary comes in the form of episodic praise for various "markers" in India's landscape: the Buddha[34] and Buddhism,[35] the Mahabharata and the Gita,[36] Ramakrishna[37] and Vivekananda.[38] Often these remarks are cursory, as when Nehru writes, "It was the ethical and social and practical idealism of Buddha and his religion that influenced our people and left their imperishable marks upon them…"[39]

Focusing away from his many disparaging remarks about religion, we can instead concentrate on positive connections Nehru sees between religion and socialism with respect to three topics: caste, solidaristic community and inward transformation. The first two resonate with thinkers discussed above concerning relationships between socialism and India's past, but with distinct twists provided by Nehru. With the third topic, Nehru makes a fresh religious theme an anchor to his socialist thought.

UNDERSTANDING AND ELIMINATING CASTE

Nehru's attitudes toward caste are neither counterintuitive nor surprising. Nehru feels little stake in defending India's religious heritage and hence no pressure to interpret caste as benevolent or misunderstood. He explains the origins of caste as a process whereby indigenous Dravidian and tribal groups got absorbed as subjugated segments by an expanding Aryan culture. Maintaining subjugation and segmentation imparted a fissiparous logic to Indian society generally. Nehru writes: "The caste divisions, originally intended to separate the Aryans from the non-Aryans, reacted on the Aryans themselves, and as a division of functions and specialization increased, the new classes took the form of castes."[41]

As to eradicating caste, Nehru ponders three different approaches. The first lies in history. India's heterodox religious movements, according to Nehru, have repeatedly attempted to dissolve the social hegemony of caste. All have failed, however, to overthrow caste in a fundamental sense.[42] For at least the more recent nineteenth century anti-caste religious movements, Nehru offers an undeveloped but suggestive diagnosis of failure. The failure lies in the "middle class" nature of those movements and in their "direct attack" on caste practices.[43] One may, based on Nehru's scattered comments elsewhere, suggest that Nehru is groping toward a Marxist or Marxish theory of how to eradicate caste.

At one point, Nehru vaguely analyzes caste with the Marxist terms "superstructure" and "base." The social attitudes and religious ideology of caste represent a cultural "superstructure" arising from a determinative foundational "base" of "economic forces." In other words, caste is fundamentally rooted in economic arrangements. The persistence or dissolution of caste depends upon the persistence or dissolution of the economic structures that undergird it.[44] This analysis seems to lie behind Nehru's view that middle-class religious attacks on caste are destined to fail. Such movements mount a "direct attack" on overt caste practices, without challenging the covert economic base that secures the system. It is not surprising that "middle class" movements fail to notice or address oppressive economic structures, where the heart of the problem lies.

This line of thought brings us to the second approach Nehru ponders for eradicating caste: socialist transformation of economic structures. He endorses this approach in an off-hand but revealing passage concerning untouchability from his 1936 presidential address to the Indian National Congress, referring to Untouchables with Gandhi's term "Harijans" (children of God):

> The problem of untouchability and the Harijans again
> can be approached in different ways. For a socialist it
> presents no difficulty for under socialism there can be

no such differentiation or victimization. Economically speaking, the Harijans have constituted the landless proletariat and an economic solution removes the social barriers that custom and tradition have raised.[45]

In this vein, Nehru thinks socialism both necessary and sufficient for eradicating caste. The caste superstructure of "custom and tradition" will not long survive once property maldistributions that facilitate economic exploitation disappear.

It is, of course, not obvious exactly how economic oppression of India's lower castes can be lifted. This brings us to the third approach Nehru ponders for eliminating caste: Gandhian action. In contrast to "direct" attacks on caste practices from "middle class" movements, Gandhi attacks caste in "indirect" fashion by mobilizing the "masses."[46] Through his focus on "uplift of the Depressed Classes and the Untouchables," Gandhi has "undermined the entire caste system."[47] In what fashion has Gandhi accomplished this uplift? Certainly Gandhi has effectuated no socialist revolution in property relationships. Nehru indicates that Gandhi's contribution lies in instigating the political organization and mobilization of India's "underprivileged and poverty-stricken." Of Gandhi, he observes: "By his technique of political action, he vitalized hundreds of millions of people, drove out fear from them, and produced in them self-respect and self-reliance."[48] Gandhian mobilization has educated India's downtrodden in habits of "cooperative action" in "resistance to oppression."[49]

In sum, Gandhi's influence has been to initiate precisely what socialism often deems necessary for economic revolution: organized political action among the oppressed. In Nehru's mind two approaches to eradicating caste—socialism and Gandhian action—converge in a unified and superior alternative to the middle class religious movements of the past. Still, Nehru judges India's religious heritage highly pertinent to caste eradication.

Nehru suggests that the success of Gandhian action in mobilizing the downtrodden stems from "stress on truth and peaceful means."[50] He thereby highlights two themes—Truth and Ahimsa—central to Gandhi's religious world view. Moreover, he argues that Gandhi's Truth and Ahimsa represent "basic principles" rooted in Indian tradition.[51] Though he portrays past religious movements as ineffectual in dissolving caste, he imagines its eventual abolition through a religious movement rooted in Indian heritage. Gandhi's religious movement, unlike those of the past, mobilizes the downtrodden.

As my discussion of thinkers above indicates, modern Indian thought has been both plagued and stimulated by ambivalence over caste. Caste represents not only oppression and hierarchy, but also solidarity and a foil to egoistic individualism. Nehru does not dwell on positive features attributed to caste by others. He comes nowhere near deploying caste, interpreted positively, as a central strand in his commentary. He nevertheless partakes modestly in interpreting caste as a locus of solidarity.

APPROPRIATING TRADITIONAL SOLIDARITY

Caste is one of three elements, along with "the autonomous village community" and "the joint family system," that Nehru identifies as fundamental within traditional Indian society. All three he portrays as incubators of communal solidarity.[52] It is not worthwhile to tarry unduly over Nehru's particular ruminations on this familiar theme. It may, however, be appropriate to record a few of his formulations. "Within each group," writes Nehru, "whether this was the village community, the particular caste, or the large joint family, there was a communal life shared together, a sense of equality, and democratic methods."[53] India's group elements nurtured "a strong sense of solidarity within each, which not only protected the group but sheltered and helped an individual member who got into trouble or was in economic distress."[54] Group frameworks fostered democratic methods of social choice. In this vein, Nehru also mentions ancient "tribal republics" and Buddhist "religious assemblies."[55] He does not make as much of these as does Aurobindo, nor view them as central to traditional Indian life.

Though he identifies a role for caste in cultivating a "democratic habit" in Indian life, Nehru strictly avoids suggesting that the caste system itself be preserved.[56] Likewise with the autonomous village community and the joint family system, he spends no energy advocating preservation. Any attempt at defense would be futile against enormous social changes sweeping India. Moreover, his critical balance prevents him from ignoring the negative aspects of caste, village communities and joint families.[57] He equates caste, village community and joint family with an overweening group orientation no more to be embraced than "the excessive individualism of the West."[58] The problem is to strike a balance, "to reconcile the respective claims of the individual and the group."[59] The point of studying traditional group structures is not to defend them against change, but to identify habits and attitudes constraining or facilitating construction of new institutions. As Nehru writes:

> In the constructive schemes that we may make, we have to pay attention to the human material we have to deal with, to the background of its thought and urges, and to the environment in which we have to function. To ignore this and to fashion some idealistic scheme in the air, or merely to think in terms of imitating what others have done elsewhere, would be folly.[60]

Though Nehru links his discussion of Indian group structure to socialism, the linkage he sees is less spiritual and more economic than that drawn by thinkers covered above. He suggests there was something quasi-socialist specifically about property arrangements within traditional Indian group structure. There was, he claims, no feudal landlordship nor private proprietorship over land.[61] Landlordism and private proprietorship came into India at a late date with the British, bringing "disastrous results."[62] Prior to British rule the property system had been "cooperative or collective," Nehru insists.[63] This is an aspect of the Indian "environment" he deems critical to "constructive schemes that we may make."

INWARD TRANSFORMATION: ADVAITA AND GANDHIAN ACTION

In guarded and unspectacular fashion, Nehru does endeavor to articulate an existential role for religion in human life. As the following passage suggests, one of his basic notions is that religion consists of an inward transformation reacting upon outside action.

> What then is religion...? Probably it consists of the inner development of the individual, the evolution of his consciousness in a certain direction which is considered good... [R]eligion lays stress on this inner change and considers outward change as but the projection of this inner development.[64]

Though Nehru stresses inward transformation and its outward effect, his sensibility is far too political to explain inward transformation in terms of private spiritual virtuosity. On the contrary, he sees inward transformation as something socially shaped and enabled. It is to Nehru obvious that "the outer environment powerfully influences the inner development." "Both act and interact on each other," he writes.[65]

In Nehru's mind, socialism entails inward transformation. Early in his career, he writes that "real socialism involves a profound transformation of the deeper habits of opinion and of character...."[66] Nehru's view of religious transformation as dialectical reciprocity between person and society manifests itself in his view of socialist transformation in personal character. "The main question for us to consider is how to create an environment and circumstances under which these deeper changes can take place," he writes.[67]

As discussion above indicates, Nehru's socialist thought richly addresses aspects of economics: investment levels, income and property distribution, unemployment and the like. Nehru insists that such concerns be central to socialist analysis. Yet he also insists that socialism requires inward transformation, even if inward transformation is not itself socialism. As he proclaims as early as 1936, "Socialism is…something even more than an economic doctrine; it is a philosophy of life…"[68] More and more in his late career, he insists that socialist politics deliberately foster inward transformation. Socialism requires "deliberately aiming at a new type of society whose chief purpose is the welfare of the people, not only in material living standards, but also in the things of the spirit."[69] In his late career, Nehru increasingly couches these concerns in traditional religious terminology. In 1964, for example, he writes that the "essential objective" of socialism is "the quality of the individual and the concept of a dharma underlying it."[70] Nehru finds much socialist thought and practice lacking in these spiritual aspects. Part of the problem, of course, lies precisely in socialism's characteristic focus on economic well-being.

> Poverty is a degradation and the obvious reaction is to get rid of it… But too much wealth and affluence, whether in an individual or a society, has also its attendant evils which are becoming evident today. The mere piling up of riches may lead to an emptiness in the inner life of man.
>
> … There is a danger that socialism, while leading to affluence and even equitable distribution, may still miss some of the significant features of life.[71]

Of all Indian religious legacies, the one with most appeal for Nehru is Advaita.He alludes approvingly to the thought of those modern

Advaitins, Vivekananda and Aurobindo, and colors his explication of Advaita in their terms. In a discussion of the Upanishads, for example, he characterizes the doctrine of identity between Self and Cosmos as a notion of "metaphysical democracy," which unites all people as equals in an "atmosphere of tolerance." He then attributes to the Upanishads a notion that any worthy endeavor entails "restraint, self-suffering, self-sacrifice" and suggests that this notion pervades Indian culture and history, including the mass movements inspired by Gandhi's leadership. At its best, Advaita posits spirituality as an experience of human solidarity, perception of a unitary and divine essence in all humanity.[72]

Unfortunately, Nehru argues, Advaita has too often failed in holding fast to its quintessential spiritual focus on solidarity. As he darkly suggests, the Upanishadic/Advaitic tradition has perhaps cultivated an overly individualistic religion, exalting private spiritual virtuosity while failing to nourish solidarity. Equally important, the tradition has failed to expand beyond minority elite boundaries. Failure to develop a relationship with "society as a whole" allows the tradition to grow "barren and sterile."[73]

Nehru's image of a stagnant tradition points to a key component of his thought about religion. True religiosity, according to Nehru, partakes of "adventure." He uses the word on many occasions to describe religiosity he admires.[74] In other ways, too, his discussion of religion suggests adventure, as when he writes that religion deals with "the uncharted realms of human experience…"[75] If true religion is spiritual adventure, bad religion is that which imprisons spiritual life in fixed and frozen formations. Nehru disparages what he sees as spirit-imprisoning religious formations, wielding images like "petrified by dogma," "static," "hindrance," "dead thought and ceremonial," and so on.[76] He refers approvingly to Aurobindo's critique of such religion and calls for an alternative.[77] For Nehru, spiritual life is first and foremost a quest. Its essence lies not in what has already been discovered but in what can be discovered behind the next event or action. Religion has no value apart from the integrity of its ever-renewing application and development.

A comprehension of Nehru's Advaita may emerge from themes of social non-dualism, adventure, anti-stagnation and reciprocity between inward and outward transformation. Advaitic spirituality does not lie in meditative contemplation of non-duality as a static insight. It lies rather in an active, never-complete quest to perceive and create union with the socially Other. It is a perpetual assault on boundaries separating humans from mutual sympathy and solidarity.

Of course, Nehru sees Gandhi as an exemplification of such spirituality. In his eyes, it is precisely such spirituality that accounts for Gandhi's socialist genius. Nehru credits Gandhi with transforming the Congress into a "socialistic" entity.[78] Gandhi took a middle-class organization and labored to unify it with the "masses."[79] He focused on language to reach the masses, issues of concern to them, membership and organizational affiliations drawn from their ranks. Nehru applauds this as an Advaitic achievement, liquefying social boundaries and creating new human unities:

> And so he set about to restore the spiritual unity of the people and to break the barrier between the small westernized group at the top and the masses, to discover the living elements in the old roots and to build upon them, to waken these masses out of their stupor and static condition and to make them dynamic.[80]

By "living elements in the old roots," Nehru refers to India's religious heritage, which Gandhi embodies, renews and restores to India's masses, quickening their own previously "static" outlook into "dynamic" spirituality. He goes on to praise Gandhi for genius in Advaitic virtue: "identification with the masses" and "community of spirit with them."[81]

Nehru's praise for Gandhian spirituality extends into analysis of village reconstruction. Such work endeavors to persuade villages to adopt new thoughts about social relationships, new habits of cooperative organization, new productive techniques. These efforts cannot succeed if new thoughts, habits, and techniques are rejected as alien, ridiculed as irrelevant, or condemned as arrogant encroachments on valued traditions. Such inertia can best be overcome if new things arise and take shape from the very midst of villages themselves. Only in this way can villagers grasp what might appear to be foreign and identify it as something intimately their own. Change thereby emerges not as self-disparagement but as self-enhancement, defanging conflict with familiar sources of identity, value and self-worth. Put another way, Gandhi's technique requires of village workers a vigilance against arrogance and an openness to the village context, so that they learn from villages even as villages learn from them. The encounter between village worker and village is one of mutual transformation, transformation with a spiritual dimension.

Nehru sums up Gandhi's approach to village work as follows:

> We should discard the air of superiority and identify ourselves with the villagers by approaching them in their dress, talking to them in their language, partaking of their food and by squatting with them on their floor. The strict official approach at once creates a wide gulf between us and the villagers and does not achieve any results.[82]

Nehru's point seems to be that Gandhian workers must *become* villagers, to identify with the village world while working for change. Nehru calls upon the Congress to enrich its organizational links with village life and movements so as to dissolve the duality between Congress and the masses.[83] The Congress should be village-ized while the villages are Congress-ized. The Congress then becomes vanguard for the masses, but in a manner tellingly different from Lenin's approach.

Lenin envisions a small, tightly-disciplined vanguard party seizing state power for the masses. The vanguard party and its use of state power are both necessary due to lack of vision and know-how among the masses. The party must therefore wield state power to effectuate revolutionized arrangements. Nehru spurns this entire scenario. His alternative retains an organizational vanguard, most likely the Congress, moving toward a transformed society. But Nehru, like Gandhi, insists that the organization itself be one of mass participation and action. As he writes, "The Congress must be not only for the masses, as it claims to be, but of the masses; only then will it really be for the masses."[84] In this Gandhian strategy, organizational development and discipline should be directed not merely at capture and use of state power, but at revolutionizing social relations on various fronts through direct action by the people. Insofar as the people so acting hold influence within it, the Congress and the new society become one and the same.

Nehru never succumbs to pure religious ideology. He sees that spiritual development cannot by itself build a better society. Progress requires specific attack on economic structures that hold people down and twist spirituality into retarded and crippled shapes. On this note he endorses satyagraha against economic injustice.[85] Yet he doubts that economic revolution can usher in a truly good society without specific spiritual effort toward inward transformation. He doubts, moreover, that a good society can truly emerge from the action of a small vanguard party wielding the state to effectuate revolution from above. Although a progressive state can and should assist in transformative change, revolution must ultimately come not from above but from below, or more precisely from within: within the bosom of every village, within the heart of each revolutionary.

PART V

Thorough Gandhian Socialism

CHAPTER 9

Lohia: General Aims, Immediacy, Heretical Gandhism

Rigorous critic and independent thinker, Rammanohar Lohia (1910-1967) came into the world at Akbarpur (U.P.), the son of a small businessman. He studied at the Universities of Bombay, Benares and Calcutta before receiving his Ph.D. in Economics at the University of Berlin in 1932 with a thesis on civil disobedience (satyagraha) in India over the salt tax.

At the age of 10, Lohia had joined Gandhi's Non-cooperation Movement, and in 1934 he became one of the chief founders of the Congress Socialist Party. At the outset of World War II, Lohia's anti-British agitations landed him in jail for more than a year. He was released and he escaped capture during the early months of the anti-British Quit India movement launched by the Congress in 1942. After directing underground activities including radio transmissions for nearly two years, he was arrested in 1944 and he then endured a second imprisonment and torture at the hands of the British. He gained release in 1946.

Lohia was elected Chairman of the Congress Socialist Party, but in 1948 the Socialists voted to leave the Congress and form an independent party. In 1949, he became the first president of the Hind Kisan Panchayat

(Indian Peasant Council), founded to work for prompt alleviation of India's agrarian poverty. In 1952, after Socialists were routed by the Congress in India's first general election, the Praja Socialist Party (P.S.P.) came together, merging the Socialist Party with the Kisan Mazdoor Praja Party. Lohia became General Secretary of the new party and Chief Minister of the first state government it was able to form, in Travancore (Kerala). He resigned from the latter post in 1954, protesting against that government's use of lethal force against demonstrators. That same year, he was arrested for his role in P.S.P.-supported peasant satyagraha over government irrigation policy. He was ultimately acquitted of charges.

In 1955, after disputes with other P.S.P. leaders over political strategy, Lohia founded a separate Socialist Party aiming opposition at Nehru's Congress. He was arrested several times thereafter for civil disobedience. He was elected to the Lok Sabha, the powerful "lower house" of India's parliament, in 1963, and he served briefly, then spent the last years of his life helping organize anti-Congress movements and governments throughout India.

As Gandhi's younger disciple, Lohia deliberately crafts his socialist thought around Gandhian themes. If J.P. Narayan (see Chapter 10) arrives at his thorough Gandhian socialism by a roundabout route, Lohia begins with Gandhian socialism and maintains it throughout. Lohia focuses his thought on articulating "socialism" as an ideology distinct from both capitalism and state-centered communism. His writings have baffled many with their slippery organization and peculiar, not to say eccentric, terminology. Main themes can easily be discerned, however, within the problematic explored here: that of juxtaposing socialist material concerns with religious or spiritual ones. In a variety of ways, using idiosyncratic phraseology, Lohia tries to frame conceptions of socialism and of spirituality dovetailing with each other.

ECONOMIC AIMS, GENERAL AIMS

One of Lohia's frequent themes is the relationship between what he calls "economic aims" and "general aims" in a social system. The term "economic aims" generally denotes material prosperity and may also refer to the economic objectives of a particular system. The particular economic aims of capitalism, for example, are "mass production and low costs and profits to owners," along with "self-interest" operating under "competition," while the economic aims of communism entail "social ownership over means of production."[1] The term "general aims" implies such universal goods as "democracy, truthfulness, good conduct, peace of the heart, and a general state of culture."[2] Basically, "economic aims" refers to material concerns, while "general aims" refers to spiritual or cultural ones. Lohia equates "economic aims" with "body" and "general aims" with "soul."[3]

The relationship of economic and general aims must be properly understood, Lohia maintains. Two opposite fallacies are possible. The first bears some affinity to what I call "materialist socialism," which imagines that establishing right economic organization will by itself secure a high quality of cultural life. Lohia attributes this error not only to communism—corresponding to what I call "materialist socialism"—but also to capitalism. Both suppose that "the general aims of society… flow out of certain economic aims."[4] He dubs this fallacy the "automotive" fallacy because it posits automatic connection between achievement of certain economic arrangements and realization of "general aims."

A second fallacy, in Lohia's words, is to suppose "that any set of general aims can be superimposed by man's effort on any set of economic aims…"[5] This fallacy, which could be called the "grafting" fallacy, comes in two varieties. One variety resembles what I call "pure religious ideology," which imagines that spiritual transformation can occur in society regardless of economic constraint. An example of this is Gandhi's doctrine of capitalist trusteeship, which tries to graft the general aims of "democracy and good conduct and moral and ethical values" onto the economic structure of capitalism. A second variety occurs not when economic constraints are ignored, but when economic transformation and general or spiritual transformation are viewed as separate tasks requiring separate methods, with results that may then be grafted into a harmonious whole. As an example of this, Lohia cites Burmese socialism, which is similar to Ambedkar's thought in simultaneously positing a socialist economic agenda and a Buddhist spiritual/moral agenda. Lohia criticizes Burmese socialism along the lines I take above in criticizing Ambedkar. The socialist and Buddhist components are added together but do not entail or reinforce each other.

As opposed to the two fallacies—automotive and grafting—Lohia argues that economic and general aims are best pursued in deliberate synchrony with each other. "An integrated relationship between the two sets of aims has to be set up by the intelligence of man," he writes. Synthesizing the two sets of aims within an "integrated harmony" provides socialism with its proper "doctrinal foundation." The two sets of aims must be "interwoven so the economic structure admits of realizing general aims and the general aims are…so construed that they can sustain the economic structure."[6]

Of the two, the automotive fallacy is more prevalent. In pursuit of particular economic aims, a system may fail to achieve and may even subvert all general aims. Against communism, which sees an ideal society emerging automatically from "social ownership over means of production," Lohia insists that general aims "do not inevitably flow out of economic aims…"[7] "Without integrated harmony," he writes, "it is generally the economic aims which command the right of way, no matter what calamity they might thereby bring." To prevent the havoc caused by single-minded focus on economic aims, he proposes that economic aims be shaped "in the image" of various "faiths" such as the "great religions" and the "creed of organized non-violence."[8].

Disproportionate stress on "economic aims" to the neglect of "general aims" pervades the ideological vice Lohia labels "environmentalism."

Environmentalism is the erroneous conceit that it is possible to create an ideal social system in which personal virtue becomes either automatic or unnecessary. Communism and capitalism are chief examples of this conceit. They both imagine social systems "where all will be automatically good. It will not be necessary for one to be good."[9]

It is, of course, puzzling for Lohia to lump capitalism together with communism and also to speak of a system where people are automatically good that is also one where it is unnecessary to be good. Lohia's inartfully expressed thought can be clarified through images from two divergent schools of thought. First, there is the Marxist notion that with communist production, humans will for the first time find it fully possible and natural to be "good," to treat each other benevolently in all spheres of life. This makes goodness, in Lohia's terminology, "automatic." Second, there is Adam Smith's notion of a capitalist market economy in which, by the magic of the "Invisible Hand," the self-serving pursuit of interest on all sides yields maximum common good. According to some formulations, though not perhaps Smith's, this makes goodness, defined as virtuous self-restraint, not "necessary." The ironic upshot, as Lohia notices, is that both communist and capitalist ideologies deny the relevance of virtue, conceived as personal self-restraint.

Lohia wants to replace this environmentalism with an approach to human change emphasizing not only social reorganization but also cultivation of personal virtue. Latent in all people, he argues, are the virtues of the "Saint," among which is capacity for "denial of the flesh." "Let us not be frightened of sainthood," writes Lohia, suggesting that practice of saintly virtues is worthwhile in two senses. First, virtue intrinsically fosters personal growth and self-realization. Second, it nourishes capacities for progressive social action. Practitioners of virtue treat themselves as both "end" and "means." They "enact virtues which do not change," while becoming "an instrument of better future…"[10]

RELIGION, GANDHI AND IMMEDIACY

Lohia's religious concerns, reflected by interest in saintly virtue, comes to him mainly through Gandhi. Lohia both admires and criticizes Gandhi's view of human change. While Gandhi merits applause for avoiding environmentalism, he errs by exaggerating too far in the opposite direction, tending to "over-emphasize the individual and underemphasize the environment," that is focusing excessively on personal virtue and slighting the need for transformed institutions. Despite his reservations, Lohia finds Gandhi without peer as agent of progressive human change. Gandhi "was the first in world history to be a revolutionary of political and social structures together with being a revolutionary of the inner world and ways of conduct." Hence, Lohia attributes to Gandhi a breakthrough in the problematic central in modern Indian thought: dialogue between socialist and religious ideas. Though these two spheres of thought, as he puts it, have previously appeared as "anti-poles," it is both worthwhile and possible to weave them into a harmonious program of "change in the environment and change in the individual, revolution and religion, social reconstruction and moral uplift..."[11]

Though styling himself a non-believer, Lohia takes great interest in religion and often appropriates religious language and metaphors to explain his ideas. Socialists, he argues, "cannot stay unconcerned about religion," despite traditional socialist disdain. Socialism's attitude toward religion should be "exploratory," not "contentious," and should not postulate an undue "antinomy" between religious and non-religious concerns. Socialism cannot, of course, tolerate religious tenets "hostile to the abolition of the enslavement of man by man or to the release of his energies in free association." Socialists can, however, embrace aspects of "religion at its best," such as "an ethical and social training in good conduct" and a "discipline of compassion and contemplation."[12]

Other Lohia themes also track our problematic. One of these Lohia calls the "dichotomy between multiplication of things and reduction of wants." The "multiplication of things" in Lohia's mind is a "materialist" approach to life, while "reduction of wants" is a "spiritual" approach. These represent two opposed responses to material scarcity. "Multiplication of things" means attempt to satiate material wants through ever-increased production. Like thinkers explored above, Lohia doubts that human contentment can ever arrive this way. "Reduction of wants" means a spiritual approach, linked by Lohia to "Gandhian doctrine," seeking to constrain material desire through heroic self-discipline. Lohia finds this latter approach, taken by itself, one-sided and unrealistic.

Like Mehta, Lohia finds a balance between the two opposed responses most appealing and he equates this balance specifically with Indian socialism. He describes the Indian socialist approach as one of "comparative multiplication of produce and comparative disciplining of wants" within a framework of social ownership and comparative equality of incomes.[13] Hence he concludes that Indian socialism entails simultaneous focus on counterbalancing elements: the economics of production and the spiritualitics of restraint. Like Mehta, he stresses that this requires at least relative equality in wealth.

The stress on equality is itself an area where Lohia explores relationships between material and spiritual concerns. Western culture, he somewhat cryptically thinks, tends to emphasize material equality, broadly including "social, political and economic." Indian culture, by contrast, cultivates "Spiritual equality," but has ignored social and economic equality. What does Lohia mean by "spiritual equality" and how has India cultivated it? He seems to mean India's contemplative spiritual techniques which bring "the joy of being one with the universe, of being equal with everything in it."[14]

Lohia argues that this sense of spiritual equality, though divorced in Indian life from material equality, in general bears affinity with it. Experience of spiritual equality propels people to at least imagine material equality with others. On the flip side, experience of material equality with others helps provoke the insight of spiritual equality. Though Indian culture proves that insight into "spiritual equality" can arise even alongside great material disparity, such insight thrives best with material equality. Excessive material disparity blunts sentiments of spiritual equality.

With these ideas in mind, Lohia explains that Indian socialism seeks a "doctrine" of "thought and action" cultivating material and spiritual equality simultaneously. In the familiar manner of an entire tradition, he portrays Indian socialism as a synthesis of Western socialism and Indian spiritualism.

In a discussion of property abolition, Lohia comments further on this convergence. Socialism seeks to abolish "property as institution," while Indian religion, at least in its "Upanishadic" strain of "non-attachment," seeks to abolish "property as emotion." Put another way, Marxism abolishes property "objectively," while religious thought like the Upanishads abolishes it "subjectively." Neither abolition suffices by itself. Lohia writes: "Let no one…make the mistake that destruction of property as emotion reduces one whit the need to abolish it as institution." Likewise, "abolition of property as institution does not reduce one whit the need to destroy it as emotion." Institutional and emotional propertylessness must reinforce each other.[15]

Emotional propertylessness and "reduction of wants" both suggest a socialist solidarity-in-austerity ethic much like Mehta's. Even under socialist economic arrangements, the "emotional lure" of material greed may fuel desire for "unequal comfort or show." An ethic of austerity must prevail so as to secure socialist economic arrangements against corruption or subversion by recalcitrant material greed.

Lohia pushes the association of socialism with Indian religion still further when he suggests "socialist ashrams" where activists could retreat "in times of spiritual need" for "creative work and creative rest." It is "Indian tradition" to build ashrams "for the training of the spirit and the spread of a doctrine." The practice of ashram living could provide the socialist movement with an "uplifting quality of the spirit."[16]

It is perhaps from Gandhi's experiments in community living that Lohia picks up the idea for socialist ashrams. In any case, he highly affirms the debt his own socialist thought owes to Gandhi. He applauds Gandhi's evolution toward socialism. Gandhi's methods and insights can be joined creatively with socialism but not with either capitalism or communism, which are "closed" to Gandhian influence. Socialist strategy should entail "rational application of Mahatma Gandhi's teaching."

Gandhi's contributions emerge in what Lohia calls the "principle of immediacy." Immediacy—directness or tangibility—carries two main and somewhat disparate Gandhian meanings. The first concerns means and ends in social struggle. The second concerns decentralized economic and political organization.

In a Gandhian view of interpenetration between means and ends, Lohia writes:

> Means are ends in the short run and ends are means in the long run. Whatever method one employs in order to achieve one's desired aim tends to become the end in the long run and whatever aim one desires to achieve…the means are piecemeal achievements of that end.[17]

"Immediacy" in this kind of means-ends sense requires that "each act of struggle should contain its own justification." Lohia ties this idea to "general aims." General aims should stand not only as "remote" ends, but also as proximate "immediate" ones. Each act of struggle must "pass the tests of general aims of society." By passing the test of general aims, satyagraha especially exemplifies "immediacy."[18] We will have more to say in a moment about Lohia's doctrine of satyagraha.

Lohia also thinks in Gandhian vein about decentralized economics and politics. This second meaning of "immediacy"—directness and decentralization in "ownership and political control," implies active and direct participation in managing terms of collective life. It requires decentralized technology, the "small-unit tool," and abolition of private productive property, except that which employs no non-owning wage labor. Socialized property should be held at various levels, including province, village and cooperative, not just that of the central state.[19] In articulating "immediacy" in "ownership and political control," Lohia focuses especially on fostering vital communal democracy in India's villages. This requires equitable redistribution of land holdings.[20]

SATYAGRAHA AND MILITANT GANDHISM

Lohia's extensive commentary on satyagraha composes an integrated theory of social action and human virtue while criticizing certain strands in Gandhian thought.

Satyagraha is, first, a method of social change, an alternative to nonviolent but often feeble parliamentary methods on the one hand and to violent revolution on the other.[21] Like most Gandhi-influenced thinkers, Lohia rejects Ambedkar's argument that constitutionally or legally valid action represents the exclusive legitimate avenue for pursuing change in a democracy. Satyagraha, he argues, is more effective than either violence or parliamentary constitutionalism, avoiding the mayhem of one and the inertia of the other.

Satyagraha is, second, a requisite atmosphere of any society that embodies and seeks justice. It should prevail not as extraordinary last resort but as habitual response by vigilant citizens to tyrannies of all kinds. A nation's freedom and commitment to justice can be measured by the number of its potential satyagrahis, practitioners of satyagraha.[22]

Satyagraha is, third, a method of cultivating virtue, "an essay in the reformation of human nature."[23] There is, to be sure, confusion over the "change of heart" that satyagraha seeks. The most important change comes in the hearts of satyagrahis, who learn sensitivity to injustice, courage in resisting it, and enhanced "determination" and "capacity for action." As Lohia sees it, changing the heart of the adversary is a decidedly secondary and seldom achieved objective. He repudiates

Gandhi's notion of capitalist trusteeship along with attempts to achieve non-violent redistribution by petitioning landlords to give land away. (This failed Gandhian movement, led by Vinoba Bhave and known as bhoodan, will receive attention in Chapter 10.)

Satyagraha is, fourth, a doctrine of class struggle. Even if wealthy people may sometimes be "declassed" by satyagraha or other factors and converted to actions or positions at odds with their own material interests, satyagraha should operate primarily as an effort by the down-trodden to increase their own power and to diminish that of elites. The point is to transform systems, not adversaries.[24] Lohia's views on this resemble Aurobindo's more than Gandhi's, except perhaps for Gandhi's late career. The purpose of satyagraha, is always pragmatic: "reduction of the power of evil and increase in the power of good."

Lohia's commentaries on satyagraha are part and parcel with claims to the Gandhian legacy. Lohia scorns forms of so-called "Gandhism" that downplay active struggle for justice: the true Gandhian legacy. Focus on converting adversaries yields a Gandhism overly "moderate" and "cozy" toward the status quo.[25] Lohia mocks this "priestly" Gandhism along with "governmental" Gandhism: ineffectual propaganda and programs. True Gandhism, "heretical Gandhism," organized non-violent action against injustice, finds its home in Indian Socialism.[26]

GANDHIAN SOCIALISM AND WORLD ORDER

To Lohia, "socialism" is an ideology distinct from both capitalism and communism and it represents the best promise of human progress today. Socialism is a Third World ideology, independent from both Western and Soviet systems, responding to specific predicaments of weak and exploited lands. Lohia coins what he calls the "theory of equal irrelevance" to criticize capitalism and communism, viewing both together as a "single complex of civilization."[27] Both systems share a bias toward capital-intensive production and aspirations for ever-higher living standards. Lohia deploys Marxist terminology to explain that though communism has different "relations of production"—patterns of ownership—from capitalism, the two share the same "forces of production"—rationalized capital-intensive organization. Socialism, he argues, seeks to transcend capitalism not only as to relations of production but also as to forces of production. Socialism requires forces of production differing from capital-intensive capitalist and communist structures. It stresses "small unit" organization.[28]

"Small-unit organization" would correspond with living standards settled at a lower level than those pursued in both capitalism and communism.[29] Socialism differs specifically from communism by adhering to "general aims" of society—non-violence—in pursuing its transformative agenda.[30] Factors distinguishing "socialism" from capitalism and communism—decentralized production, modest living standards, and non-violent transformation—are all Gandhian. Socialism *is* Gandhian socialism.

India and the the Third World, Lohia thinks, must reject both capitalism and communism. One reason for this is that both systems fail to harmonize economic aims with general aims. Both sacrifice general aims to economic aims. A second reason is that economic aims shared by both systems—capital-intensive production—simply cannot be achieved in the Third World. Third World socialism must think about problems very different from those imagined in traditional socialist theory. Such theory often imagines socialism simply commandeering capital-intensive production already developed by capitalism. But in the Third World, capital-intensive production does not exist and cannot foreseeably exist on a widespread scale. Prohibitively massive amounts of new capital would be needed to raise Third World capitalization to heights achieved under capitalism and communism. Third World socialism must therefore adhere to lower-capital production.

Third World plight, according to Lohia, stems directly from the rise of capitalism in the West. Capitalism and imperialism have been intertwined from the start. Capital accumulation in the West has been a process of extracting value from both home and colonial labor. Colonial surplus value has been extracted in two ways: through direct employment of colonial wage labor by Western capital and through trade advantages asymmetrically favoring the West. The latter point requires brief elaboration.

According to Lohia, it takes less labor for an advanced country than for a colonial one to produce the goods exchanged in trade. Advanced high-capital countries expend less labor power in producing a trade item than low-capital colonized ones do in producing its exchange equivalent. In trade with colonial countries, advanced countries trade lesser labor expenditures for greater and thereby appropriate the labor of poor countries. Foreign trade therefore represents a transfer of congealed labor-power or surplus-value from current or former colony to advanced country, yielding capital accumulation there. High capital levels in advanced countries, giving power to extract labor value from poor ones, itself stems from past colonial exploitation. Lohia explains that, "in the current produce of labor in West-European factories, appears the saved labor of many generations of colonials."[31]

Though possibly circular (assuming capitalization disparities in explaining how they arise) this picture accounts for Lohia's skepticism that Third World lands can achieve Western affluence levels. Such affluence embodies wealth extraction from the Third World. With no equivalent field for exploitation, the Third World cannot hope to match it. To equalize world wealth distribution requires equalizing capitalization worldwide. Lohia doubts this can be done on the basis of capital-intensive production. Evenly-distributed low-capitalization must become the worldwide socialist pattern. Of course, this lower capitalization will spell lower living standards than those currently enjoyed in wealthy lands, but Third World living standards will rise.

His views on capitalist accumulation convince Lohia that a Gandhian pattern of production must prevail not only in India but throughout the world.[32] Like other thinkers in the modern Indian tradition, he sees a bridge linking India's spiritual genius to the world's progressive future. Gandhian socialism is that bridge.

CHAPTER 10

J.P. Narayan: Socialist Gandhism

Idea-hungry and firm in integrity, Jayaprakash Narayan (1902-1979) (J.P.) was born to a lower middle-class family in Sitabdiara village, located now in Uttar Pradesh. He left Patna College in 1921 without receiving his science degree in order to participate in Gandhi's anti-British Non-cooperation campaign. He soon resumed his education, however, studying at several American state universities before securing bachelor's and master's degrees in sociology in 1929.

Forsaking a possible academic career in India, J.P. became active in the Congress. He assumed the role of Acting General Secretary when its top leaders were arrested in 1932 during a civil disobedience campaign. J.P. was himself imprisoned later that year. After his release, he helped launch the Congress Socialist Party in 1934. He served as General Secretary of that organization for many years.

In 1940, J.P. landed in jail for delivering a speech advocating non-cooperation with the British war effort. He escaped from prison in 1942 and pursued underground anti-British activities for nearly a year before being captured, jailed again, and subjected to torture and solitary confinement. He gained release in 1946.

In 1954, J.P. shocked India's socialist movement, announcing his departure from the Praja Socialist Party to devote himself full time to bhoodan (land-gift), Vinoba Bhave's rural campaign aimed at persuading large landholders to donate tracts to land-poor peasants. He retained his stature as an admired public spokesman, and in the 1970s gradually returned to a more militant stance on economic and political change. He turned his energies toward organizing non-violent popular actions to provoke economic transformation and to check retardation of democratic institutions under the rule of Mrs. Gandhi's Congress.

In 1974, J.P. assumed leadership of a popular dissent movement in Bihar, which he hoped might extend itself into a pan-Indian movement for non-violent revolution. Criticism of Mrs. Gandhi's regime mounted up, eventually provoking her 1975 Emergency decree, resulting in censorship and the detention of opposition leaders, including J.P. His failing health impelled J.P.'s release from jail in late 1975. His poor health did not prevent him from playing a critical role in the 1977 consolidation of the Janata Party to contest general elections called by Mrs. Gandhi in false confidence she would win. Though J.P.'s preeminent stature made him a natural choice for official leadership of the Janata, he declined that role and declined also to serve as Prime Minister after the Janata's election victory. J.P. died as the Janata coalition, stitched together from opposition fragments ranging from communists to Hindu chauvinist parties, began to unravel, paving the way for Mrs. Gandhi's return to power.

J.P. is perhaps modern India's most accomplished, comprehensive and representative social thinker. His thought is the best synthesis of major themes in modern Indian thought, culminating the tradition launched by Vivekananda and carried in various directions by thinkers explored above.

MARXISM MODIFIED

J.P. begins his career as straightforward Marxist. There is "only one theory of socialism—Marxism," he writes in his 1936 publication, *Why*

Socialism? J.P. portrays socialism as a doctrine of social and economic reorganization, abolishing private ownership of productive property in favor of social ownership. There is nothing "religious" about socialism: "It is not a code of personal conduct; it is not something which you and I can practice."[1] Socialism will create a society of material abundance where people will find no strain in practicing virtue.

> ... (L)et us consider the nature of the society they would be living in. There would be full security of life and work: provision for old age, sickness, child birth, etc... In a society like this, what motive could the individual have to hoard things? He would get what he needed, whenever he wanted.[2]

J.P. scorns pure religious ideology in favor of materialist socialism. Progress lies not through reform of humanity's "so-called spirit," which can affect only stray individuals, but through change in the "social environment," which requires chiefly the revolutionary capture of state power to eradicate exploitative economic structures.[3]

J.P. mounts specific attacks against both Gandhism and Bhagavan Das. He hits hard at the Gandhian doctrine of trusteeship, that "bog of timid economic analysis, good intentions and ineffective moralizing." Trusteeship by the wealthy for the poor is only superficially non-violent, according to J.P., because it ignores the violence and exploitation through which the wealthy have acquired their riches. Gandhism does not press for abolition of wealth inequality because "the existence of paupers is essential for the working out of Gandhism ethics," which is, he suggests, that rich people get to practice "deeds of high-minded philanthropy and thus prove the Hindu conception of human nature!"[4] The Gandhian "change-of-heart" philosophy cannot sustain social improvement if carried on in the face of an economic system imbued with exploitative norms.[5]

J.P. also rebukes Das's Manu-ite socialism. He accuses Das of mis-casting Marxist "materialism" as an ideology incompatible with self-sacrifice. He explains that according to Das, self-sacrifice can emerge only from a "mystical" or religious viewpoint. He insists that Marxist materialism allows the possibility of self-sacrificial action, but merely attributes it to social environments.[6]

J.P. gives Das credit for at least the intention of transcending pure religious ideology: that is, to work out a practical scheme of social or-ganization that embodies moral values. But he sees no way to imple-ment Manu's four-varna order in contemporary society, and strongly suggests that it could not in any case resolve problems of economic ex-ploitation. In the end, as he points out, the Manu-ite scheme for so-cialism depends not on an economic organization intrinsically antagonistic to exploitation but rather on a moral atmosphere that Das hopes will radiate from a spiritual elite. J.P. places no faith in this vision, which is of course a version of pure religious ideology. Like Gandhism, the Manu-ite scheme depends finally on "persuasion."

Within four years of penning *Why Socialism?*, J.P.'s socialist thought begins to shift. In 1940, J.P. writes critically of the "Marxist" viewpoint that socialization of economic life will "automatically" create "socialist morality." He argues that "planned progress" in moral character-build-ing is needed for national well-being and that economic restructuring cannot be stable without it. He comments positively on the detailed planning of moral life attributed by Das to Manu and suggests that so-cialists cultivate a kind of planned spiritual development, replete with defined moral standards. Despite evident changes from his 1936 posi-tion, J.P. in 1940 still stations himself substantially apart both from ex-plicit religion and from Gandhi. He sees promotion of socialist morality as primarily a "secular" effort and rejects Gandhi's doctrine that "moral purposes" must never be pursued through "immoral means."[9]

During the course of the 1940s, J.P. continues to modify his so-cialism and articulates the germs of many themes that he will carry forward through his career. On the economic front, he envisions a variety of new arrangements, which can be summarized briefly. There is, first, agrarian reform aimed at organizing villages as self-governing co-operatives, with farm-linked industry to absorb surplus labor. There is, second, an industrial economy mixing state-owned large enterprise with small-scale worker-owned and municipality-owned enterprise. J.P. stresses small-scale enterprise both for maximizing employment and for avoiding monopoly economic power in the hands of the state.[10]

J.P. favors democratic over violent means to capture state power for socialism. Peaceful means, he argues, lead to "democratic socialism," while "violent revolution" leads to the "bureaucratic state."[11] Though he favors peaceful revolution, he maintains that ruling class repression may be so severe as to justify violent overthrow and subsequent dictatorship by the previously exploited.[12]

Through this period, J.P. continues to develop his theme of socialist moral virtue: "strict adherence to certain human values and standards of conduct." He now embraces, in contrast to earlier views, the Gandhian dictum that "means are ends" and that "nothing but good means" can bring socialism to pass. He argues that virtuous persons become so "by training" and that socialist work must include moral tutelage as well as pursuit of power. In fact, he repudiates his view as voiced in 1936 that capture of state power must predominate in socialist transformation. He begins to call for "spiritual regeneration," though he continues to deny any personal religious orientation:

> I have no knowledge of matters spiritual, if the term is understood in a religious or metaphysical sense. I have not suddenly come to acquire faith in something called the spirit or the soul of Brahma. Such philosophy as I have is earthy and human.[13]

In short, J.P. develops through the 1940s a deepening interest in cultivating socialist virtue, meanwhile growing sympathetic to socialist agendas other than state capture, especially if such capture entails violence and centralized administration. His respect for Gandhi grows.

RELIGION RECONSIDERED

In the early 1950s, J.P. navigates what can best be called a religious crisis, dramatized by a three-week fast at Poona in 1952. The result as he explains it is that he comes to reject "materialism as a philosophical outlook."[14] He gravitates toward an increasingly religious cast of mind, with religious imagery appearing more and more heavily in his writing. In the aftermath of this moment, his enthusiasm for Gandhi rises dramatically and he enlists in the famous bhoodan or land-gift campaign led by the Gandhian disciple, Vinoba Bhave.

The religious question preoccupying J.P. at this stage is: what motivates or provides incentive to human virtue? In past history, as he argues, such incentive came from "religion" or belief in some "higher moral force." In modern days, however, religion dissipates, leaving only "materialism" as an outlook on life.[15] This troubles him. In contrast with his 1936 view, J.P. now finds Marxist "materialism" inconsistent with human virtue.

> For many years I have worshipped at the shrine of the goddess—Dialectical Materialism—which seemed to me intellectually more satisfying than any other philosophy. But while the main quest of philosophy remains unsatisfied, it has become patent to me that materialism of any sort robs man of the means to become truly human. In a material civilization man has no rational incentive to be good.[16]

J.P. writes that humanity must go "beyond the material" to find the "incentives to goodness" needed for social reconstruction.

Materialism confines human vision of enjoyment and success. J.P. insists that an alternative must be found but does not seek it in any particular school of religion or moral doctrine. Instead, his rejection of materialism leads to what could be called existential openness to transcendence, an "endeavor to realize" one's "true nature." This openness, not any particular religious system, strikes him as key to spiritual growth.

Spiritual endeavor leads in its "natural course" to the "good and the true," to "certain basic values which are absolute and eternal."[17] J.P. sometimes associates moral growth with cultivation of something like the Advaitic insight as interpreted by Vivekananda and Aurobindo:

> It is only in the ultimate spiritual experience that this dualism is shed and the seer and seen become one. The root of morality lies in the endeavor of man to realize this unity of existence or, to put it differently, to realize his self. For one who has experienced this unity, the practice of morality becomes as natural and effortless as the drawing of breath.[18]

By and by, as J.P.'s religious orientation deepens, he increasingly portrays socialism itself as something inseparable from religious attitude. In 1959, for example, he proclaims:

> Socialism for me was always a way of life. It represented a set of values to which we owed allegiance voluntarily and which we tried to put into practice in our lives. These values we didn't see developing anywhere as a result of merely institutional changes, whether economic or political.[19]

Striking here is J.P.'s insistence that he has "always" conceptualized socialism as a "way of life" and "set of values" to be "put into practice in our lives." He does not even recall his 1936 position in *Why Socialism?* explicitly rejecting notions of socialism as a way of life and affirming that "institutional changes" in economics and politics suffice to usher in a worthwhile socialist order.

DESIGN FOR COMMUNITY

Before focusing on the bhoodan and "total revolution" phases in J.P.'s, career, it is worthwhile to explore two works—*A Plea for Reconstruction of Indian Polity* and *Swaraj for the People*—penned by J.P. in the late 1950s and early 60s. These offerings merit close inspection for two reasons. First, they represent culmination of J.P.'s reflections on how to structure a humane socialist society. Second, within the wider context of modern Indian thought, they represent the single most unified and systematic statement of Gandhian socialism's principles and goals. If Gandhian socialism is modern India's quintessential idiom in political thought, these two works embody a crystallization of modern Indian social vision.

A Plea for Reconstruction of Indian Polity opens with reflections on democracy. J.P. finds deficiencies in indirect or representative democracy, "the ability of a people to choose and dismiss a government." This form of democracy is wan and incomplete in his evaluation, eliciting disparagements like "elected oligarchy" and "democratic oligarchy." In characterizing parliamentary democracy as incomplete, J.P.'s point is not to repudiate it as inherently counter-progressive or to confine it under party rule as in state socialist systems. He means rather to counteract the oligarchic character of representative democracy by embedding it in a structure where crucial social decisions emerge in more direct democratic fashion.

What representative democracy lacks is widespread existential contact with rich feelings of self-mastery, responsibility, solidarity and active power over social decisions. This "glow and satisfaction of self-government" is a spiritual experience that J.P. places at the heart of democratic values. Fostering that spiritual experience guides design of what J.P. calls "participating democracy."[20]

Creating such a democracy, he argues, is not mainly a problem of governmental systems. It is instead a "moral" problem and perhaps a religious one, that of fostering particular "spiritual qualities" necessary to democracy. J.P. offers a list of these virtues, including non-violence, love of liberty, courage against tyranny and oppression, tolerance, belief in equality, cooperative spirit, and willingness to sacrifice private interest for general well-being.[21]

J.P. makes several points about this cluster of virtues. First, they are not innate, but emerge only through painstaking education and practice. Second, the needful tutelary process looms far too large, challenging and crucial for simple entrustment to the state. The entire social fabric must be such that it "inculcates these values in its members." Institutions of various sorts must work together to reinforce "the necessary moral climate for democracy to thrive." Third, the whole cluster of democratic virtues sits menaced by one monumental vice: material greed.[22] As an antidote to greed, democracy requires the practice of one pivotal virtue: "voluntary limitation of wants." Without this, none of the other democratic virtues can flourish. As J.P. explains it, material greed fosters intractable social conflicts impervious to democratic resolution. It also gives rise to productive systems of excessive size and complexity, inimical to democratic control and oversight. The inevitable result is "bureaucratic oligarchy."[23]

Both capitalism and certain forms of socialism contradict true democracy because they fuel materialist greed and thus subvert democratic virtue.[24] A further problem is that typical socialist organizational forms— "the centralized State" and "large-scale industrialization"—specifically defy participatory democracy.[25] Though J.P. rebukes prevailing socialist formations, his vision of democratic society remains crucially socialist.

J.P. finds two organizational forms essential to democratic life. These forms, "voluntary associations"[26] and "self-governing communities,"[27] are both instruments of popular participation and influence. J.P. seems to have picked up some Tocqueville.

In "self-governing communities," J.P. suggests, social life can be "*deliberately* organized for self-government," deliberately designed, that is, to foster democratic experience and virtues. "Voluntary associations" cannot be so designed, but come as caboose behind the engine of "self-governing communities." J.P. believes that a society's democratic tenor resides in the quantity and quality of its voluntary associational activity. Structural design can at best encourage such independent associational action. J.P. imagines his "self-governing communities" as maximally compatible with free associational activity. J.P.'s "self-governing communities" are themselves a species of voluntary association in that political life within them is an exercise in social creativity. They are creativity by design.

A Plea for Reconstruction of Indian Polity and *Swaraj for the People* primarily seek to outline a social system conducive to self-governing communities. Many elements are familiar from discussions of thinkers above and need not be belabored here in detail. The chief value of these two works lies in their synthesized and unified presentation of themes expounded by others less cohesively.

Like others, J.P. begins by hearkening back to antecedents. He draws explicitly on Aurobindo's discussion of "organs of popular democracy" in ancient India. India's ancient republics, so prominent a theme in Aurobindo, likewise suggest to J.P. that "India was perhaps the earliest home of democracy." J.P. quotes extensively from Aurobindo, emphasizing that the essence of Indian social organization was "the principle of an organically self-determining communal life," seeking "not so much an individual as a communal freedom." This principle, embodied prominently in the republics, was later preserved in the "territorial community" of the "self-governing village" and in "the functional or occupational community, the varna."[28]

Like others, J.P. argues that both territorial communities—self-governing villages—and functional communities—the varna system—have gone into decline since days of old. He blames British imperialism for the eclipse of village communities. Without great detail, he suggests that Britain followed a "deliberate policy" of undermining self-governing villages that might otherwise have sapped British hegemony. On the eclipse of varna as occupational communities, he supplies no analysis, commenting simply that the system "has been so depraved and distorted that there would be few defenders of it now."[29]

Though rare in his early career, explicit religious imagery characterizes J.P.'s thought after his crisis in the early fifties. J.P. wields a traditional religious notion, decline of dharma, to summarize ills brought by dissolution of self-governing villages and by varna system decadence. By dharma, J.P. means "social ethics,"[30] internalized notions of upright action, integrity and responsibility that Rousseau and Tocqueville call "mores."

The vitality of dharma, J.P. suggests, depends upon the degree to which a society manifests "organic self-regulation," organization "on the basis of self-determining and mutually co-ordinating and integrating communities."[31] But if dharma depends on "organic self-regulation" in social arrangements, the reverse is also true. Such organic self-regulation can be achieved only to the degree that dharma already flourishes. "The ancient concept of dharma has to be revived and the appropriate dharma for a democracy has to be evolved," J.P. writes.[32] There can be no substitute for deliberate cultivation of democratic virtue. It is equally true that democratic dharma cannot grow or be practiced in a vacuum. Its flourishing depends reciprocally on construction and maintenance of self-governing communities. Organic self-regulation and dharma reinforce each other positively, as does their absence negatively.

The democratic Indian society J.P. envisions takes the reconstructed village as its chief institution. "The foundation of this polity," as he writes, lies in "self-governing, self-sufficient, agro-industrial, urbo-rural, local communities," based largely on "reconstruction" of existing villages.[33] This orientation owes a great deal to Gandhi, of course. J.P.'s particular contribution lies in thinking through certain aspects of the vision with special articulateness.

J.P. pays particular attention to issues of economic organization. Of decisive importance is his insistence on "economic decentralization," which requires that the village be economically "self-sufficient" to a maximum possible degree. It should be able to produce within itself the "necessaries of life" such as food, clothing, shelter, and so on, while also ensuring that each resident finds "useful employment."[34] Local self-sufficiency will maximize the experience of participatory democratic control over affairs.

J.P. remains Marxist enough to see that self-government is chimerical unless it includes mastery over economic decisions that fundamentally shape social conditions and possibilities. Self-government therefore excludes strong reliance on markets or on large techno-bureaucratic organization private or public for economic decision-making. Such mechanisms are neither transparent nor responsive to popular will. They therefore defy the life of deliberative participation, while subjecting local communities to distant and possibly destructive forces. These considerations convince J.P. that for primary needs at least the village economy should be one of local production for local consumption.[35]

J.P. goes on to delineate certain fundamental features of a democratic and self-sufficient village economy. Like Gandhi and Lohia, he emphasizes developing new and appropriate technologies utilizing small-scale machinery and labor-intensivity so as to avoid unemployment. He also stresses maximum reliance on local resources human and material, preserving manageable local scope for planning and coordination.[36] Technological research and resource surveys would support small-scale machinery and local resource mobilization. Though wary of detailed central planning as in party-state socialism, J.P allows for higher-level planning on matters beyond local self-sufficiency.[37] As to natural resources, J.P. stresses two features. One is common ownership and allocation by democratic processes to their various uses. Another is reliance on renewable resources, so as to conserve non-renewables.

Democratic virtue in limitation of wants would constrain consumption demands and facilitate sustainability through renewables.[38]

In what J.P. calls the "agro-industrial community," light industry would engage in immediate processing of agrarian products and manufacture of consumer and producer goods for direct local use.[39] Such agro-industrial development coincides with local self-sufficiency and planning without undue dependence on markets or central hierarchies.

Social ownership of productive wealth is crucial. In villages, landholdings must be redistributed "so that each person in the village becomes an equal share-holder in the landed wealth of the village."[40] Beyond this, social ownership of productive enterprise could appear in various guises and be articulated at various levels. In village communities, J.P. seems to imagine two sorts of social ownership: 1) enterprises owned by the whole community and governed by boards representing both enterprise workers and the community at large; and 2) enterprises owned and governed by their workers within regulatory frameworks established in their communities.[41] Both forms promote participatory democratic decision-making and experiences of collaborative solidarity. J.P. allows for some privately owned enterprise employing wage labor.[42] A village economy with worker-owned and privately-owned firms would seem to require some sphere of market relations. J.P. sidesteps investigating how such market relations could fit within the overall planned scheme.

J.P. recognizes aspects of economic life beyond the scope of village self-sufficiency, large-scale irrigation, power supply, and manufacture of production goods among them.[43] Economic coordination for such matters requires administrative organs at remove from village life.[44] J.P. offers several observations on ownership and management of higher-level enterprise. His remarks are suggestive but unclear as to how his proposals fit together.

Large-scale enterprise might be either privately or socially owned. Once again, J.P. sidesteps questions on what play of markets, ownership, regulation and planning would prevail in trans-village production, distribution and exchange. He seems to imagine large private enterprise as a minor portion so that few would work as non-owning wage labor. He calls for worker representation in governing large-scale enterprise private or public.[45]

A Plea for the Reconstruction of Indian Polity musters surprisingly kind words for Das,[46] much in contrast to J.P's early-career dismissal. J.P. revives Das's attempt to connect notions of varnadharma with ideas from guild socialism. He suggests that various productive functions and occupations be organized into political bodies, each engaged in substantial self-regulation of internal affairs and represented within government. "These Associations and Councils would be the modern varna organizations and their rules the modern varnadharma," he writes.[47]

His conception of a "modern varnadharma," combined with village-centered democracy, yields a picture of integrated occupational/functional and territorial democracy reminiscent of ancient India as J.P. portrays it. Fortunately, J.P. does not follow Das's lead in taking ancient Manu-ite varnadharma as a specific blueprint. It remains unclear how he would integrate his village/territorial democracy with his occupational/functional one.

Though J.P. attends to tasks of trying to articulate institutional structures for socialism, he insists socialism cannot be founded upon mere institutional transformation, what he calls "social engineering."[48] He explicitly rejects "state socialism" for its institutionalist bias, which I call "materialist ideology." "The old faith that state ownership of the means of production, distribution, and exchange plus planning will bring about socialism has been falsified," he observes.[49]

On the contrary, socialism's crucial and most difficult challenge is the same as democracy's: cultivating an appropriate spiritual climate, without which it cannot sustain itself. J.P. calls this the "spirit of community."[50] As he explains in a 1961 speech, such spirit requires that the rich in every village practice a "sense of responsibility" for the "uplift of the weak and backward."[51] This sounds like tip-toeing toward Gandhi's trusteeship. Even as he stresses socialism's spiritual aspect, however, he remains Marxist enough to avoid pure religious ideology. Socialism poses specifically spiritual challenges, but "[t]he task also is one of social engineering," he maintains.[52] Specifically, he stresses that the spirit of community cannot thrive in the face of excessive economic disparity.[53] As he puts it: "How can there be such a spirit when the village is so divided into hostile economic classes...one trying to live off the other?"[54] As indicated, he insists that no village community can flourish without equitable land redistribution. Spiritual and economic transformation require each other.

METHODS OF TRANSFORMATION

After the late 1950s and early 60s when J.P. pens *A Plea for Reconstruction of Indian Polity* and *Swaraj for the People*, his picture of a democratic social structure remains essentially unchanged. The two works condense and restate certain key themes in Gandhian socialism. J.P.'s thought does not rest, however, with articulation of what Gandhian socialism, once attained, would look like. In his last quarter-century, J.P. works through twists in conceptualizing transformative methodology: how to bring Gandhian socialism into being.

Land reform, redistribution from landlords to poor peasants, is widely seen as key to successful Third World development. It may be blocked by elite domination of high-level government and of localities. One Asian example of ambitious land reform came in China during early years of communist rule. Carried out by a revolutionary party and government along with mobilized peasants, it spawned terrific violence, killing perhaps hundreds of thousands.[55]

Less violently, Japan, South Korea and Taiwan have implemented substantial land reform in recent decades. Despite legislation and off-stated intentions, independent India has achieved only minimal land reform, except notably in West Bengal and Kerala with their communist-centered elected governments. This is not the place to rehearse vicissitudes in Indian land reform efforts. Suffice it to say that the Indian state has proved largely ineffectual and that this was foreseen by sensitive observers from a very early post-Independence stage.

In the early 1950s, a distinctive Indian land reform movement arose, called bhoodan (land-gift). Led by the Gandhian disciple Vinoba Bhave, bhoodan asked wealthy land-owners to donate holdings to land-poor neighbors. Vinoba's movement organized volunteers to tramp the country seeking land gift pledges. Estimates have it that during the 50s, pledges for nearly a million acres came in.[56]

J.P. threw himself fervently into bhoodan. He characterizes it as a revolutionary method avoiding both violence and ineffectual "parliamentary action."[57] Bhoodan is Gandhian revolution by non-violent mass action.[58] J.P. comes to view bhoodan as the main vehicle not only for land reform, but also for what Gandhi had called "constructive work" in village transformation: introduction of new institutions, attitudes, techniques and productive arrangements. He sees the bhoodan movement as spearhead of "Lok Sevak Sangh," the mass organization for rural transformation Gandhi had envisioned as future for the Congress.[59]

During this period, J.P. scorns socialist efforts to win and hold state power through party politics. Even a democratic and nominally socialist state, he maintains, remains a "Leviathan" of centralized power, inconsistent with true democracy. Preoccupation with state politics is therefore self-defeating for socialism. Socialists should focus on what J.P., following Vinoba, calls *lokniti* (politics of the people) not *rajniti* (politics of the state). As J.P. summarizes:

> [T]he remedy is to create and develop forms of socialist living through the voluntary endeavor of the people, rather than seek to establish socialism by the use of the power of the State. In other words, the remedy is to establish people's socialism rather than State socialism.[60]

Borrowing Marxist phrasing, J.P. explains that emphasis on lokniti will yield a "real withering away of the State," without awaiting some distant day when the revolutionary state shall have constructed conditions for its own dissolution.

J.P.'s enthusiasm for bhoodan coincides with his turn toward increasingly religious sensibilities after his 1952 epiphany. He interprets bhoodan from a distinctly religious standpoint. He portrays Vinoba as a sannyassin in the tradition of Indian renouncers. In a description echoing Vivekananda's ruminations on sannyassins of service, he explains that Vinoba acts in pursuit of "spiritual ends," not for any "social, economic, or political" ends. He reveres Vinoba as "a rishi," "a seer," "a man of God."[61] Like its leader, bhoodan is religious to its core in J.P.'s view. The religious component J.P. sees is bhoodan's pursuit of spiritual transformation. As he writes, "Bhoodan is essentially a moral movement, or a movement to solve socio-economic problems by moral means and thereby to bring about the moral transfiguration of man."[62]

J.P. adopts Gandhi's term sarvodaya to name the philosophy of life and change into which bhoodan fits. Sarvodaya's philosophy of change, as he explains it, is grounded in religious transformation, based on "the principle of change of heart." He invokes Advaitic theology to explain how religious transformation in social relations may be possible. "That is so, because all of us are essentially one, fragments of the same Almighty Father," he explains.[63] Like Vivekananda and Aurobindo, J.P. posits Advaitic insight as cognitive foundation for social ethics:

> Why should we want the good of all?... The philosophical answer is that this difference which we experience today is only an appearance, and an unreality. In reality all of us are one... My real "I" and your real "I" are the same... My good is your good, and your good is mine...[64]

Premised on moral conversion of landholders, bhoodan manifests the outlook behind Gandhi's notion of trusteeship. Indeed, during this period and occasionally through the rest of his life, J.P. comments favorably on trusteeship, in contrast with his scathing 1936 denunciation.[65] In rejecting the materialist ideology of state socialism, does J.P. fall prey to pure religious ideology, positing moral/religious conversion as a sufficient transformative methodology?

J.P.'s scattered favorable references to trusteeship should not be overstated. J.P. never elaborates in detail on trusteeship and certainly does not stress it as a major component of his vision. His favorable references to trusteeship probably signify genuflection to Gandhi, expressing pious hope that private wealth-owners might come to act more charitably.

In one sense, bhoodan partakes less than does trusteeship in pure religious ideology. Unlike trusteeship, bhoodan is materialist enough at least to insist that alleviating deprivation requires actual wealth redistribution. Redistribution depends, however, on moral conversion. It seems doubtful that virtue could ever be summoned enough to accomplish meaningful redistribution this way. In his early infatuation with bhoodan, J.P. sometimes seems to ensnare himself in pure religious ideology. As times goes by, however, he begins to recognize this and his posture toward bhoodan grows increasingly critical.

Most problematic in Vinoba's bhoodan is rejection of satyagraha in seeking land redistribution. Satyagraha—in the form of strikes by landless workers, symbolic non-violent confrontations or otherwise—could possibly have been deployed in support of bhoodan. Though Vinoba applied the label satyagraha to bhoodan, he made clear his rejection of techniques that might entail "coercion." He went so far as to characterize certain Gandhian campaigns as "negative" satyagraha, in contrast to "constructive" satyagraha as embodied in bhoodan.

In rejecting confrontational applications of satyagraha, Vinoba's movement seemingly became a false heir to the Gandhian legacy. To be sure, Vinoba's squeamishness about "coercion"—his desire to proceed exclusively on the basis of conversion—follows Gandhi's own somewhat muddled discussions of satyagraha. Fortunately, Gandhi's deeds in satyagraha were not unduly hampered by his tendency to confuse nonviolence with non-coercion. Moreover, as Chapter 5 indicates, Gandhi moved in his late career toward conceptualizing oppressive economic structures as embodiments of violence against which satyagraha must be directed in the name of ahimsa.

Meanwhile, Gandhi's reconceptualization of trusteeship as a legal institution, not just a moral injunction, also revealed his increasing distance from pure religious ideology. These trends in Gandhi's thought, combined with Gandhi's actual deeds, suggest that the true Gandhian philosophy is more "militant" than what Vinoba espoused. A truer and more militant Gandhian approach is what J.P. ultimately embraces.

Within a few years after its inception, bhoodan began revealing itself as a failure. The quantum of arable land permanently redistributed was small despite the impressive momentum of early pledges. Much pledged land was never actually transferred or was taken back forcibly or with aid of law when donors or their families developed second thoughts. Land permanently transferred was often poor-quality or in plots too small to provide an adequate living.[67]

J.P. finds himself vexed by bhoodan's failure because he deeply doubts whether the Indian state apparatus can carry through serious land reform. With the deficiencies of both bhoodan and land reform legislation before him, he takes the position that the two efforts must be pursued in tandem. He wavers on which effort should get priority. At some points he gives primacy to bhoodan because legislative effort has achieved little success.[68] Bhoodan could maybe help create a transformed spiritual atmosphere where land reform becomes enforceable and sustainable in local settings.[69] At other moments he admits that bhoodan has achieved only negligible redistribution and suggests legislation may be more efficacious. In that case, bhoodan becomes valuable mainly for its spiritual atmospherics, which J.P. hopes will encourage religious "change of heart" in village relations.[70]

Even in the period of his greatest infatuation, J.P. worries that bhoodan by itself might take too long in accomplishing land reform. He fears that violent methods might inevitably come to the fore should bhoodan not quickly succeed.[71] Meanwhile, J.P. comes under fire from socialist comrades, notably Lohia, for pursuing bhoodan efforts doomed to failure. Though he resists these criticisms at the time, J.P. later concedes their central thrust: that bhoodan must fail due to shortfall of "struggle"—active confrontation between the land-poor and landlords.[72]

As time goes by, J.P. grows increasingly critical of bhoodan and the philosophy of change behind it. He disparages it as "ineffectual" and consigns it to the "limbo of history," concluding it can "never get off the ground."[73] Its focus on "spiritual and moral appeals" retards systemic change which can only emerge through "struggle."[74]

As J.P. distances himself from Vinoba, his move is toward confrontational satyagraha. Where he had once seen bhoodan as the middle-way alternative to both violent revolution and parliamentary democracy, he now assigns that place to confrontational satyagraha.[75] He begins to contemplate large-scale and widespread satyagraha applied for various purposes.[76]

J.P. begins to criticize Vinoba's overly "gentle" approach as an erroneous construal of Gandhi. Even more striking, he begins to view non-violence as a more relative, less absolute, value in revolutionary morality. He claims that his opposition to violent revolution is not based on "moral grounds" but merely on "practical considerations." Though that overstates his true position, J.P. wants to remove himself in no uncertain terms from the pure religious ideology that nearly overtook him. He writes:

> My Sarvodaya friends and my Gandhian friends will be
> surprised to read what I publicly say now. I say with a

> due sense of responsibility that if convinced that there
> is no deliverance for the people except through vio-
> lence, Jayaprakash Narayan will also take to violence.[77]

As J.P. puts bhoodan behind him, he begins to advocate an ideology of change he calls "total revolution." Total revolution embodies certain distinct ideas, but it also can be used to refer to the general drift of J.P.'s thoughts in his last decade. It takes shape against a background of political events—the Bihar Movement, Mrs. Gandhi's Emergency involving J.P.'s imprisonment, the consolidation and election of the Janata Party—in which J.P. played pivotal roles.

J.P.'s most distinct idea in total revolution is that social transformation be analyzed in terms of action within various "spheres" of society. J.P. does not concern himself with defining these spheres precisely. Typical statements identify six or seven spheres, some of which go under different names at different times. In one version, for example, he identifies the "social, economic, political, cultural, educational and moral" spheres.[78] In another version, he repeats the first five but does not mention the "moral" sphere, instead mentioning two spheres—the "ideological or intellectual" and the "spiritual"—not included on the other list. We should take J.P.'s word that these variations are insignificant in and of themselves.[79]

J.P.'s point is that achieving a decent society requires revolution in each of the various spheres.[80] He calls attention in Marx-like fashion to issues of harmony and contradiction among spheres. Social stability and social change are explicable in terms of these relationships. He does not follow Marxism in singling out the economic sphere as determining the rest. He seems to think such econocentrism detrimental to balanced transformative thought and practice. At the same time, he avoids the opposite error: downplaying the importance of economic transformation.

Though he articulates these multiple spheres for revolutionary action, J.P. does not systematically explain particular actions he envisions for each sphere. His most detailed comments focus on the "moral-spiritual" sphere and the "economic" sphere.[81] In fact, J.P.'s "total revolution" seems mainly an update on the "dual revolution"—spiritual and economic/structural—he had conceptualized years earlier, praising Gandhi as its key exponent and practitioner.[82] There is nothing especially new in J.P.'s position on the key interdependent spiritual and economic components of "total revolution." The spiritual component emphasizes a "moral" orientation toward "voluntary limitation" on "consumption" and "material development." The economic component stresses an "appropriate technology" of "small industry" and "rural industry." It emphasizes various forms of "social ownership"—including village ownership, worker and cooperative ownership, and public company ownership—while also including "self-employed producer" ownership, small-scale capitalist ownership employing small numbers of wage workers, and a small number of larger capitalist enterprises, closely regulated. The economic component also entails worker participation in management. This adds some detail to what he had earlier sketched in *A Plea for Reconstruction of Indian Polity* and *Swaraj for the People*. It also leaves the same knotty issues unresolved.[83]

To grasp the specific character of J.P.'s "total revolution" outlook, one needs to look not at J.P.'s specific explications but at J.P.'s emerging positions on several related matters. First, as mentioned, comes increasing advocacy of militant satyagraha. J.P. calls for large-scale and widespread satyagraha action against a range of deleterious institutions and practices. Like Gandhi, he sees satyagraha yielding both structural transformation and spiritual development.[84] Like Gandhi also, he continues to see village reconstruction work, sarvodaya, as satyagraha's twin component in transformative effort.[85]

Meanwhile, renewed emphasis on transformative use of state power characterizes J.P.'s total revolution phase. In his bhoodan period, as indicated, J.P. had portrayed fixation on state power as positively detrimental to socialism's best possibilities. Socialist efforts, as he argued then, should focus away from rajniti, state politics, and toward lokniti, mobilizing the downtrodden for direct construction of new arrangements. By the last decade of his career, he reconsiders the degree of this anti-statist emphasis. The reign of Mrs. Gandhi's Congress has impressed him with ways in which the state, even if nominally socialist, can frustrate popular mobilization and construction, repress them or deflate them through pseudo-socialist reform. Mrs. Gandhi's supression of J.P.'s "Bihar movement," her anti-democratic emergency regime and her nationalization efforts offer key lessons. J.P. never abandons his insistence on popular organization efforts. He does, however, revive his pre-bhoodan stance that popular efforts will bear fruit slowly unless linked to a popular political party organized to capture and wield state power in support of grass-roots action. Diverse state initiatives suggest themselves, including support for unions, especially agrarian ones, marketing assistance, cooperative rural credit unions, irrigation aid, soil conservation, land reclamation and so on.[86]

Hence, J.P. plays a critical role in organizing the Janata Party to contest the 1977 election against Mrs. Gandhi. The official Janata "creed," as he explains it, is "Gandhian socialism." He envisions the Janata drawn into an increasingly close mutually transformative relationship with popular organizations, much the same relationship Gandhi and sometimes Nehru had once envisioned as future of the Congress.[87]

As J.P. turns his attention this way, two themes receive special stress. Both concern things he feels the state should *not* prioritize. First, he warns against over-emphasizing nationalization of capitalist enterprise. Nationalization should not be confused with genuine socialism. It tends to produce little more than state bureaucracy, which he goes so far as to call "state capitalism." He comments: "There is no element or trait of socialism in all this… It is a pity that our socialists very largely equate socialism with nationalization." True socialism requires "economic democracy" or "industrial democracy," J.P.'s conceptions of which are outlined above. Better the state should assist in constructing institutions compatible with "economic democracy" than pursue pseudo-socialism as in Mrs. Gandhi's nationalization.[88] J.P.'s skepticism about the fanfare does not mean he opposes nationalization in principle.[89] He merely ranks it low in socialist priority. Meanwhile, he never wavers in supporting stronger land reform legislation.[90]

Secondly, J.P. continues to stress that socialist spiritual transformation lies largely outside state competence. State action should focus on institutional change, leaving spiritual effort to popular organizations.[91] Sometimes he walks back close to a quasi-Marxist notion that institutional transformations must complete themselves, with spiritual change to follow.[92] Elsewhere, however, he envisions spiritual revolution as spearhead of change.[93]

In transition from bhoodan to total revolution, J.P. re-appropriates two notions critical to an adequate Gandhian socialist vision. One, confrontational satyagraha, he draws from Gandhi. The other, state action to help effectuate transformation, he draws from Marxism. Both notions depart from pure religious ideology by insisting on wielding power against injustice. Consistently, however, J.P. integrates these notions within an overall outlook stressing direct effort toward spiritual transformation.

During his bhoodan period, J.P. immerses himself in spiritual efforts, but his Marxist sensibilities ultimately judge bhoodan wanting as a philosophy of change. In the integrity of his quest for an appropriate transformative philosophy as well as in the soundness of his matured intuitions, J.P. reveals himself as India's best Marxist and truest Gandhian.

CONCLUSION

The discussion above has pursued three overarching objectives: to high-light the existence and nature of a persistent problematic in modern Indian thought, that of considering religious themes alongside socialist ones; to offer interpretations of the various thinkers examined in terms of this problematic; and to explicate the development of Gandhian socialism as the quintessential resolution of it.

If the discussion above accomplishes these objectives, there is little to add here. It is worthwhile, however, to reflect briefly on this whole tradition of thought from the standpoint of issues left unexplored above. I will do so with respect to four such issues: the Hindu-centered religiosity of the tradition; the reasons for shifts among Indian Marxists toward increasing sympathy with Gandhi; the significance of India's failure to pursue Gandhian socialism; and Gandhian socialism's current world-historical significance.

The Hindu-centered religiosity of the tradition can be explained in terms of several overlapping factors, including: Hinduism's numerical and cultural dominance in India; preoccupation among Muslim leaders and thinkers with Pakistan's nationalism and the place of Muslim identity in a Hindu-dominated polity; and Indian nationalism's need for a usable past, leading it to stress the ancient and indigenous religiosity over its late-coming non-indigenous rivals.

It is appropriate to ask what responsibility this Hindu-centered intellectual tradition may bear for generating the religious strife that has racked India for the past century. Strife has fed on Hindu nationalism and Muslim fears of subjugation and cultural effacement. The tradition of thought explained here may perhaps be reproached for over-preciousness in exaltation of Hindu themes. Were its Hindu-oriented visionaries sufficiently aware that the subtleties of their religious interpretations might get lost or distorted when heard by chauvinist Hindus or anxious Muslims?

If such a charge has merit, it obviously sticks most heavily to Gandhi, due to his oft-proclaimed Hinduism and outsize influence. Of course Gandhi is not alone to blame for Hindu-Muslim antagonism. But it may be fair to assign Gandhi and perhaps other thinkers covered here with some fair share of responsibility while recognizing that historical circumstances may have been inevitably tragic.

Experience of colonial subjugation created need for a nationalist ideology impelling India towards freedom. In its vastness and diversity, India lacked unifying ethnic, racial, political, and linguistic identities that have elsewhere energized nationalist movements. India was unified, if at all, only through the reach of Hindu religiosity which, though extensive and predominant, was by no means universal. The visionaries leading India toward liberation might have labored long and hard before managing to forge a nationalist identity not rooted in Hindu themes. Did Gandhi choose rightly or should he have been less Hindu and in less of a hurry? Given Gandhi's outlook, such alternatives are almost unimaginable.

Socialist thought may at least sometimes benefit when it uses religious sensibilities to supplement Marxist and other economic analytics. Several of the thinkers explored here—Mehta, Deva, Nehru, and, most compellingly, J.P.—moved in parallel ways through their careers from an economically-centered, state-oriented, Marxist "scientific" socialism toward a more religiously-tinged, grass-roots Gandhian socialism. They did so without abandoning certain key Marxist perspectives for analysis. In doing so, they managed, especially J.P., to forge a distinctive and important socialist vision.

One may wonder why these thinkers all manifested these parallel perspectival shifts. Personal biography, touched upon here only lightly, may have weighed significantly. Other factors can be considered as well.

First, Gandhi's charismatic leadership and political effectiveness brought his methods and viewpoints onto center stage, making it increasingly impossible for any prominent thinker to dismiss them wholesale. Second, as suggested in Chapter 5, Gandhi's increasing clear-headedness in grasping socialist analysis in his late career made him more and more accessible to socialist minds. Third, persistently negative features of the Soviet state system fueled attempts to envision both a socialist order and a transformative program explicitly concerned with avoiding those features. Fourth, India's character as a deeply challenged Third World agrarian economy provoked an impulse to focus theoretically on village reconstruction. Fifth, the Third World experience imparted a sense of damages and dangers from economic growth, thereby fostering search for a prosperity not overly growth-biased. Sixth, despite Marxism's frequent skepticism of consumerism, Indian thinkers found the socialist tradition inadequate and their own spiritual tradition valuable for picturing an egalitarian economy not subverted by competitive greed and materialism.

All these factors made it increasingly imperative for leading Indian Marxists to convince Gandhi into thinking seriously about socialism, rather than simply dismissing him as a hopeless bourgeois romantic, as in some of their early careers. Gandhi's response, though diffident, ultimately sufficed to draw Marxist pupils toward perceiving an integrity in the project of "Gandhian socialism."

India's inferior development since Independence certainly cannot be counted as the failure of Gandhian socialism. The extent to which

India's political economy could ever have been designated "socialist" at all is debatable. Whatever its name, India's current order appears to realize Gandhi's nightmare for India's future: crushing mass poverty, illiteracy and ill-health alongside dazzling wealth and a state apparatus ineffectual in crucial tasks of progressive development. It seems to manifest all the negatives of socialism, capitalism and feudalism combined. It is what Gandhi expected for an India that failed to pursue systemic satyagraha and sarvodaya in pursuit of transformation.

Had he lived longer, Gandhi's charisma might possibly have been enough to lead independent India along his envisioned course of systemic non-violent village-centered transformation. In the early Independence years, India's nationalist elan was perhaps at high enough pitch to support significant mobilization for rural reconstruction. Nothing could have succeeded short of simultaneous effort by both the state and a highly mobilized citizenry. By the mid-50s, even at the height of Vinoba's bhoodan, the moment may already have been lost. A political economy driven by interlinkages between concentrated wealth and state power had fixed its grip. J.P. increasingly saw this, which impelled his activities during the 70s. But the time for Gandhian socialism in India was no longer ripe, if it ever was, and it may not be ripe (again?) for quite some time.

Circumstances like those at present may yield a dark conclusion that Gandhian socialism is irrelevant or impossible. Even highly diminished practice of satyagraha and sarvodaya may consequently wither. That would be unfortunate. We cannot know if or when circumstances may emerge in which such practice might bloom into transformative scope and potential. If that happens, those who have kept effort alive will deserve thanks.

The revolutions in Eastern Europe three decades ago may highlight the ongoing relevance of Gandhian socialism. First, they underscore state socialism's limited capacity in fostering human fulfillment. Second, they prove how resisters and visionaries may sometimes harvest surprising fruit when circumstances turn advantageously.

By nature of its focus, Gandhian socialism does not on its own go deep on race, sex/gender, immigration, environment and other important concerns. Some may say that Gandhian socialism grapples inadequately with markets in positive functions like facilitating rational pricing and promoting innovation through competition. Reconciling Gandhian socialism with "market socialism" remains a task for another day. Envisioning how it could integrate with welfare-state social democracy in wealthy countries is another. Additional agenda items could include conceptualizing sarvodaya for non-village communities, training for satyagraha, and studying satyagraha's usefulness for divergent situations.

Of course, no one can say whether a robust Gandhian socialism will ever come to pass. The world is no Indian village even for myriad millions who live in one. Any dream of organized, disciplined nonviolent mobilization against injustice and of spiritualized productive communities must reckon with vast complexity. By all means, consider viewpoints specifically contrary to Gandhian socialism: that capitalism's orderly acquisitiveness helps subdue unruly and violent passions; that producing consumer luxuries provides jobs for the poor; that urbanism alleviates farm pressure on habitats. Still, there is reason to suppose that neither India nor the world at large can ever reach a humane, sustainable and fulfilling prosperity for all without some quotient of Gandhian socialism. It is hard to shrug off J.P.'s insistence that active citizenship yields spiritual experience that no one should miss and that such citizenship is found best in an order of vibrant direct community and organized non-violent action for justice. Is it plausible we could attain such a state from where we are now? Gandhian socialism suggests that we foster local production units owned or governed by democratic communities and that we do so in part through non-violent citizen confrontation toward recalcitrant wealth and power. For the sake of human fulfillment, justice and concord, we should ponder these suggestions.

FOOTNOTES

CHAPTER 1

Vivekananda: Socialism and the Reconstruction of Hindu Religion

Primary source notes on Vivekananda will refer to the volumes listed below, and will be cited in specific notes by the volume number.
The Complete Works of Swami Vivekananda, Mayarati Memorial Edition, (Calcutta: Advaita Ashram)
a. Vol. I, Fifteenth Ed., 1977.
b. Vol. II, Fourteenth Ed., 1983.
c. Vol. III, Twelfth Reprint, 1979.
d. Vol. IV, Eleventh Ed., 1978.
e. Vol. V, Eleventh Reprint, 1979.
f. Vol. VI, Tenth Ed., 1978.
g. Vol. VII, Ninth Reprint, 1979.
h. Vol. VIII, Sixth Ed., 1977.

1 Vol. VI, p. 381.
2 A.V. Rathna Reddy, *The Political Philosophy of Swami Vivekananda*, (New Dehli: Sterling Publishers Private Ltd., 1984). p. 71.

3   B.R. Purohit, *Hindu Revivalism and Indian Nationalism*, (Sagar M.P.: Sathi Prakashan, 1965). pp. 66-67.

4   Vol. I, pp. 75-77, 111, Vol. VI, pp. 417-418, Vol. IV, p. 144.

5   Vol. V, pp. 245, 308, 418; Vol. VII, p. 9.

6   Vol. VI, p. 395.

7   Vol. V, pp. 357, 245.

8   Vol. III, p. 216.

9   Vol. III, pp. 215-216.

10   Vol. III, pp. 213-216.

11   Vol. IV, p. 362.

12   Vol. V, pp. 441-42.

13   Vol. IV, p. 362.

14   Vol. V, p. 354.

15   Vol. V, p. 525.

16   Vol. VII, pp. 148-49.

17   Vol. VIII, pp. 475-76.

18   Vol. VIII, p. 476.

19   VII, p. 280.

20   Vol. VIII, p. 476.

21   Vol. V, p. 65.

22   Vol. V, p. 17.

23   Vol. VI, pp. 254-55.

24   Vol. VI, p. 288.

25   Vol. VI, pp. 289-90.

26   Vol. VII, p. 183.

27   Vol. VI, p. 460.

28   Vol. VI, p. 427.

29   Vol. V, p. 215.

30   Vol. IV, p. 468.

31   Vol. V, p. 380.

32   Vol. VI, p. 381.

33   Vol. IV, pp. 451-52.

34   Vol. VI, p. 381.

35   Vol. VI, p. 381.

36   Vol. VI, p. 381.

37   Vol. V, p. 202.

38   Vol. V, p. 213.

39   Vol. III, p. 189.

40   Vol. I, p. 110.

41   Vol. II, pp. 51-53, 62-66, 173-74, 234.

42   Vol. II, p. 339; Vol. I, p. 409; Vol. VI, p. 44.

43   Vol. II, p. 196; Vol. VI, pp. 34, 44; Vol. VII, pp. 32, 38.

44   Vol. VIII, pp. 26-27.

45   Vol. VII, p. 102.

46   Vol. V, p. 428.

47   Vol. VIII, p. 22.

48   Vol. VI, p. 505.

49   Vol. VIII, p. 26.

50   Vol. II, p. 85.

51   Vol. III, pp. 147-48, 177, 369.

52   Vol. III, pp. 139, 146-159, 171-182, 204, 277, 314, 317; Vol. IV, pp. 155, 362-368, 402, 476.

53   Vol. V, p. 308.

54   Vol. VI, p. 462.

55   Vol. III, p. 158.

56   Vol. III, p. 182.

57   Vol. III, p. 182.

58   Vol. III, p. 139.

59   Vol. V, p. 216.

60   Vol. III, pp. 344-45.

61   Vol. III, p. 153.

62   Vol. IV, p. 368.

63   Vol. III, pp. 171-172.

64   Vol. IV, p. 368.

65 Vol. I, p. 22.

66 Vol. IV, p. 200; Vol. V, pp. 311, 525; Vol. VI, p. 114; Vol. VIII, p. 205.

67 Vol. III, p. 271.

68 Vol. III, p. 167.

69 Vol. VIII, pp. 61-62.

70 Vol. V, pp. 307, 537.

71 Vol. III, p. 205.

72 Vol. IV, p. 161.

73 Vol. IV, p. 161.

74 Vol. VI, p. 394.

75 Vol. V, p. 198.

76 Vol. V, p. 214.

77 Vol. IV, p. 299.

78 Vol. V, p. 214.

79 Vol. IV, p. 299.

80 Vol. III, p. 245.

81 Vol. III, p. 245.

82 Vol. IV, p. 372; Vol. VI, p. 114.

83 Vol. VI, pp. 210, 247, 317-18; Vol. VII, p. 173.

84 Vol. V, p. 214.

85 Vol. V. p. 214.

86 Vol. III, pp. 198, 296.

87 Vol. VI, p. 428.

88 Vol. III, p. 297; Vol. V, p. 214.

89 Vol. III, p. 297; Vol. V, p. 214.

90 Vol. IV, p. 441.

91 Vol. IV, p. 441.

92 Vol. IV, p. 440.

93 Vol. IV, pp. 439-440.

94 Vol. IV, p. 442.

95 Vol. VIII, p. 68.

96   Vol. IV, p. 442.

CHAPTER 2
Bhagavan Das: Theosophy and Guild Socialism

1   Bhagavan Das, *Ancient versus Modern "Scientific Socialism"*, cited below as *AVMSS*, (Madras: Theosophical Publishing House, 1934), pp. 5-6.
2   *AVMSS*, pp. 6-7.
3   *AVMSS*, p. 29.
4   *AVMSS*, p. 29.
5   *AVMSS*, pp. 156, 161-162; Bhagavan Das, *The Science of Social Organisation*, 2 ed. (3 Vols., published separately in 1932, 1935, 1948), cited below as *SSO*, by volume), (Madras: Theosophical Publishing House), Vol. I, pp. 199-200.
6   *AVMSS*, p. 154.
7   *SSO* Vol. I, pp. 146-147.
8   *AVMSS*, pp. 28-29.
9   *SSO* Vol. III, pp, 783, 878; Vol. I, p. 164.
10   *AVMSS*, p. 58.
11   *AVMSS*, pp. 2-3, 31-32, 41, 45; *SSO* Vol. III, p. 1205.
12   *SSO* Vol. II, p. 678.
13   *AVMSS*, pp. 28-29.
14   *SSO* Vol. II, p. 678.
15   *SSO* Vol. II, p. 678; *AVMSS*, p. 29.
16   *SSO* Vol. III, p. 1181.
17   *AVMSS*, pp. 4-5.
18   *SSO* Vol. II, p. 681.
19   *SSO* Vol. III, p. 822.
20   *AVMSS*, p. 29.
21   *SSO* Vol. II, p. 1222.

22   *AVMSS*, pp. 29-31; *SSO* Vol. III, pp. 1185-86, 1223.

23   *SSO* Vol. III, pp. 783, 878; AVMSS, p. 57.

24   *SSO* Vol. III, p. 821.

25.   *SSO* Vol. III, p. 1075.

26   *SSO* Vol. III, p. 1180.

27   *AVMSS*, p. 132.

28   *AVMSS*, p. 71.

29   *SSO* Vol. I, p. 145 f.n. 1.

30   *AVMSS*, pp. 71-72.

31   *SSO* Vol. III, pp. 783, 878; Vol. I, p. 164.

32   *AVMSS*, pp. 150-52; *SSO* Vol. I, p. 164.

33   *AVMSS*, pp. 58-59.

34   *SSO* Vol. III, p. 808.

35   *AVMSS*, pp. 69-70. *SSO* Vol. I, pp. 162-63.

36   *SSO* Vol. III, pp. 787, 781.

37   *SSO* Vol. III, pp. 781-82, 806.

38   *SSO* Vol. III, p. 787.

39   *SSO* Vol. III, p. 788.

40   *SSO* Vol. III, p. 807.

41   *SSO* Vol. III, pp. 788, 819, 822.

42   *SSO* Vol. I, p. 157.

43   *AVMSS*, p. 80; *SSO* Vol. II, p. 551; Vol. III, 81.

44   *SSO* Vol. I, p. 160.

45   *SSO* Vol. I, p. 160.

46   *SSO* Vol. III, pp. 800, 807, 817.

47   *SSO* Vol. III, pp. 788, 792, 819.

48   *AVMSS*, pp. 138-39.

49   *AVMSS*, pp. 69-71.

50   *SSO* Vol. I, p. 199; Vol. III, p. 821.

51   *SSO* Vol. III, pp. 787, 821-22; *AVMSS*, p. 165; *SSO* Vol. I, p. 199.

52   *SSO* Vol. III, pp. 782, 821.

53   *SSO* Vol. III, p. 782.

54   *SSO* Vol. III, p. 807.

55   *SSO* Vol. III, p. 821.

56   *AVMSS*, pp. 66-67, 108-110; *SSO* Vol. III, pp. 783-84.

57   *SSO* Vol. III, p. 784.

58   *AVMSS*, pp. 156, 161-62; *SSO* Vol. I, pp. 199-200.

59   *AVMSS*, p. 71.

60   *AVMSS*, pp. 183-84, quoting G.R.S. Taylor, *The Guild State*.

61   *AVMSS*, p. 166.

62   *SSO* Vol. III, p. 1185.

63   *SSO* Vol. II, pp. 433-35; Vol. III, p. 1074.

64   *SSO* Vol. III, p. 1204.

65   *AVMSS*, p. 31.

66   *AVMSS*, p. 31.

67   *SSO* Vol. III, p. 1185.

68   *AVMSS*, pp. 126-27; *SSO* Vol. I, p. 301; Vol. III, p. 1185.

69   *SSO* Vol. III, p. 1185; *AVMSS*, p. 126.

70   *AVMSS*, pp. 126-127.

71   *AVMSS*, p. 127; *SSO* Vol. III, p. 1204.

72   *SSO* Vol. III, pp. 787, 801, 1185, 1209, 1222-23.

73   *SSO* Vol. I, pp. 432-36; Vol. III, pp. 1074, 1204, 1223.

74   *SSO* Vol. III, p. 787.

75   *SSO* Vol. III, p. 1075.

76   *SSO* Vol. I, p. 301.

77   *SSO* Vol. III, p. 1075.

78   *SSO* Vol. III, p. 835; Vol. II, p. 628.

79   *AVMSS*, pp. 5-6.

80   *SSO* Vol. III, p. 1070.

81   *AVMSS*, pp. 112, 132-33.

82   *AVMSS*, p. 67; *SSO* Vol. II, pp. viii, 556; *SSO* Vol. III, pp. 861, 989, 738-59.

83   *AVMSS*, p. 67; SSO Vol. III, p. 1059.

84   *AVMSS*, pp. 109-110.

85   *AVMSS*, p. 110.

86   *SSO* Vol. I, p. 275; Vol. III, p. 780.

87   *SSO* Vol. II, pp. 442, 626; Vol. III, p. 1153.

88   *SSO* Vol. I, pp. 276-77.

89   *SSO* Vol. III, pp. 831, 1155; Vol. II, p. 441.

90   *SSO* Vol. III, p. 1154.

91   *SSO* Vol. III, p. 1153; Vol. I, p. 163.

92   *SSO* Vol. III, pp. 770, 781-82; 805, 819.

93   *AVMSS*, pp. 4-5; *SSO* Vol. I, pp. 15-23; Vol. II, pp. 471-472, 553; Vol. III, 1128-1133.

94   *SSO* Vol. III, pp. 1130-32.

95   *SSO* Vol. II, pp. 432-34.

96   *SSO* Vol. II, pp. 432-36; 469, 548; Vol. III, pp. 1074-75, 1132.

97   *SSO* Vol. II, pp. 432-36; Vol. III, 1074-75.

98   *SSO* Vol. III, pp. 1132, 1224.

99   *SSO* Vol. III, pp. 1075, 1130-33, 1223-24.

100 *AVMSS*, p. 208; *SSO* Vol. II, p. 584; Vol. III, pp. 1130-33, 1223-24.

101 *SSO* p. 1224.

102 *SSO* pp. 1205-1211.

103 *SSO* pp. 1189-1201, 1210.

104 *AVMSS*, pp. 135-36.

105 *SSO* Vol. III, pp. 1196-1202.

CHAPTER 3

Aurobindo and Pal: Hegelian Hinduism and Federal Socialism

1   Sri Aurobindo, *Bande Mataram: Early Political Writings* (Pondicherry: Sri Aurobindo Ashram, 1973), cited below as *Bande Mataram*, pp. 81, 918.

2   Bipinchandra Pal, *Swadeshi and Swaraj*, cited below as *Swadeshi*

and Swaraj, (Calcutta: Yugayatri Prakashak Limited, 1954), p. 291.

3   *Swadeshi and Swaraj*, p. 146.

4   *Bande Mataram*, p. 86.

5   *Bande Mataram*, pp. 114-128

6   *Bande Mataram*, p. 91.

7   *Bande Mataram*, pp. 12-13, 101; Sri Aurobindo, *The Human Cycle, The Ideal of Human Unity, War and Self-Determination*, cited below as *Cycle, Unity, War* (Pondicherry: Sri Aurobindo Ashram, 1977), pp. 305-315.

8   *Bande Mataram*, p. 91.

9   *Bande Mataram*, pp. 534-35.

10   *Bande Mataram*, pp. 16-18, 35.

11   *Bande Mataram*, pp. 30-45.

12   *Bande Mataram*, p. 652.

13   *Bande Mataram*, pp. 66-71, 117, 125-26, 216, 655-665, 701, 855.

14   *Bande Mataram*, p. 661.

15   *Ideal of the Karmayogin*, p. 34.

16   Sri Aurobindo, *Foundations of Indian Culture*, cited below as *Foundations*, (Pondicherry: Sri Aurobindo Ashram, 1959), pp. 74-75.

17   *Ideal of the Karmayogin*, p. 37; *Foundations*, pp. 74-75.

18   *Cycle, Unity, War*, pp. 21-55.

19   *Cycle, Unity, War*, pp. 23, 40, 52, 54-55.

20   This subjective/objective distinction as Aurobindo conceives it indicates as do other features of his thought a familiarity with Hegel. See Hegel, Raymond Plant, (Bloomington: Indiana Univ. Press, 1973), pp. 33-34.

21   Aurobindo mentions neither Hobbes nor Kant, but clearly has Hobbesian and Kantian notions in mind, especially in the paragraph on p. 50 of *Cycle, Unity, War*. He does not comment on a third typical response to the liberal dilemma of order: the idea of a harmony of selves emerging through the spontaneous workings of the market. See also *Cycle, Unity, War*, pp. 603-604.

22 Durkheim draws roughly this distinction between his own view of morality and Kant's, which it resembles in other respects. Hegel, too, criticizes Kant along these lines. See G.W.F. Hegel, *Philosophy of Right*, paragraph 135; Emile Durkheim, *Moral Education*, Ch. 7-8.

23 *Cycle, Unity, War*, p. 53.

24 *Foundations*, pp. 104-107, 114-115, 335-344.

25 *Cycle, Unity War*, p. 1-28.

26 *Cycle, Unity, War*, pp. 337-340.

27 *Foundations*, pp. 352-359.

28 *Foundations*, pp. 324-333.

29 *Foundations*, p. 343.

30 See Alexis Tocqueville, *Democracy in America*, (Garden City, New York: Anchor Books, 1969), p. 60

31 *Cycle, Unity, War*, p. 263.

32 *Cycle, Unity, War*, p. 346.

33 *Cycle, Unity, War*, pp. 336-337.

34 *Cycle, Unity, War*, pp. 340-341.

35 *Cycle, Unity, War*, pp. p. 341.

36 *Cycle, Unity, War*, p. 522.

37 *Cycle, Unity, War*, p. 399.

38 *Cycle, Unity, War*, pp. 61-63, 398-400.

39 *Cycle, Unity, War*, pp. 398-399.

40 *Cycle, Unity, War*, p. 347.

41 *Bande Mataram*, pp. 738-39; see also *Foundations*, pp. 370-71.

42 *Bande Mataram*, p. 537.

43 *Foundations*, pp. 347-356.

44 *Bande Mataram*, pp. 536-37.

45 *Bande Mataram*, pp. 534-538.

46 *Bande Mataram*, pp. 16, 559; *Cycle, Unity, War*, pp. 183-187, 269-270, 371-380, 448-449.

47 *Bande Mataram*, p. 37; *Cycle, Unity, War*, pp. 183-187, 645.

48   *Ideal of the Karmayogin*, pp. 32, 38.

49   *Cycle, Unity, War*, pp. 188-190, 390.

50   *Cycle, Unity, War*, pp. 646-648.

51   *Cycle, Unity, War*, p. 188-190.

52   *Cycle, Unity, War*, pp. 189-199, 362, 390, 449.

53   *Cycle, Unity, War*, pp. 192-200.

54   *Cycle, Unity, War*, pp. 49-51.

55   *Cycle, Unity, War*, p. 51.

56   *Cycle, Unity, War*, pp. 464-466.

57   *Cycle, Unity, War*, p. 648.

58   *Cycle, Unity, War*, pp. 649-653.

59   *Cycle, Unity, War*, pp. 650-654.

60   *Cycle, Unity, War*, p. 205.

61   *Cycle, Unity, War*, pp. 181, 187-189, 359-360, 545-547.

62   *Cycle, Unity, War*, p. 204.

63   *Cycle, Unity, War*, p. 205.

64   *Cycle, Unity, War*, pp. 205-206.

65   *Cycle, Unity, War*, p. 206.

66   Sri Aurobindo, *The Superamental Manifestation Upon Earth*, (Pondicherry: Sri Aurobindo Ashram Press, 1952), pp. 67, 52.

67   *Cycle, Unity, War*, p. 524.

68   *Cycle, Unity, War*, p. 207.

69   *Cycle, Unity, War*, p. 540-544.

70   *Cycle, Unity, War*, p. 544.

71   *Cycle, Unity, War*, pp. 545-47.

72   *Cycle, Unity, War*, p. 545.

73   *Cycle, Unity, War*, pp. 545-554.

74   *Cycle, Unity, War*, p. 554.

75   *Cycle, Unity, War*, p. 554.

76   *Cycle, Unity, War*, p 554.

77   *Cycle, Unity, War*, p. 211.

78   *Cycle, Unity, War*, p. 211.

79   *Cycle, Unity, War*, p. 211.

80   *Cycle, Unity, War*, p. 211, 229.

81   *Cycle, Unity, War*, pp. 232-233.

82   *Cycle, Unity, War*, pp. 232-233.

83   Bipinchandra Pal, *Swadeshi and Swaraj*, (Calcutta: Yugayatri Prakashak Limited, 1954), pp. 33-34, 174.

84   *Swadeshi and Swaraj*, pp. 33-34, 174.

85   *Swadeshi and Swaraj*, pp. 162-167.

86   *Swadeshi and Swaraj*, pp. 19-21.

87   *Swadeshi and Swaraj*, pp. 55(a).

88   Bipinchandra Pal, *Writings and Speeches, Vol. I*, cited below as *Writings and Speeches*, (Calcutta: Yugayatri, 1958), pp. 22-24.

89   Bipin Chandra Pal, *Nationality and Empire*, cited below as *Nationality and Empire*, (Calcutta: Thacker, Spink & Co., 1916), p. 6.

90   *Nationality and Empire*, p. xi.

91   *Nationality and Empire*, pp. x, xi.

92   *Nationality and Empire*, p. xiii.

93   *Nationality and Empire*, p. xix.

94   *Nationality and Empire*, pp. xv and xvi.

95   *Swadeshi and Swaraj*, p. 147.

96   *Swadeshi and Swaraj*, pp. 29-31.

97   *Nationality and Empire*, p. xxx.

98   *Nationality and Empire*, p. xvii.

99   *Nationality and Empire*, p. 11.

100   Bipin Chandra Pal, *The Soul of India*, (Madras: Tagore and Co.), pp. 78-79.

101   *Soul of India*, p. 13; *Swadeshi and Swaraj*, pp. 37-38.

102   *Writings and Speeches*, p. 168; *Swadeshi and Swaraj*, p. 201.

103   *Soul of India*, pp. 126-146.

104   *Nationality and Empire*, pp. 31-33; Soul of India, p. 126; *Swadeshi and Swaraj*, p. 147.

105   Bipin Chandra Pal, *An Introduction to the Study of Hinduism*, (Cal-

cutta: Yugayatri Prakashak Limited, 1968), PP. 61-77.

106 Bipinchandra Pal, *Shree Krishna*, (Calcutta: 1964), p. 44.

107 Bipinchandra Pal, *Bengal Vaishnavism*, (Calcutta: Yugayatri Prakashak Ltd., 1962), p. 12.

108 *Bengal Vaishnavism*, pp. 10-11; *Shree Krishna*, p. 100-101.

109 *Nationality and Empire*, pp. 52, 75, 146.

110 *Shree Krishna*, p. 90.

111 *Bengal Vaishnavism*, p. 2.

112 *Bengal Vaishnavism*, pp. 25-27, 107; *Soul of India*, pp. 168, 173.

113 *Bengal Vaishnavism*, pp. 40-41.

114 *Bengal Vaishnavism*, pp. 32-33, 88-89.

115 Bipin Chandra Pal, *The New Economic Menace to India*, (Madras: Ganesh and Co.), p.247.

116 *Nationality and Empire*, pp. 56-58, 122.

117 *Nationality and Empire*, pp. 56-59; Writings and Speeches, pp. 151-55.

118 *Soul of India*, pp. 63-65, 34.

119 *Nationality and Empire*, p. 28.

120 *Nationality and Empire*, pp. 28-29.

121 *Nationality and Empire*, p. 30.

122 *Swadeshi and Swaraj*, pp. 34-39.

123 *Swadeshi and Swaraj*, p. 16.

124 *Soul of India*, pp. 108-109.

125 *Nationality and Empire*, p. 35.

126 *Nationality and Empire*, pp. 114-116.

127 *Swadeshi and Swaraj*, pp. 106-107; *Soul of India*, pp. 32-33

128 *Soul of India*, p. 106.

129 *Soul of India*, pp. 95-108.

130 *Nationality and Empire*, pp. 9-11.

131 *Nationality and Empire*, pp. 8-10, 17, 26-27.

132 *Nationality and Empire*, pp. 8-11, 27.

133 *Writings and Speeches*, p. 150.

134 *New Economic Menace*, pp. 2, 65-66, 79.

135 *Swadeshi and Swaraj*, pp. 223-225; *New Economic Menace*, pp. 29, 6142, 95, 101, 196-198, 203-209.

136 *New Economic Menace*, pp. 71-76, 101, 107.

137 *New Economic Menace*, pp. 115-127, 138, 150-165.

138 *Nationality and Empire*, p. 82; *New Economic Menace*, pp. 125, 170-188, 203. 139 *New Economic Menace*, pp. 110-115, 204-206.

140 *New Economic Menace*, pp. 214, 225-32.

141 *Nationality and Empire*, p. 40.

142 *Nationality and Empire*, p. 40.

143 *Swadeshi and Swaraj*, p. 232.

144 *Swadeshi and Swaraj*, p. 232; *New Economic Menace*, pp. 71-76, 101, 107.

145 *New Economic Menace*, pp. 243, 196-202.

146 *New Economic Menace*, pp. 236-237.

147 *New Economic Menace*, pp. 206-210.

148 *New Economic Menace*, pp. 211-212.

149 *Swadeshi and Swaraj*, p. 128.

150 *New Economic Menace*, pp. 209-210.

151 *Swadeshi and Swaraj*, pp. 247-248.

152 *Nationality and Empire*, pp. 228-229.

CHAPTER 4
Ambedkar: (A)-Political Buddhism and State Socialism

1 B.R. Ambedkar, *Annihilation of Caste*, (Jullundur: Bheem Patrika Publications), p. 92, *Thus Spoke Ambedkar*, Vol. I, Ed. Bhagwan Das (Jalandhar: Buddhist Publishing House, publication date unavailable), p. 46.

2 B.R. Ambedkar, *Thus Spoke Ambedkar*, Vol. II, (Jullundur: Bheem Patrika Publications 1969), p. 186; *Thus Spoke Ambedkar*, Vol. I, p.46.

3   *Thus Spoke Ambedkar*, Vol. II, p. 187.

4   *Annihilation of Caste*, p. 92.

5   *Thus Spoke Ambedkar*, Vol. I, p. 72.

6   B.R. Ambedkar, *The Buddha and His Dhamma*, (Bombay: Siddharth Publication, 1984), p. 234.

7   *Thus Spoke Ambedkar*, Vol. I, p. 73.

8   *Thus Spoke Ambedkar*, Vol. I, p. 62.

9   B.R. Ambedkar, Dr. Babasahem Ambedkar: *Writings and Speeches*, Vol. I, (Bombay: Education Dept., Govt. of Maharashtra, 1979), p. 412, 186-87.

10 B.R. Ambedkar, Speech to G.I.P. Railway Depressed Class Workmen's Conference at Manmad, Feb. 12, 13 1938, Quoted in G.S. Lokhande, *Bhimrao Ramji Ambedkar: A Study in Social Democracy*, (New Delhi: Sterling Publishers Pvt., Ltd.), p. 208.

11 B.R. Ambedkar, *Who Were the Shudras?* (Bombay: Thackers, 1946), p. 7; *Annihilation of Caste*, p. 23.

12 *Writings and Speeches*, p. 408; *Thus Spoke Ambedkar*, Vol. I, p. 22.

13 *Writings and Speeches*, pp. 409-410.

14 B.R. Ambedkar, *Gandhi and Gandhism*, (Jullundur: Bheem Patrika Publications), pp. 139-144.

15 B.R. Ambedkar, *Thus Spoke Ambedkar*, Vol. III, Ed. Bhagwan Das (Bangalore: Ambedkar Sahitya Prakashana), pp. 142-146; *Thus Spoke Ambedkar*, Vol. I p. 55.

16 *Annihilation of Caste*, pp. 23, 29.

17 *Annihilation of Caste*, pp. 23-24; *Who Were the Shudras?* p. 56.

18 B.R. Ambedkar, *Mr. Gandhi and the Emancipation of the Untouchables*, pp. 31-40.

19 *Annihilation of Caste*, pp. 40, 49, 111.

20 *Annihilation of Caste*, pp. 81-83.

21 *Annihilation of Caste*, p. 74.

22 *Gandhi and Gandhism*, pp. 128-133, 144-149; *Annihilation of Caste*, p. 126.

23   B.R. Ambedkar, *Buddha and the Future of His Religion* (Jullundur: Bheem Patrika Publications, 1980), pp. 10¬12.

24   *Annihilation of Caste*, pp. 123-26.

25   *Who Were the Shudras?* p. xvii.

26   *Annihilation of Caste*, p. 123.

27   *Annihilation of Caste*, p. 123-128.

28   B.R. Ambedkar, *Thus Spoke Ambedkar*, Vol. IV, ed. by Bhagwan Das, (Bangalore: Ambedkar Sahitya Prakashana, publication date unavailable), pp. 61.

29   *Thus Spoke Ambedkar*, Vol. IV, Ed. Bhagavan Das (Bangalore: Ambedkar Sahithya Prakashana, publication date unavailable), pp. 58-65.

30   B.R. Ambedkar, *The Buddha and His Dhamma*, p. 299; *Thus Spoke Ambedkar*, Vol I, p.50; *Thus Spoke Ambedkar*, Vol. II., pp. 134, 184.

31   *The Buddha and His Dhamma*, pp.231-234; *Buddha and the Future of His Religion*, pp. 5-6. For some of the considerable evidence of Ambedkar's familiarity with Durkheim, see *The Untouchables*, p. 125.

32   *The Buddha and His Dhamma*, p. 231.

33   *The Buddha and His Dhamma*, pp. 369-370; *Thus Spoke Ambedkar*, Vol. II, pp. 127-138.

34   *Thus Spoke Ambedkar*, Vol. II, p. 162.

35   *Thus Spoke Ambedkar*, Vol. II, pp. 132-134, 184.

36   *Who Were the Shudras?* pp. xii, 56, 233.

37   *Who Were the Shudras?* pp. 84-108, 120, 146.

38   *Who Were the Shudras?* pp. 170, 194, 214-218, 235-237.

39   B.R. Ambedkar, *The Untouchables*, (New Delhi: Amrit Book Co.), pp. v, 31, 117, 119, 127, 147.

40   *The Untouchables*, pp. 90-93, 100, 117-121.

41   *The Untouchables*, pp. 80, 122-128.

42   *The Buddha and the Future of His Religion*, p. 13.

43   *The Buddha and His Dhamma*, pp. 5-6.

44 *The Buddha and His Dhamma*, p. 14.

45 *The Buddha and His Dhamma*, pp. 8-9.

46 *The Buddha and His Dhamma*, p. 45.

47 *The Buddha and His Dhamma*, pp. 45, 83.

48 *The Buddha and His Dhamma*, pp. 159, 226.

49 *The Buddha and His Dhamma*, pp. 202, 256-259, 285-286.

50 *The Buddha and His Dhamma*, pp. 17, 50, 82, 156, 164-168.

51 *The Buddha and His Dhamma*, pp. 318-319.

52 *The Buddha and His Dhamma*, pp. 318-319.

53 *The Buddha and His Dhamma*, pp. 308-318.

54 *The Buddha and His Dhamma*, p. 41.

55 G.S. Lokhande, *Bhimrao Ramiji Ambedkar: A Study in Social Democracy*, cited below as "Lochande," (New Delhi: Sterling Publishers Pvt. Ltd. 1977), p. 191.

56 *Thus Spoke Ambedkar*, Vol. II, pp. 200-201.

57 *Writings and Speeches*, pp. 396-397, 408.

58 *Writing and Speeches*, pp. 409-412.

59 For example, see "Lokhande," pp. 170-76.

60 *Thus Spoke Ambedkar*, Vol. II, pp. 175-76.

61 "Lokhande," pp. 175-76.

62 *Thus Spoke Ambedkar*, Vol. I, p. 61.

63 *Thus Spoke Ambedkar*, Vol. I, pp. 46-47.

64 B.R. Ambedkar, *Mr. Ghandi and the Emancipation of the Untouchables*, (Jullundur: Bheem Patrika Publications, publication date unavailable), pp. 42-43.

65 *Thus Spoke Ambedkar*, Vol. I, p. 160.

66 *Thus Spoke Ambedkar*, Vol. I, p. 160.

67 *Writings and Speeches*, pp. 409-410.

68 *Writings and Speeches*, pp. 455-479.

69 *Mr. Gandhi and the Emancipation of the Untouchables*, pp. 31-40.

70 *Thus Spoke Ambedkar*, Vol. I, p. 132; Vol. II, pp. 89-90.

71 *Thus Spoke Ambedkar*, Vol. III, pp. 186-187.

72   *Thus Spoke Ambedkar*, Vol. III, pp. 129-130; *Mr. Gandhi and the Emancipation of the Untouchables*, pp. 16-17, 35-40.

CHAPTER 5
Gandhi: The Social Logic of Ahimsa

1   M.K. Gandhi, *In Search of the Supreme*, 3 Vols., Ed. V.B. Kher, (Ahmedabad: Navajivan Publishing House, 1961), Vol. I, p. 11, Vol. II, p. 10.

2   *In Search of the Supreme*, Vol. II, p. 27.

3   M.K. Gandhi, *Sarvodaya*, Ed. Bharatan Kumarappa, (Ahmedabad: Navajivan Publishing House, 1954), p. 11.

4   M.K. Gandhi, *Democracy: Real and Deceptive*, Ed. R.K. Prabhu, (Ahmedabad: Navajivan Publishing Rouse, 1961), p. 9. M.K. Gandhi, *Economic and Industrial Life and Relations*, 3 Vols., Ed. V.B. Kher, (Ahmedabad: Navajivan Publishing House, 1957), pp. 151, 189; Sarvodaya, pp. 9, 55, 151.

5   *Sarvodaya*, p. 16.

6   M.K. Gandhi, *Hind Swaraj or Indian Home Rule*, (Ahmedabad: Navajivan Publishing House, 1982), pp. 60-62, 94-97.

7   *Democracy: Real and Deceptive*, pp. 9-18.

8   *Democracy: Real and Deceptive*, pp. 1-6.

9   *Sarvodaya*, p. 38.

10   M.K. Gandhi, *Panchayat Raj*, Ed. R.K. Prabhu, (Ahmedabad: Navajivan Publishing House, 1959), p. 19-23, 29; *Sarvodaya*, p. 129.

11   *Economic and Industrial Life and Relations*, Vol. II, pp. 158-165; *Sarvodaya*, p. 54; *Panchayat Raj*, pp. 33-34.

12   *Sarvodaya*, pp. 121-123.

13   Jayaprakash Narayan, *A Revolutionary's Quest*, Ed. Bimal Prasad, (Delhi: Oxford Univ. Press, 1980), p. 314.

14   M.K. Gandhi, *Village Industries*, (Ahmedabad: Navajivan Publish-

ing House, 1960), p. 10-11. *Economic and Industrial Life and Relations*, Vol. I, pp. 22-23.

15   *Panchayat Raj*, p. 11.

16   *Economic and Industrial Life and Relations*, Vol. II, pp. 197.

17   M.K. Gandhi, *Political and National Life and Affairs*, 3 Vols. Ed. by V.B. Kher, (Ahmedabad: Navajivan Publishing House, 1967), Vol. I, pp. 5-6, 125.

18   M.K. Gandhi, *My Socialism*, Ed. R.K. Prabhu, (Ahmedabad: Navajivan Publishing House, 1959), p. 44.

19   *Economic and Industrial Life and Relations*, Vol I, p. 42, 69-70, 148.

20   Buddhadeva Bhattacharyya. *Evolution of the Political Philosophy of Gandhi*, (Calcutta: Calcutta Book House, 1967), p. 233.

21   *Economic and Industrial Life and Relations*, Vol. I, p. 45.

22   M.K. Gandhi, *My Theory of Trusteeship*, (Bombay: Bharatiya Vidya Bhavan, 1970), p. 51.

23   *Sarvodaya*, p. 89. See also, *Democracy: Real and Deceptive*, p. 15.

24   *Economic and Industrial Life and Relations*, Vol. I, p. 171. *National Life and Affairs*, Vol. III, pp. 171.

25   *Political and National Life and Affairs*, Vol. III, pp. 79, 148, 184.

26   *Sarvodaya*, p. 82.

27   *Political and National Life and Affairs*, Vol. III, pp. 73, 113.

28   *Sarvodaya*, p. 85.

29   *Economic and Industrial Life and Relations*, Vol. I, p. 146.

30   *Economic and Industrial Life and Relations*, Vol. I, pp. 70, 72, 86, 146.

31   *Economic and Industrial Life and Relations*, Vol. I, p. 40; *Sarvodaya*, p. 19.

32   *Economic and Industrial Life and Relations*, Vol. I, p. 72.

33   *My Theory of Trusteeship*, p. 51.

34   *Economic and Industrial Life and Relations*, Vol. I, p. 157.

35   *Economic and Industrial Life and Relations*, Vol. I, p. 87.

36   *Economic and Industrial Life and Relations*, Vol. I, pp. 69, 87.

37   M.K. Gandhi, *Capital and Labor*, (Bombay: Bharatiya Vidya Bhavan, 1970), pp.37-75.

38   *Economic and Industrial Life and Relations*, Vol. I, p. 194.

39   *Capital and Labor*, p. 83.

40   *Capital and Labor*, pp. 47-52, 55-56, 62, 67, 74, 75.

41   *Sarvodaya*, p. 97.

42   *Economic and Industrial Life and Relations*, Vol. I, pp. 158-166.

43   *Sarvodaya*, p. 43; *My Theory of Trusteeship*, pp. 50-52; *Economic and Industrial Life and Relations*, Vol. I, p. 159; *My Socialism*, p.44.

44   *My Socialism*, p. 12; *Economic and Industrial Life and Relations*, Vol. I, p. 162.

45   *My Socialism*, pp. 30, 41-45; *Sarvodaya*, p. 93; *Economic and Industrial Life and Relations*, Vol. I, p. 152.

46   *Economic and Industrial Life and Relations*, Vol. I, p. 152.

47   *Panchayat Raj*, pp. 10-11; *Economic and Industrial Life and Relations*, Vol. I, pp. 46-49, 164.

48   M.K. Gandhi, *In Search of the Supreme* (3 Vols.), Ed. V.B. Kher, (Ahmedabad: Navajivan Publishing House, 1961) Vol. III, pp. 115-116.

49   *In Search of the Supreme*, Vol. III, p. 94.

50   M.K. Gandhi, *Varnashramadharma*, Ed. R.K. Prabhu, (Ahmedabad: Navajivan Publishing House, 1962.), p. 5-27.

51   B.R. Ambedkar, *Gandhi and Gandhism*, (Jullundur: Bheem Patrika Publications), (publication date unavailable). p. 129.

52   *Varnashramadharma*, pp. 9-10.

53   Ambedkar, *Gandhi and Gandhism*, p. 129; *In Search of the Supreme*, Vol. III, p. 147.

54   *Varnashramadharma*, p. 11.

CHAPTER 6

Asoka Mehta: Gandhi as Utopian Socialist

1   Asoka Mehta, *Socialism and Gandhism*, (Bombay: The Congress Socialist Publishing Co., Ltd., 1935), pp. 4-5, 14, 17-18.

2   *Socialism and Gandhism*, pp. 4, 12-13.

3   *Socialism and Gandhism*, pp. 8, 12, 22.

4   Asoka Mehta, *Studies in Socialism*, (Bombay: Bharatiya Vidya Bhavan), 1964, pp. 53, 56, 89.

5   *Studies in Socialism*, pp. 56-98, 61, 69.

6   *Studies in Socialism*, pp. 54, 55.

7   *Studies in Socialism*, pp. 90-91.

8   *Studies in Socialism*, p. 73.

9   *Studies in Socialism*, pp. 74-79.

10   *Studies in Socialism*, pp. 211-218.

11   *Studies in Socialism*, p. 81.

12   *Studies in Socialism*, p. 89.

13   *Studies in Socialism*, p. 219; Asoka Mehta, *Democratic Socialism: Mid-Twentieth Century Synthesis*, (Hyderabad: Chetana Prakashan Limited, 1951), pp. 195-96.

14   *Socialism and Gandhism*, pp. 5, 14.

15   *Studies in Socialism*, p. 80.

16   *Democratic Socialism*, pp. 170-71; *Studies in Socialism*, pp. 79-80.

17   *Democratic Socialism*, p. 144.

18   *Democratic Socialism*, pp. 123-125, 197.

19   Asoka Mehta, *Towards Socialism*, (Bombay: Socialist Party, publication date unavailable), pp. 4-8.

20   *Democratic Socialism*, pp. 6-8.

21   *Socialism and Gandhism*, pp. 17-18.

22   *Democratic Socialism*, pp. 181-182, 202; *Towards Socialism*, p. 8

23   Asoka Mehta, *Tasks of Social Democracy in Asia*, (New Delhi: Praja Socialist Publication, 1961), p. 8.

24   *Studies in Socialism*, pp. 89-98.

25   *Studies in Socialism*, p. 98.

26   *Democratic Socialism*, p. 199.

CHAPTER 7
Narendra Deva: Gandhi and Democratic Socialism

1   Acharya Narendra Deva, *Towards Socialist Society*, Ed. by Brahmanand, (New Delhi: Centre of Applied Politics, 1979), pp. 46-53.

2   *Towards Socialist Society*, pp. 183-202.

3   *Towards Socialist Society*, pp. 194-199.

4   *Towards Socialist Society*, p. 221.

5   Acharya Narendra Deva, *Democratic Socialism in India*, Ed. by Chandrodaya Dikshit, (New Delhi: S. Chand & Co. (Pvt.) Ltd., 1971), p. 71.

6   *Towards Socialist Society*, pp. 302-304.

7   *Towards Socialist Society*, pp. 302-306.

8   *Towards Socialist Society*, p. 298.

9   *Towards Socialist Society*, pp. 344-345, 402-403.

10   *Towards Socialist Society*, pp. 218, 278, 283.

11   *Towards Socialist Society*, pp. 442-443.

12   *Towards Socialist Society*, p. 305.

13   *Democratic Socialism in India*, p. 61.

14   *Democratic Socialism in India*, p. 59.

15   *Towards Socialist Society*, pp. 277-79.

16   *Towards Socialist Society*, pp. 298-99; *Democratic Socialism in India*, p. 61.

17   *Towards Socialist Society*, pp. 293, 344, 349.

18   *Towards Socialist Society*, p. 248.

19   *Democratic Socialism in India*, p. 61.

20   *Towards Socialist Society*, pp. 232, 236, 287, 346, 430.

21   *Towards Socialist Society*, pp. 176, 229.

22   *Towards Socialist Society*, pp. 392-393.

23   *Towards Socialist Society*, pp. 287, 347-348, 392.

24   *Democratic Socialism in India*. p. 61.

25   *Towards Socialist Society*, pp. 250, 267, 337.

26   *Towards Socialist Society*, p. 427.

27   *Towards Socialist Society*, p. 362.

CHAPTER 8
Nehru: The Advaita of Non-Violent Revolution

1   Jawaharlal Nehru, *India's Independence and Social Revolution*, (New Dehli: Vikas Publishing House Pvt. Ltd., 1984), p. 55.

2   Jawaharlal Nehru, *India's Freedom*, (London: Unwin Books), (Publication date unavailable), pp. 24-25; Jawaharlal Nehru, *The Discovery of India*, New Delhi: Oxford Univ. Press, 1983, pp. 284-306.

3   Nehru, *India's Freedom*, pp. 31-33.

4   *India's Freedom*, p. 25; Jawaharlal Nehru, *Glimpses of World History*, (New Delhi: Oxford Univ. Press, 1984), pp. 881-886.

5   Jawaharlal Nehru, *An Anthology*, Ed. by Sarvepalli Gopal, (Delhi: Oxford Univ. Press, 1983), p. 98.

6   Jawaharlal Nehru, *Towards a Socialistic Order*, (New Delhi: All India Congress Committee, 1956), pp. 40-41; Nehru, *India's Independence and Social Revolution*, p. 150.

7   Jawaharlal Nehru, *India's Independence and Social Revolution*, pp. 33-34.

8   Nehru, *Towards a Socialistic Order*, p. 3; see also pp. 48-49, 59.

9   Jawaharlal Nehru, *Jawaharlal Nehru on Community Development, Panchayati Reg. and Co-operation*, (New Delhi: Patiala House, 1969), p. 43; Nehru, *An Anthology*, p. 307.

10   Jawaharlal Nehru, *Nehru on Socialism: Selected Speeches and Writings*, (New Delhi: Perspective Publications (Pvt.) Ltd., 1964), p. 82.

11   Nehru, *Anthology*, p. 245; *India's Independence*, p. 98.

12   Nehru, *Community Develoment*, p. 39.

13   *Community Development* , p. 39; *Towards a Socialistic Order*, p. 30; Jawaharlal Nehru, *India Today and Tomorrow*, (New Delhi: Indian

Council for Cultural Relations, 1959(?)), p. 30.

14   *Towards a Socialistic Order*, p. 12; *India Today and Tomorrow*, pp. 30-31.

15   *India Today and Tomorrow*, p. 31; *Community Development*, p. 43.

16   *India's Independence*, p. 98; *Anthology*, p. 318.

17   *India's Independence*, p. 58; *Glimpses of World History*, pp. 858-882.

18   *India's Independence*, p. 57.

19   *Towards A Socialistic Order*, p. 63.

20   *Nehru on Socialism: Selected Speeches and Writings*, p. 80.

21   *Towards a Socialistic Order*, pp. 6-7.

22   *Towards a Socialistic Order*, p. 6.

23   Donald Eugene Smith, *Nehru and Democracy: The Political Thought of an Asian Democrat*, (Bombay: Orient Longmans, publication date unavailable), pp. 134-137.

24   *Nehru and Democracy: The Political Thought of an Asian Democrat*, p. 135.

25   *Nehru and Democracy: The Political Thought of an Asian Democrat*, p. 122; *Towards A Socialistic Order*, pp. 39-42.

26   Jawaharlal Nehru, *An Autobiography*, New Delhi: Oxford Univ. Press, 1980, p. 192.

27   Jawaharlal Nehru, *Nehru on Socialism*, Ed. by V.B. Singh, (New Delhi: Publications Division, Ministry of Information and Broadcasting, Government of India, 1977), p. 40.

28   *India's Independence*, p. 114, 153; *The Discovery of India*, pp. 398, 522; *Towards a Socialistic Order*, p. 26.

29   *Towards a Socialistic Order*, pp. 9, 43; *Nehru on Socialism: Selected Speeches*, p. 119; *India Today and Tomorrow*, p. 28.

30   *Towards a Socialistic Order*, p. 26; Smith, *Nehru and Democracy*, p. 109.

31   Nehru, *An Autobiography*, pp. 12-16.

32   *An Autobiography*, p. 374.

33   *An Autobiography*, 379; *India's Freedom*, p. 23.

34   *Anthology*, p. 577.

35   *The Discovery of India*, pp. 98, 175-178.

36   *The Discovery of India*, pp. 106-110.

37   *Anthology*, pp. 594-595.

38   *Anthology*, p. 595; *The Discovery of India*, pp. 336-339.

39   *The Discovery of India*, p.175.

40   *The Discovery of India*, pp. 89-96.

41   *The Discovery of India*, p. 85.

42   *The Discovery of India*, pp. 120-121.

43   *The Discovery of India*, p. 121.

44   *The Discovery of India*, pp. 246-247.

45   *India's Independence*, p. 34.

46   *The Discovery of India*.

47   *India Today and Tomorrow*, pp. 6-7.

48   *India Today and Tomorrow*, p. 7.

49   *Nehru on Socialism*, Ed. by Singh, p. 50.

50   *India Today and Tomorrow*, p. 7.

51   *India Today and Tomorrow*, p. 7.

52   *The Discovery of India* 7.

53   *The Discovery of India*, p. 255.

54   *The Discovery of India*, p. 251.

55   *The Discovery of India*, pp. 98, 256.

56   *The Discovery of India* 256.

57   *The Discovery of India*, pp. 248-257.

58   *The Discovery of India*, p. 246.

59   *The Discovery of India*, pp. 246-247.

60   *The Discovery of India*, p. 247.

61   *The Discovery of India*, pp. 249, 253.

62   *The Discovery of India*, p. 249.

63   *The Discovery of India*, p. 249.

64   *The Discovery of India*, p. 379.

65   *The Discovery of India*, p. 379.

66   *Nehru on Socialism*, Ed. by Singh, p. 26.

67   *Nehru on Socialism*, p. 26.

68 *India's Independence*, p. 32.

69 *India's Independence*, p. 127.

70 *Anthology*, p. 318.

71 *India Today and Tomorrow*, p. 26.

72 *The Discovery of India* 73 *The Discovery of India*, pp. 93-96.

74 For example, see *The Discovery of India*, p. 514.

75 *The Discovery of India*, p. 26.

76 *The Discovery of India*, pp. 510-511; *Anthology*, p. 499.

77 *The Discovery of India*, pp. 511-515.

78 *Towards a Socialistic Order*, p. 22.

79 *India's Independence*, p. 62; *The Discovery of India*, pp. 360-63.

80 *The Discovery of India*, p. 363.

81 *The Discovery of India*, p. 363.

82 *Community Development*, p. 38.

83 *Nehru on Socialism: Selected Speeches*, pp. 79-82.

84 *India's Independence*, pp. 28-29.

85 *India's Freedom*, p. 26; *Towards a Socialistic Order*, pp. 55-56.

CHAPTER 9
Lohia: General Aims, Immediacy, Heretical Gandhism

1 Rammanohar Lohia, *Marx, Gandhi and Socialism*, (Hyderabad Rammanohar Lohia Sanata Vidyalaya Nyasa, 1978) pp. 322-334.

2 *Marx, Gandhi and Socialism*, p. 112.

3 *Marx, Gandhi and Socialism*, p. 329.

4 *Marx, Gandhi and Socialism*, p. 334.

5 *Marx, Gandhi and Socialism*, p. 341.

6 *Marx, Gandhi and Socialism*, pp. 116, 334, 340-41.

7 *Marx, Gandhi and Socialism*, p. 334.

8 *Marx, Gandhi and Socialism*, p. 341.

9 *Marx, Gandhi and Socialism*, p. 136.

10   *Marx, Gandhi and Socialism*, p. 137.

11   *Marx, Gandhi and Socialism*, p. 137.

12   *Marx, Gandhi and Socialism*, pp. 173, 374-75, 428.

13   *Marx, Gandhi and Socialism*, pp. xiv, xv, 199-204, 480.

14   *Marx, Gandhi and Socialism*, p. 224.

15   *Marx, Gandhi and Socialism*, pp. xv-xvi, 117.

16   *Marx, Gandhi and Socialism*, p. 351.

17   *Marx, Gandhi and Socialism*, p. 123.

18   *Marx, Gandhi and Socialism*, pp. 112, 128-131, 195, 326-331, 418.

19   *Marx, Gandhi and Socialism*, pp. 128-131, 326-331.

20   *Marx, Gandhi and Socialism*, pp. 402, 480.

21   *Marx, Gandhi and Socialism*, p. 302.

22   *Marx, Gandhi and Socialism*, pp. xxi, 345, 493.

23   *Marx, Gandhi and Socialism*, p. 432.

24   *Marx, Gandhi and Socialism*, pp. 157, 346.

25   *Marx, Gandhi and Socialism*, pp. 116, 135.

26   *Marx, Gandhi and Socialism*, pp. xxxiii-xxxv.

27   *Marx, Gandhi and Socialism* pp. 108, 142-248.

28   *Marx, Gandhi and Socialism*, pp. 108-110.

29   *Marx, Gandhi and Socialism*, pp. 106.

30   *Marx, Gandhi and Socialism*, pp. 109-112.

31   *Marx, Gandhi and Socialism*, pp. 21-27.

32   *Marx, Gandhi and Socialism*, pp. 285, 466.

CHAPTER 10

J.P. Narayan: Socialist Gandhism

1   Jayaprakash Narayan, *A Revolutionary's Quest: Selected Writings of Jayaprakash Narayan*, Ed. by Bimal Prasad, (Delhi: Oxford Univ. Press, 1980), p. 6.

2   *A Revolutionary's Quest: Selected Writings of Jayaprakash Narayan*, p. 33.

3   *A Revolutionary's Quest: Selected Writings of Jayaprakash Narayan*, p. 44.

4   *A Revolutionary's Quest: Selected Writings of Jayaprakash Narayan*, p. 39.

5   *A Revolutionary's Quest: Selected Writings of Jayaprakash Narayan*, p. 43.

6   Jayaprakash Narayan, *Why Socialism?* (Benares: All India Congress Socialist Party), 1936, p. 113.

7   *Why Socialism?*, p. 114.

8   *Why Socialism?* pp. 74, 111-125.

9   Narayan, *A Revolutionary's Quest*, pp. 116-118.

10   *A Revolutionary's Quest*, pp. 122-124.

11   *A Revolutionary's Quest*, p. 128.

12   *A Revolutionary's Quest*, p. 132.

13   *A Revolutionary's Quest*, pp. 142-144

14   *A Revolutionary's Quest*, p. 192; Jayaprakash Narayan, *Socialism to Sarvodaya*, (Madras: Socialist Book Centre, 1956), p. 30.

15   *Socialism to Sarvodaya*, p. 29.

16   *Socialism to Sarvodaya*, p. 30.

17   *Socialism to Sarvodaya*, pp. 32-33.

18   *A Revolutionary's Quest*, p. 194.

19   Jayaprakash Narayan, *The Dual Revolution*, (Tanjore: Sarvodaya Prachuralaya, 1963), p. 17.

20   Jayaprakash Narayan, *A Plea for Reconstruction of Indian Polity*, (*Reconstruction*)(Kashi: Akhil Bharat Sarva Seva Sangh Prakeshan, 1959), p. 2; Jayaprakash Narayan, *Swaraj for the People,*(*Swaraj*) (Varanasi: Akhil Bhavat Sarva Seva Sangh), 1961, p. 3.

21   Narayan, *Reconstruction*, pp. 2-3, 8.

22   *Reconstruction*, pp. 3-4.

23   *Reconstruction*, pp. 4-6.

24   *Reconstruction*, p. 4.

25   *Reconstruction*, pp. 8-9.

26   *Reconstruction*, p. 8.

27   *Reconstruction*, pp. 43-44.

28   *Reconstruction*, pp. 15-19.

29   *Reconstruction,* pp. 19-20.

30   *Reconstruction,* p. 23.

31   *Reconstruction,* p. 23.

32   *Reconstruction,* p. 23.

33   *Reconstruction,* p. 63; see also p. 67.

34   *Reconstruction,* pp. 55-56; *Swaraj for the People (Swaraj)* p. 19.

35   *Reconstruction,* p. 56; *Swaraj.* pp. 19-20.

36   *Reconstruction* pp. 55-58; *Swaraj,* pp. 9-10, 20-21.

37   *Reconstruction,* pp. 55-57; *Swaraj,* pp. 13, 20.

38   *Reconstruction,* pp. 54-55, 57.

39   *Reconstruction,* pp. 55-56; *Swaraj,* p. 21.

40   *Swaraj,* p. 13.

41   *Reconstruction,* pp. 59-60; *Swaraj,* p. 21.

42   *Reconstruction,* p. 59.

43   *Reconstruction,* p. 43.

44   *Reconstruction,* pp. 42-43.

45   *Reconstruction,* p. 59.

46   *Reconstruction,* pp. 72, 76.

47   *Reconstruction,* pp. 59-60.

48   *Reconstruction,* p. 80.

49   *Reconstruction,* p. 64.

50   *Reconstruction,* pp. 66, 80.

51   Jayaprakash Narayan, *Communitarian Society and Panchayati Raj,* Ed. by Brahmanand, (Varanasi: Navachetan Prakashan, 1970), p. 102.

52   *Reconstruction,* p. 80.

53   *Reconstruction,* p.57.

54   *Communitarian Society and Panchayati Raj (Communitarian Society),* p. 130.

55   For a perhaps romanticized account of China's land reform period, see William Hinton, *Fanshen,* (New York: Vintage Books, 1966).

56   Ajit Bhattacharjea, *Jayaprakash Narayan: A Political Biography*, (New Delhi: Bell Books, 1975), pp. 152,153.

57   Jayaprakash Narayan, *Towards Total Revolution*, (4 vols.) Ed. by Brahmanand, (Bombay: Popular Prakashan, 1978), Vol. I, pp. 159-160.

58   Narayan, *Towards Total Revolution*, Vol. I, p. 160.

59   *A Revolutionary's Quest*, pp. 196-200, 280-282; Jayaprakash Narayan, *A Picture of Sarvodaya Social Order*, (Tanjore: Sarvodaya Prachuralaya, 1957), p. 130.

60   *A Revolutionary's Quest*, pp. 196-200, 280-282; *A Picture of Sarvodaya Social Order*, p. 130.

61   Jayaprakash Narayan, *The Dual Revolution*, (Tanjore: Sarvodaya Prachuralaya, 1963), pp. 5-6.

62   Jayaprakash Narayan, *Socialism to Sarvodaya*, (Mylapore: Socialist Book Centre, 1956), pp. 65-66.

63. Jayaprakash Narayan, *A Picture of Sarvodaya Social Order*, pp. 6 50, 72.

64   *A Picture of Sarvodaya Social Order*, p. 77.

65   *A Picture of Sarvodaya Social Order*, p. 12; *Reconstruction*, p. 6; Jayaprakash Narayan, *Total Revolution*, (Varanasi: Sarva Seva Sangh Prakashan, 1975), p. 5.

66   Bhattacharjea, *Jayaprakash Narayan*, p. 153; Vinoba Bhave, *Democratic Values and the Practice of Citizenship*, (Varanasi: Sarva Seva Sangh Prakashan, 1977), pp. 115-122.

67   Bhattacharjea, *Jayaprakash Narayan*, p. 156.

68   *A Revolutionary's Quest*, p. 317.

69   *A Picture of Sarvodaya Social Order*, p. 13.

70   *A Picture of Sarvodaya Social Order*, pp. 63-64.

71   *A Picture of Sarvodaya Social Order*, p. 31.

72   *A Revolutionary's Quest*, p. 363; Bhattacharjea, *Jayaprakash Narajan*, p. 163.

73   Narayan, *Towards Total Revolution*, Vol. IV, p. 191; *A Revolutionary's Quest*, pp. 319, 359, 363.

74 *A Revolutionary's Quest*, p. 363.

75 *A Revolutionary's Quest*, pp. 282-287,

76 *A Revolutionary's Quest*, pp. 314, 356-357.

77 *A Revolutionary's Quest*, p. 285.

78 *Total Revolution*, p. 68.

79 *Towards Total Revolution*, Vol. IV, pp. 192-193.

80 *Total Revolution*, p. 68; Jayaprakash Narayan, *Prison Diary 1975*, (Bombay: Popular Prakashan, 1977), pp. 33, 61-64; *Towards Total Revolution*, Vol. IV pp. 192-197.

81 *Prison Diary*, pp. 61-64; *Towards Total Revolution*, Vol. IV, pp. 192-197.

82 See generally, *The Dual Revolution*.

83 *Prison Diary*, pp. 61-64; *Total Revolution*, pp. 92-95; *Towards Total Revolution*, Vol. I., p. 159, Vol. IV, pp. 192-197.

84 *A Revolutionary's Quest*, pp. 282, 314, 349, 357; *Towards Total Revolution*, Vol. IV, pp. 182, 185; *Prison Diary*, pp. 29-30.

85 *A Revolutionary's Quest*, pp. 280-282, 368, *Towards Total Revolution*, Vol. IV, p. 185.

86 See, e.g, Narayan, *Communitarian Society*, p. 54.

87 *A Revolutionary's Quest*, pp. 364-366, 377, 387.

88 *Prison Diary*, p. 32; *Total Revolution*, pp. 5-7, 110.

89 *Total Revolution*, p. 110.

90 *A Revolutionary's Quest*, p. 307; *Prison Diary*, p. 33.

91 *A Revolutionary's Quest*, p. 341.

92 *Prison Diary*, p. 21.

93 *Total Revolution*, pp. 73, 88.

Bibliography

A. PRIMARY SOURCES

B.R. Ambedkar

1. *Annihilation of Caste*. Punjab Jalandhar: Bheem Patrika Publications (publication date unavailable).

2. *Buddha and the Future of his Religion*. Punjab Jullundur: Bheen Patrika Publications, Third Ed, Aug. 1980.

3. *The Buddha and His Dhamma*. Bombay: Siddharth Publication, Third Ed, 1984.

4. *Dr. Babasaheb Ambedkar: Writings and Speeches, Vol. I*. Bombay: Education Dept. Govt. of Maharashtra, 1979.

5. *Gandhi & Gandhism*. Jullundur, Punjab: Bheem Patrika Publications (publication date unavailable).

6. *Mr. Gandhi and the Emancipation of the Untouchables*. Jullundur, Punjab: Bheem Patrika Publications (publication date unavailable).

7. *Poona Pact: An Epic of Human Rights*. Jalandhar, Punjab: Buddhist Publishing House (publication date unavailable).

8. *Thus Spoke Ambedkar Vol. I*. Ed. by Bhagwan Das, Jalandhar, Punjab: Buddhist Publishing House (publication date unavailable).

9. *Thus Spoke Ambedkar Vol. II.* Ed. by Bhagwan Das. Jullundur, Punjab: Bheem Patrika Publications, 1969.

10. *Thus Spoke Ambedkar Vol. III.* Ed. by Bhagwan Das Bangalore: Ambedkar Sahitya Prakashana (publication date unavailable).

11. *Thus Spoke Ambedkar Vol. IV.* Ed. by Bhagwan Das, Bangalore: Ambedkar Sahitya Prakashana (publication date unavailable).

12. *The Untouchables: Who Were They and Why They Became Untouchables.* New Delhi: Amrit Book Co. (publication date unavailable).

13. *Who Were the Shudras? How They Came to be the Fourth Varna in the Indo-Aryan Society.* Bombay: Thackers, 1970.

Sri Aurobindo

1. *Bande Mataram: Early Political Writings.* Pondicherry: Sri Aurobindo Ashram, 1973.

2. *The Ideal of the Karmayogin.* Pondicherry: Sri Aurobindo Ashram, 1977.

3. *The Human Cycle, The Ideal of Human Unity, War and Self-Determination.* Pondicherry: Sri Aurobindo Ashram (Fifth Combined Edition)(Facsimile) 1977.

4. *Foundations of Indian Culture.* Pondicherry: Sri Aurobindo Ashram, Sixth Edition (facsimile in reduced size). Second Impression, 1980.

Bhagavan Das

1. *Ancient versus Modern "Scientific Socialism" or Theosophy and Capitalism, Fascism, Communism.* Adyar Madras: Theosophical Publishing House, 1934.

2. *The Science of Social Organization or The Laws of Man in the Light of Atma-Vidya.*
   a. Second Edition Vol. I. Adyar Madras: Theosophical Publishing House, 1932.

b. Second Edition vol. II. Adyar Madras: Theosophical Publishing House, 1935

c. Third Edition Vol. III. Banares: Ananda Publishing House, 1948.

Acharya Narendra Deva

1. *Democratic Socialism in India.* Ed. by Chandrodaya Dikshit. New Delhi: S. Chand & Co. Ltd., 1971.

2. *Towards Socialist Society.* Ed. by Brahmanand. New Delhi: Centre of Applied Politics, 1979.

M.K. Gandhi

1. *Capital & Labor.* Ed. by Anand T. Hingorani. Bombay: Bharatiya Vidija Bhavan, 1970.

2. *Democracy: Real and Deceptive.* Ed. by Anand T. Hingorani. Ahmedabad: Navajivan Trust, 1961.

3. *Economic and Industrial Life and Relations* (3 Vols)., Ed. by V. B. Kher. Ahmedabad: Navajivan Publishing House, 1957.

4. *Hind Swaraj.* Ahmedabad: Navajivan Publishing House, 1938.

5. *In Search of the Supreme.* (3 Vols) Ed. by V. B. Kher. Ahmedabad: Navajivan Publishing House, 1962.

6. *Man v. Machine.* Ed. by Anand T. Hingorani. Bombay: Bharatiya Vidya Bhavan, 1966.

7. *Modern v. Ancient Civilization.* Ed. by Anand T. Hingorani. Bombay: Bharatiya Vidya Bhavan, 1970.

8. *My Theory of Trusteeship.* Ed. by Anand T. Hingorani. Bombay: Bharatiya Vidya Bhavan, 1970.

9. *Panchayat Raj.* Ahmedabad: Navajivan Publishing House, 1959.

10. *Political & National Life and Affairs.* Ed. by V. B. Kher. Ahmedabad: Navajivan Publishing House, 1967.

11. *Sarvodaya.* Ed. by Bhavatan Kumarappa. Ahmedabad: Navajivan Publishing House, 1954.

12. *Varnashramadharma*. Ed. by R. K. Prabhu. Ahmedabad: Navajivan Publishing House, 1962.

13. *Village Industries*. Ed. by R. K. Prabhu. Ahmedabad: Navajivan Publishing House, 1960.

14. *Village Reconstruction*. Ed. by Anand T. Hingorani. Bombay: Bharatiya Vidya Bhavan, 1966.

Rammanohar Lohia

1. *Fragments of a World Mind*. Calcutta: Maitrayani (publication date unavailable).

2. *Marx, Gandhi and Socialism*. Hyderabad: Rammanohar Lohia Samata, Vidyalaya Nyasa, 1978.

Asoka Mehta

1. *Democratic Socialism; Mid-Twentieth Century Synthesis*. Hyderabad: Chetana Prakashan Ltd., 1951.

2. *Socialism v. Gandhism*. Bombay: Congress Socialist Publishing Co. Ltd., 1935.

3. *Studies in Socialism*. Bombay: Bharatiya Vidya Bhavan, 1964.

4. *Tasks of Social Democracy in Asia*. Praja Socialist Publication (no other publication information available).

5. *Towards Socialism*. Bombay: (no other publication information available).

Jayaprakash Narayan

1. *Communitarian Society and Panchayati Raj*. Ed. and with an Introduction by Brahmanand. Varanasi: Navachetna, 1970.

2. Jayaprakash Narayan, *The Dual Revolution*, (Tanjore: Sarvodaya Prachuralaya, 1963).

3. Forward to Folkert Wilken, *New Forms of Ownership in Industry*. Varanasi: Sarva Seva Sangh Prakashan, Second Edition, 1969.

4. *A Picture of Sarvodaya Social Order*. Tanjore: Sarvodaya Prachuralaya, 1957.

5. *A Plea for Reconstruction of Indian Polity*. Rajghat, Kashi: Sarva Seva Sangh Prakashan, 1959.

6. *Organic Democracy*. (publication information unavailable).

7. *Prison Diary*. Ed. with an Introduction by A.B. Shah, 1975. (additional publication information unavailable).

8. *A Revolutionary's Quest: Selected Writings of Jayaprakash Narayan*. Ed. with an Introduction by Brimal Prasad. Delhi: Oxford Univ. Press, 1980.

9. *Socialism to Sarvadaya*. Madras: Socialist Book Centre. (Publication date unavailable).

10. *Swaraj for the People*. Varanasi, Madras: Socialist Book Centre, 1961.

11. *Total Revolution*. Varanasi: Sarva Seva Sangh Prakashan, 1975.

12. *Towards Total Revolution*. (Four Vols.). Ed. by Brahmanand. Bombay: Popular Prakashan, 1978.

13. *Why Socialism?* Benares: All India Congress Socialist Party, 1936.

Jawaharlal Nehru

1. *An Anthology*. Delhi: Oxford University Press, 1983.

2. *An Autobiography*. New Delhi: Oxford University Press, 1980.

3. *The Discovery of India*. New Delhi: Oxford University Press, 1983.

4. *Glimpses of World History*. New Delhi: Oxford University Press, 1984.

5. Pamphlet including "The Right Approach to the People," Development Commissioners' Conference, Mussourie, April 29, 1957 and "The Basic Approach," AICC Economic Review, August 15, 1958.

6. *India's Freedom*. London: Unwin Books (publication dateunavailable).

7. *India's Independence and Social Revolution*. New Delhi: Vikas Publishing Hse. Pvt. Ltd., 1984.

8. *Nehru and Democracy: The Political Thought of an Asian Democrat*. Ed. by Donald Eugene Smith. Bombay: Orient Longmans (publication date unavailable).

9. *Nehru on Socialism: Selected Speeches and Writings*. New Delhi: Perspective Publications, 1964.

10 *Nehru on Socialism*. Ed. by V.B. Singh. New Delhi: Govt. of India, Ministry of Information and Broadcasting Publications Division, 1977.

11. Forward to *Socialism in Indian Planning* by Shriman Narayan. Bombay: Asia Publishing House, 1964.

12. *Soviet Russia: Some Random Sketches and Impressions*. Bombay: Chetana, 1949.

13. *India: Today and Tomorrow*. New Delhi: Indian Council for Foreign Relations, (publication date unavailable).

14. *Towards A Socialistic Order*. New Delhi: Indian National Congress, 1956.

Bipin Chandra Pal — also Bipinchandra Pal

1. *Bengal Vaishnavism*. Forward by Hirendranath Datta. Calcutta: Yugayatri Prakashak Ltd., 1962.

2. *An Introduction to the Study of Hinduism*. Calcutta: Yugayatri Prakashak Limited, 1968.

3. *Nationality & Empire: A Running Study of Some Current Indian Problems*. Calcutta & Simla: Tracker, Spink & Co., 1916.

4. *The New Economic Menace to India*. Madras: Ganesh & Co. 1920.

5. *Shree Krishna*. Calcutta: 1964. (additional publication information unavailable).

6. *The Soul of India*. Madras: Tagore & Co. (additional publication information unavailable).

7. *Swadeshi & Swaraj: The Rise of New Patriotism*. Calcutta: Yugay-adri Prakashak Ltd. 1954.

8. *Writings and Speeches. Vol. I*. Calcutta: Yugayatri (publication date unavailable).

Vivekananda

1. *The Complete Works of Swami Vivekananda*, Mayarati Memorial Edition, Calcutta: Advaita Ashram
   a. Vol. I, Fifteenth Ed., 1977.
   b. Vol. II, Fourteenth Ed., 1983.
   c. Vol. III, Twelfth Reprint, 1979.
   d. Vol. IV, Eleventh Ed., 1978.
   e. Vol. V, Eleventh Reprint, 1979.
   f. Vol. VI, Tenth Ed., 1978.
   g. Vol. VII, Ninth Reprint, 1979.
   h. Vol. VIII, Sixth Ed., 1977.

B. SECONDARY SOURCES

1. Arora, V.F. *Rammanohar Lohia and Socialism in India*. New Delhi: Deep & Deep Publications, 1984.

2. Bhattacharyya, Buddadeva. *Evolution of the Political Philosophy of Gandhi*. Forward by Normal Kumai Bose. Calcutta: Calcutta Book House, 1967.

3. Bondurant, Joan. *Conquest of Violence: The Gandhian Philosophy of Conflict*. Bombay: Oxford University Press, 1959.

4. Desai, A. R. *Social Background of Indian Nationalism*. Bombay: Popular Prakashan, 1984.

5. Kuber, W.N. *Ambedkar: A Critical Study*. New Delhi: People's Publishing House, 1979.

6. Lokhande, C.S. *Bhimrao Ramji Ambadkar: A Study in Social Democracy*. New Delhi: Sterling Publishers Private Ltd. 1977.

7. Markandan, K.C. *Directive Principles of the Indian Constitution.* Bombay: Allied Publishers Private Ltd. 1966.

8. Mehrotra, N.C. *Lohia: A Study.* Forward by Madhu Limaye. Delhi: Atma Ram & Sons, 1978.

9. Pradhan, Benudhar. *The Socialist Thought of Mahatma Gandhi* (Two Vols). New Delhi: GDK Publications, 1980.

10. RathnaReddy, A.V. *Political Philosophy of Swami Vivekananda.* New Delhi: Standing Publishers Pvt. Ltd., 1984.

11. Sharma, M.L., *Gandhi as a Socialist.* New Delhi: Deep & Deep Publications, 1980.

12. Singh, Shail Kumari. *Religious and Moral Pholosophy of Swami Vivekanada.* Delhi: Janaki Prakashan, 1983.

13. *Satprem Sri Aurobindo or The Adventure of Consciousness.* Pondicherry: Sri Aurobindo Astram, 1968.

14. Varma, V.P. *Modern Indian Political Thought.* Agna: Lakshmi Narain Agarwal, 1980.

15. Varma, V.P. *The Political Philosophy of Sri Aurobindo.* Delhi: Motilal Banarsidas, 1976.